McCANN

WAR & PEACE IN NORTHERN IRELAND

EAMONN McCANN

books

First published October 1998 by Hot Press Books,
13 Trinity St, Dublin 2.

British Library Cataloguing in Publication Data is available for this book.

ISBN No:
0 9524947 4 4 (paperback)
0 9524947 3 6 (hardback)

Design by Simon Roche and Paula Nolan
Cover Photograph: Colm Henry
Cover Design: Simon Roche

Printed by Colour Books, Baldoyle Industrial Estate, Dublin 13.

Thanks to Mette, Chris, Niall, Liam, Simon and all at Hot Press. And to Goretti, Vanessa and Hilary.

Eamonn McCann writes a fortnightly column in Hot Press. He also contributes to other publications in Ireland and Britain.

Secretary of the North-West Ulster branch of the National Union of Journalists and a member of the NUJ's Irish Executive Council, he is also a member of the executive committee and a past chairman of Derry Trades Union Council. He is a member of the Derry-based Campaign for Decent Wages and sits on the management committee of the cross-border Low Pay Unit. Eamonn is a member of the Bloody Sunday Campaign, and of the Socialist Workers' Party.

CONTENTS

INTRODUCTION by Paul Foot

WANDERING THROUGH SCRUBLAND IN Derry in the week after the police riot on 5th October, 1968, I was introduced to Eamonn McCann, a young man in a rage. He had come from a meeting in which Nationalist councillors had swamped the energetic and effective Derry Housing Action Committee. The Nationalist grandees, he fumed, were "middle-class, middle-aged and middle-of-the-road". They had, once again, strangled the breath out of the people they pretended to represent. I listened in stunned admiration, and observed that the young man's eyes, as they flashed with fury, seemed to twinkle at the same time with merriment.

Most young firebrands lose their early passions and mellow into respectable and respectful citizens. In the 30 years since that dramatic October, Eamonn McCann's indignation has not subsided an inch. He is as outraged now as he ever was by the condition of the working people in the North of Ireland, and in his native Derry. He refuses to accept that these people remain divided forever by ancient religious shibboleths which have no relevance to their real lives.

Though his obsessional knowledge of the Bible and the intricacies of Christian religion border on the macabre, he sees his fellow countrymen and women not as Protestants and Catholics but as human beings whose aspirations for a fulfilled life are frustrated, as they are everywhere else in the world, by much more relevant divisions: divisions between rich and poor, between employers and workers, between the few with their many mansions and the many with their rotten housing, stunted education and dead-end jobs.

This unusual approach gives Eamonn a refreshingly sharp insight into political developments in the North. He is entirely free of the sectarianism which suffocates almost all the political analysis and dialogue in that most political of territories. Above all, his writing style never loses that most elusive but vital quality: clarity. So many political commentators, including socialist ones, insult their readers – and lose them – in jargon, obfuscation and swank.

Even at the peak of his indignation, Eamonn never loses the capacity to explain, and to amuse and entertain at the same time. His book War And An Irish Town remains by far the clearest account of the origin of what later became known as "the Troubles". His analysis of the 1972 Bloody Sunday massacre in Derry – a masterpiece of informed and passionate investigative journalism – helped to persuade the Irish and British governments to set up a full-scale inquiry. In recent months, the BBC, casting around desperately for an analysis of events which is not stained with sectarianism, have repeatedly fallen back on the "extremist" Eamonn McCann to help their viewers out of the maze.

Hot Press has done the Irish people a profound service by publishing Eamonn McCann's political column on the North of Ireland over the last sixteen years – and an even greater service by bringing the best of these columns together in this collection. I can guarantee the reader that when finishing reading this book – and it is impossible to start it without finishing it – he or she will have learned far more about the politics of Northern Ireland than could have been gleaned from a thousand sermons or their political equivalent.

PREFACE

E VERYBODY STILL AROUND AGREES, it doesn't seem like 30 years. October 5th, 1968. So long ago 'Those Were The Days' was number one.

Sifting through the back issues of HOT PRESS preparing this book, I'm struck by how fast some figures have faded, how vivid some others are still. It's jolting to be reminded that Peter Barry, who makes an early appearance here, was a key figure in North-South relations just a few years ago. Patrick Mayhew, at the Northern Ireland Office as recently as 1997, seems, in my mind's eye, a picture from the far distant past, while Bernadette at the barricades in 1969 was only yesterday.

It's neat to say we've come full circle, and not entirely fanciful. From one perspective, the question raised by the civil rights movement was whether the Catholic minority could be incorporated into the Northern State on terms congenial to itself. Thirty years on we are, perhaps, at the edge of an answer.

If the Belfast Agreement ends violence between Protestant Unionists and Catholic Nationalists there'll be few quibbles. Only the politically deranged could want sectarian war. Not that "sectarian war" is an adequate formulation: it denies the combat-ant role of the State, erases the torture and murder which its forces perpetrated in the course of our tangled history.

People's view of the '60s reflects their interests and needs. Those who have given up on revolution need to rubbish revolu-tionary ideas.

One reason that certain of the '60s generation now propound a view of the period in line with what the ruling class said then is that they, themselves, have become agents of the ruling class in the interim.

They depict the civil rights movement as, at best, an innocent crusade led by dizzy idealists, at worst, a series of provocations certain to prompt a revival of armed-struggle Republicanism.

But the fact that things worked out the way they did doesn't mean they couldn't have worked out differently.

There was nothing giddy or guileful about associating the campaign for reform of the North with the black struggle in the US, the workers' fight in France, the resistance of the Vietnamese to imperialism, the uprising against Stalinism in Czechslovakia.

We said, One world, One struggle, because, then as now, it was true.

I remember Bernadette Devlin touring the US and having a run-in with Richard Daley, mayor of Chicago back then, and the most powerful Irish-American politician not called Kennedy. Daley had unleashed his cops against anti-war protesters during the 1968 Democratic Party convention.

Scheduled to meet him, Bernadette refused, comparing the Chicago police's use of CS gas to the RUC's against the Bogside. Told that Daley was the key to raising money in Chicago, she shot back: "I wouldn't shake his corrupt boss' hand for the whole US Treasury".

Black militants and anti-war activists in Chicago rejoiced at her remarks, while corporate interests were enraged.

Daley's son and political heir, US Commerce Secretary William Daley, was in the North this year, heading a delegation of US business executives. Gerry Adams wrote in the *Irish News*: "I am looking forward to meeting him again, and talking to him about jobs and investment".

Mr. Adams recounted that on a recent US visit "I had a number of discussions with President Clinton, senior investment bankers, financiers, Wall Street brokers and others, all of whom I found keen to offer help to consolidate the peace process in Ireland. On a visit to Wall Street, I especially found an enormous heightened awareness of the efforts for peace in Ireland and a desire to help".

One world, One struggle still, and still, perforce, we all take sides. That's just the way it is.

The Belfast Agreement offers an end to war: but to class war, too, on terms auspicious for capital, ill-omened for labour.

That may be the way it is – but it doesn't mean that's the way it has to be.

The world is getting stranger
We'll never lose heart.
We can't wait for the old world to die
Before we make a new start.
Bring on the revolution
Keep the pressure on
Don't want to die for nothing.
I hear your children sing
Freedom will ring
Freedom will ring.

(From 'Revolution' by Chrissie Hynde, on the album *The Last Of The Independents*, 1994)

– Eamonn McCann, October 1998.

01

The Birmingham 6 Are Innocent. Peter Barry Says So

"I AM MORE THAN EVER convinced of the innocence of the Birmingham Six," former Foreign Affairs minister Peter Barry told the *Sunday Tribune* the week before last. Mr. Barry had been a member of a delegation of TDs which met with the Six in Long Lartin prison.

What was the evidence which so significantly strengthened Mr. Barry's belief in the men's innocence?

. . . "You just couldn't believe that these men would be the kind of men who would do the things they were convicted of. The only offences you could imagine them being guilty of were parking offences or maybe drinking in a pub after hours." In other words, they seemed like decent fellows and decent fellows don't plant bombs in crowded pubs. Ergo, The Birmingham Six are innocent.

Isn't it a great pity in these days of fiscal rectitude that nobody has ever thought of saving the State the cost of operating the

Special Criminal Court by the expedient of having Mr. Barry chat up terrorist suspects, so as to detect which are pleasant peaceful sorts and therefore innocent, and which are personifications of evil and therefore guilty? Apparently he can handle a batch of six in one hour flat.

The underlying assumption is, of course, that terrorists are a breed apart; that they involve themselves in shooting and bombing on account of the type of people they are, rather than on account of the circumstances in which they find themselves.

This is a very common assumption, discernable in the ritual denunciations of the Provos which follow every IRA operation and in oft-used phrases such as "Men of Violence". The assumption is common because it's so handy. Once accepted, it liberates us from the awkward necessity of investigating, and of seeking to eliminate, the circumstances which propel perfectly decent people towards shooting and bombing.

The Birmingham Six were not convicted because the British courts made a mistaken estimation of their individual personalities. They were convicted because they were stitched up by the British State, the stitch-up involving torture, perjury and a wide-ranging conspiracy to pervert the course of justice.

But Peter Barry, anxious to be regarded as a friend by the British State, would rather not see it like that.

* * * * *

There's another reason Barry has to resort to banalities when dealing with the Birmingham Six. The last effort to reopen the case followed the acquittal of a group of warders stationed at Winston Green prison in Birmingham, who had been charged with assaulting the six men. The warders' defence rested on a claim that the injuries which the men had sustained had been inflicted prior to their arrival at prison – while they were in police custody. This seemed to buttress the Six's allegation – rejected at their trial – that the confessions which were crucial to their conviction had been beaten out of them by the cops.

However, when lawyers sought on this ground to have the case brought back to court their argument was rejected, in January 1980, by Lord Justice Denning who held that the Six, because they had previously exhausted the normally-available avenues of appeal, were now estopped from proceeding further.

In December 1984 the Irish State entered a defence in the High Court against a claim by Nicky Kelly for damages. Kelly's case was that the confession which formed the basis of his conviction for the Sallins mail train robbery had been beaten out of him by gardaí. The State's defence dealt not at all with the substance of Kelly's claim. Instead, it argued that, because he had already exhausted the usual machinery of appeal, he was estopped from going ahead. Mr. Justice Rory O'Hanlon accepted the State's argument.

The only precedent cited by the Irish State to support this line of defence was Denning's ruling in the case of the Birmingham Six.

Not only did the government of which Peter Barry was a senior member do sweet f.a. for the Birmingham Six, it used the case of the Birmingham Six to prevent justice being obtained by a citizen convicted in very similar circumstances in its own courts.

* * * * *

The Attorney General who devised the stratagem of using the Birmingham precedent was Peter Sutherland. This oily operator is now an EEC Commissioner, in which capacity he has been publicly warning the voters back home not to dare "let down our friends in Europe" by presuming to vote against the Single European Act.

"Bunter" Sutherland and his fellow Paddy-bureaucrats in Brussels have been feverishly feeding the message back to Ireland that the entire populations of the eleven other member-States are apoplectic with anger at the Twenty-Six County curmudgeons screwing up the Single-Europe scheme for capricious constitutional reasons, and might be minded to cut the oul' country off without a Eurodollar if the voters don't behave responsibly on referendum day. Not so, according to all the reliable evidence, e.g. that of the *Irish Times* man in Brussels, Colm Boland.

The only people in Brussels noticeably agitated about the affair are the aforementioned Paddy-bureaucrats. What's unnerved these super-annuated pen-pushers is the distant possibility of a break between the Free State and the Community requiring them to remove their snouts from the Euro-trough.

This, on its own, is sufficient reason for voting against the proposed constitutional amendment.

Vote No and sicken a Euro-yuppie!

* * * * *

Is the phrase "Paddy-bureaucrat" sexist?

I suppose it is.

Mind you, "Biddy-bureaucrat" might be even worse.

Nothing's simple.

"Men of violence" is certainly sexist. I enclosed it in quotation marks above to make clear that it isn't mine. Indeed, I'm surprised that, despite my past pleadings, campaigners for women's rights haven't focused on this foul phrase which writes so many women out of contemporary history.

"Paramilitary godfathers" is another shockingly sexist phrase. One of my best mates is a fiery godmother who is fast running out of patience. Unless more moderate politicians (Where are you, Ms. Fennell? Speak up, Monica Barnes!) can provide a constitutional means of ending this discrimination, I don't see how the woman in question can be blamed if she resorts to Other Methods.

23 April '87

02

What Do We Want? Three Judges! When Do We Want Them? Now!

THIS CONTROVERSY ABOUT REFORM OF the Diplock Courts in the North is as odd as Eamon Dunphy.

A couple of weeks ago Maggie's man at Stormont Castle, Tom King, let it be known that her Majesty's Government was "not presently persuaded" that the number of judges in the no-jury Diplock courts should be upped from one to three. The result was instant outrage from the likes of P. Barry, D. Spring, S. Mallon and other glittering stars from the crazy world of constitutional politics.

I should, I suppose, make it clear here and now exactly where I stand on this issue. Idly by, is where I stand.

Indeed, differ as we might on this or that matter, you and I can agree that the question of whether there is one judge or three – or even a whole bevy of bewigged elderly men – on the bench up in Belfast is not nearly as important for the future happiness and prosperity of the plain people of this island as is the question whether WEA are really going to sign The Carrellines and thus re-release the remarkably youthful ex-Undertones skin-slapper Billy Doherty on the long-deprived musical masses.

Not so in the minds of P. Barry, etc.

Mr. Barry was out of the starting blocks with an agility that would have made Ben Johnson look arthritic to complain that Tom King's intransigence was down to Fianna Fáil: the weak-kneed wimps around C.J. Haughey hadn't piled on enough pressure to force the Brits to back off. If only he, Peter Barry, were still heading up our side at the Anglo-Irish Conference there'd have been action on the three-judges front long ago.

Next into the news bulletins was Labour boss Spring, with the dramatic announcement that if King didn't change his tune he, Dick Spring, might feel constrained to turn the opposable digit down in December when the Leinster House lot vote on the implementation of the new extradition act.

Meanwhile, up here, Johnny Hume's adjutant Seamus Mallon was fretting in public that if the British persisted with the single-judge system, the entire edifice of the Anglo-Irish Agreement might collapse onto the heads of the suffering citizenry.

Such was the kerfuffle that the BBC News solemnly reported "a new crisis in Anglo-Irish relations".

Now I read that the three-judge issue sits ominously at the top of the agenda for next month's meeting of the Anglo-Irish Conference.

So what's it all about, eh?

In advancing the demand for three judges, Messrs. Barry, Spring etc. are fulfilling the role allotted to them in the Hillsborough agreement – they speak as "representatives" of the Northern nationalists, as, more directly, does Mr. Mallon.

Now then. Another thing we might both agree on is that Northern nationalists are not one bit bashful about alerting anybody who cares to listen as to which aspects of life displease them. In fact, some would say that they never give over. Northern nationalists are great ones for inscribing references to the perceived causes of their discontents on cardboard placards and parading with these through the public streets. Alternatively, they gather in numbers and give expression to these discontents in the form of pithy phrases shouted in unison.

When's the last time you saw a placard or a picture of a placard reading "Three judges now!"? Or heard vibrant chants of the same or a suchlike phrase? Have you ever heard tell of a march or a meeting, a picket or protest rally, designed to call attention to this desire?

Me neither.

I'll tell you what I think. I think that Barry, Spring and the rest of them want three-judge courts introduced as a demonstration of their ability to have three-judge courts introduced. The fact that this change would make not a blind bit of difference to the day-to-day life of Prod, Taig or decent Pagan figures not at all in their thinking.

Aren't they desperate eejits?

10 September '87

03

Poor John Cushnahan Is Not A Tragic Case

"IF WE WANT SO MUCH TO see peace restored in the North, and a return to parliamentary democracy, we must be prepared to pay a price. That price must be one by which we ensure the Cushnahans of Northern Ireland can engage in politics without having to worry about the tyranny of making an independent living . . ."

Thus John Healy in the *Irish Times* on September 12 commented on the retirement of Alliance Party leader John Cushnahan. Mr. Cushnahan had explained that he was pulling out of politics because there wasn't a decent living in it. And what's more, given the evident inability of the SDLP and Unionist leaderships to agree terms for devolved government, there was little chance of getting a start as a paid parliamentarian in the foreseeable future.

In the same week the chief executive of the Official Unionist Party, Frank Millar, announced that he, too, was leaving Northern politics, and indeed leaving the North – for a job as a researcher with London Weekend Television. Mr. Millar had been co-author of the Unionist Task Force report, and was the most vocal Unionist advocate of the devolved government strategy recommended in the report.

Others who have recently thrown in the linen towel include Nigel Hamilton, general secretary of the Democratic Unionist Party, Will and Pip Glendenning, Alliance members of Belfast City Council, and SDLP research officer John Kennedy. What these people had in common is that all were under 40 and involved in constitutional politics. As things stand, they had as little hope as Mr Cushnahan and Mr. Millar of rapid political advancement.

This small exodus had generally been taken as depressing evidence of how obdurate the Northern problem still is and of the intolerable frustration felt by bright, young(ish) politicians for whose talents there is no ready outlet.

In his *Times* piece, Mr. Healy suggested as a solution that the British government set up a fund to subsidise the political parties in the North. Drawing on the fund, the parties could pay the likes of Mr. Cushnahan salaries sufficient to prevent them being lured out of politics by offers of lucre elsewhere.

And speaking of subsidies . . .

The most recent change in the social welfare system in the North involves the abolition of Child Benefit and Family Income Supplement. The Child Poverty Action Group estimates that this will mean an average loss of £2.54 a week to families on Supplementary Benefits, the total amount to be withdrawn from claimants this year being around £25 million. (The long-term unemployed will lose £11.6 million, single parents will lose £1.5 million and pensioners £12.3 million.)

This is happening in an area of the "United" Kingdom which is already the worst off in terms of infant mortality, average unemployment, personal income, average wages, housing amenities, dependency on social security and just about any other index of economic misery you care to mention.

The defining characteristic of life in large areas of the North is not sectarianism, the activity of paramilitaries, or the security presence. It is poverty, and the desperation associated with it.

This is as big a factor as any other in keeping hearts and minds here hard.

There is a "tragedy" here, sure enough. But it doesn't lie in the departure of "the best and the brightest" *(Irish Times)*, alias "the Young Turks *(Sunday Tribune)*, aka "the generation of hope" *(Belfast Telegraph)*, any more than the "tragedy" of starvation in the Third World could be said to lie in the inability of aid organisations to generate good jobs for caring young executives.

Indeed, the admiration which the media have heaped on Mr. Cushnahan and the rest of the what's-in-it-for-me? mob as they wish us luck and wave politics goodbye, is indicative only of the distance between the reporting of the North and the reality.

Mr. Healy's suggestion implies that some of the money "saved" by making the North's poor even poorer might usefully be used to protect the likes of John Cushnahan from "having to worry about the tyranny of making an independent living . . ."

24 September '87

04
———

No Time For Love On The *Late Late Show*

BIG HUGO MEENAN WON'T BE sellotaping the reviews of his debut television appearance into a leather-bound family album or looking forward to reading them out in years to come to awe-stricken grandchilder gathered around an as-advertised Bord Na Móna blaze. At least, I don't think so.

Big Hugo was the hirsute, darkly-handsome fellow who filled

the final guest-spot on *The Late Late Show* on the Friday before last. He'd been invited onto the show to talk about his just-published book, *No Time For Love.*

Strangely enough – if you still find these things strange – neither Mr. Gay Byrne nor anyone else mentioned the subject of Hugo's book or directed a single question to him about it. No Time For Love.

Was it, perhaps, a treatise on the "bangbang and g-night now" approach to sex? Or, possibly, a candid exposé of the anti-musical methodology of upswinging '50s big bandsman Geoff Love? Or maybe a novel about the North taking its title from the brilliant Jack Warshaw song which upset Bill Graham so much when it was included on Moving Hearts' first album?

"They call it the law we call it apartheid, internment, conscription, partition and silence/It's the law that they make to keep you and me where they think we belong/They hide behind steel and bullet-proof glass, machine guns and spies/And they tell us who suffer the teargas and the torture that we're in the wrong/No time for love when they come in the morning . . ."

It's the best novel of its kind that I've ever read, because it's the only one. It's written from deep inside. It's about a former British paratrooper who leads a breakaway Republican paramilitary group in Derry in the early '70s. Hugo, a former British paratrooper, was active in the armed wing of the Workers' Party, (the "Official IRA") in Derry in the early '70s.

There was a number of very obvious, and, I would have thought, interesting questions which might have been put to Hugo. How much of the book is factually-based? Why did he write it? To expunge the memory? Or to celebrate the period? What might his former associates, a couple of whom are readily recognisable from the text, make of it?

Instead, Hugo was presented as a rare and exotic specimen. The director hit him repeatedly with BCUs – Big Close-Ups – framing his face so that it filled the screen, lending the appearance of significance to every eye flicker and facial twitch. It was a very unusual shot indeed for *The Late Late Show.* No such shot was used on any of the night's other guests, Spike Milligan, Maeve

Binchy and Colm Tóibín. There was one slowish dissolve from a two-shot of Hugo and Gay Byrne to a BCU of Hugo which was pure cinema. Hugo, the television audience was being instructed to understand, was a strange being, to be studied closely.

And that's the way the national press reviewers saw him. One terribly agitated woman told readers of the *Sunday Indo* that if Section 31 were ever repealed, beings like Hugo Meenan would be popping up on RTE screens all the time! They'd become TV stars!

I watched the programme in the Dungloe Bar in the company of Terry, Tommy, Don, Cathy, Pat, Seamus and the rest of the gang who drink with Hugo when he's in town. I'm afraid the reviews were pretty bad in the Dungloe, too. Don remarked: "He's making it all soft to get people to buy his book."

A few hours before *The Late Late Show* was transmitted, the results were announced of two City Council by-elections in West Belfast. The by-election had been caused by the resignations of Pippa and Will Glendenning of the Alliance Party, two of the bright young moderates who, to the deep distress of media commentators, have withdrawn from the political scene in the North.

The 1985 local government election figures indicated that Sinn Féin would win in Lower Falls and the SDLP in Upper Falls. In the event, Fra McCann romped home for SF in Lowers Falls and Mairtín O'Muilleoir of the same party won the other area handily enough. Unlike Hugo Meenan, Fra McCann and Mairtín O'Muilleoir give unequivocal support to the IRA campaign now.

So are the people of the Falls – a voting majority of them – even stranger and more exotic specimens of humanity than Hugo?

Take a dander down the Falls Road some time (it's statistically safer than O'Connell Street) and look and listen for yourself. I think you'll find that Falls people have as much time for love and decent values in their daily lives as the people of any other area of the island.

So there must be some other explanation why they think the way they do – other than the explanation *The Late Late Show* contrived to offer.

But then, what really goes down well on RTE, and in the

Southern media generally, is Colm Tóibín describing how he tiptoed daringly along the entire length of the border without ever putting a foot down on either side. This is what's called "balance".

5 November '87

05
_____

Enniskillen And The Blood On Mourning Margaret's Hands

SICKO SIGHT OF THE YEAR was Mrs Margaret Thatcher in mourning dress at the Enniskillen war memorial on November 22nd, acting as if she cared about the eleven people killed by the IRA bomb.

It can be said with certainty that Mrs Margaret Thatcher is in no way opposed to, or emotionally perturbed by, the killing of people, military or civilian, in small or large numbers, for political reasons.

Margaret Thatcher wafted around Westminster in 1982, immured in a phosphorescent glow of pleasure at the horrible deaths of more than 350 Argentine sailors who perished with the sinking of the Belgrano. The information which has emerged since, extracted to the fury of Mrs Thatcher from a reluctant bureaucracy by the persistent questioning of Mr. Tam Dalyell MP and others, leaves no room for doubt that the Belgrano was sunk for straightforwardly political reasons and not out of any military "necessity".

In April of last year, Mrs Thatcher supported and directly involved herself in the organisation of the no-warning bombing of Tripoli and Benghazi in which more than 50 civilians were blown to bits. She treated all political or moral objection to that massacre with derisive contempt.

Immediately after leaving the remembrance service at St McCartin's Cathedral in Enniskillen, Mrs Thatcher flew to Paris for a *tête-a-tête* with the French Premier, M. Jacques Chirac. This, I should make clear in order to avoid confusion, is the same Jacques Chirac who a few months ago, travelled 18,000 miles to visit a remote island in the South Pacific in order to greet and, in his own words, "to honour" the two members of the French intelligence service who, in July 1985, killed a Greenpeace volunteer worker on board the Rainbow Warrior in Auckland, New Zealand.

En route to Paris, Mrs Thatcher would have had time to catch up on coverage of the US Congressional report on the Iran/Contra affair. A passage in that report which has attracted remarkably little attention from the British and Irish media, but which Mrs Thatcher will have read with close interest, describes the secret purchase from Britain by Col. Oliver North of Belfast-manufactured Blowpipe surface-to-air missiles for use by the Contras. The report clearly implies that the purchase, although "secret" in that the operation was clandestine, was not secret from the British government.

The activities of the Contras are illegal, both in terms of the law of the country in which the killings are taking place and in international law, but when it comes to slaughtering innocent people for political reasons, legally means as little as morality to Margaret Thatcher.

And we could go on . . . El Salvador, Mozambique, Guatemala, Namibia, Angola, Indonesia, Kampuchea, you name it. Anywhere real big-time slaughter of civilians takes place, it's quite likely that Mrs Margaret Thatcher is cheering on the killing squads – and, possibly, enquiring whether they need fresh ammo.

And lest we imagine that there's a limit to the numbers of people Mrs Thatcher would contentedly have killed to further her political ends, she has told us herself that she would willingly order a nuclear bomb dropped on Moscow.

And yet, there was something exactly appropriate about this amoral woman wearing a death-mask face, and with a blood-red emblem affixed to her pitch-black lapel, standing before a war memorial at a re-enactment of Remembrance Sunday. Remembrance Day falls every year on the Sunday before November 11th because it began as, as in large measure it remains, a day of remembrance of the dead of the First World War – which ended with formal surrender by Germany on that day in 1918. It is this which gives Remembrance Day its special significance here in the North.

Tens of thousands of Northern Protestants, including virtually the entire membership of the Ulster Volunteer Force which had been raised by Edward Carson to resist Home Rule, joined the British Army once war was declared. They fought with ferocious courage and died in droves.

It is absolutely right that this should be remembered, not just ceremoniously once a year, but all year, every year – remembered with rage against those responsible.

The First World War was fought between two competing and equally vicious sets of capitalists for mastery over the world's trade routes and for "rights" in the exploitation of the colonial world. It had nothing to do with "the freedom of small nations": no historian, of the Right, Left or Centre, argues that line now. The interests of the working-class people of Britain, Germany, Russia, France, Ireland, Belgium, the United States, anywhere, didn't register a feather's weight in the balance. Whipped up into a froth of enthusiasm by the patriotic rantings of Church and State, the role of those who rallied to the flags was to supply the required suffering. The generals on both sides flung them to their deaths like fistfuls of chaff.

This is what is remembered with pomp and sombre pride on Remembrance Day. No complaint or whisper of protest is ever permitted at the ceremony. The few who remain who can still remember, and their descendants, are urged again to believe – and for many no doubt it's a genuine comfort – that it was sweet and fitting to fall at the Somme, Gallipoli or Passchendaele. The blood-soaked old lies are saluted again.

"Blessed are the peacemakers," the Church of Ireland Archbishop, Dr. Robin Eames, began at St. McCartin's on November 22nd, and I wouldn't doubt that he meant it. He went on: "We have come here today to remember with dignity and humility those who made the supreme sacrifice in defence of freedom and democracy in two world wars." Flanders and the Somme were included among battlegrounds to be held in "sacred memory". Small wonder that Mrs Thatcher was able, as she listened, to tremble her lip for the cameras.

Planting the bomb at Enniskillen on November 8th was a rotten, lousy thing for the Provos to do. But I do not believe that we should take any lectures from Mrs Margaret Thatcher, who has no entitlement to comment on the morality of anybody's political violence.

I am not, as I am often at pains to explain, a Republican, or indeed a nationalist, of any sort. But if I have to make a choice – and indeed I do – between Mrs Margaret Thatcher and Mr. Gerry Adams, I am content, because I want to be associated with the side which has the lesser amount of blood on its hands, to take my stand with Gerry Adams.

3 December '87

06

Sectarianism: Time For Trade Unions To Divide And Conquer

I DON'T IMAGINE THAT THE blood of many HOT PRESS readers spurted with excitement at the announcement that the Northern

Ireland Youth Committee of the Irish Congress of Trade Unions launched a new campaign against sectarianism.

It's odds-on a lot of you missed the announcement altogether. Personally, I wasn't even aware that such a body as the NIYC of the ICTU existed. Perhaps it's been called into existence for the purpose of organising this campaign.

It wouldn't be a bad reason. The trade union movement is better placed than any other to purge the politics of this island of sectarianism. No other institution brings Catholic and Protestant workers together on a regular basis in pursuit of a common purpose which is antipathetic to sectarianism. And younger trade unionists are obviously the right people to involve, if a new start is to be made.

A pity, then, that there is no possibility whatever of the campaign succeeding. Sad that so much honest energy and organisational ability is about to be frittered away.

I'm open to correction here, but I make this the ninth anti-sectarian initiative launched by the trade union movement since the outbreak of the troubles twenty years ago.

In 1969 there was the Programme For Peace And Prosperity In Northern Ireland.

The Better Life For All campaign came in 1976.

And so on up to the Trade Union Alternative document (1983), Peace, Work And Progress (1986), and thence to this latest youth campaign announced on January 31st.

Each of these initiatives was based on a strategy for combating sectarianism which has been popular not only with trade union leaders but in leftish and liberal circles generally. Trade unionists were called on to forswear violence as a means of achieving political ends and to reject "extremists on both sides", in the meantime lobbying the British government to adopt economic policies which would eradicate poverty and thus eliminate the social conditions in which "terrorism" was assumed to be rooted.

Say it quickly without pausing for breath and it sounds sensible enough. In practice, what it has meant is that the trade unions have consistently and determinedly avoided grappling with the issues which divide Protestants from Catholics.

Take discrimination. Pretty divisive business, it can scarcely be denied. Yet not only have the unions failed to mount vigorous resistance, they have tacitly condoned the exclusion of Catholics from workplaces and even, on occasion – at Belfast shipyard, for example – participated actively in the process of discrimination.

The excuse/explanation traditionally offered has been that to raise the issue of anti-Catholic discrimination within the trade union movement would be . . . divisive, a version of Catch 22 which was entertaining Northern trade union officials long before Yossarian sussed out that in wartime only lunatics can prove themselves sane.

Determination to avoid being "divisive" resulted in the unions in the North becoming so hysterically tight-lipped when internment without trial was introduced in 1971 that, afterwards, the entire movement had to be put under an anaesthetic and a surgeon called in to open its mouth again. The union historian Andrew Boyd claims that the Northern Committee of the ICTU was the only representative union body in all of Europe, East or West, which failed to condemn internment. (To be fair, the Committee did issue a statement asking, in vain, that the pension rights of interned trade unionists should be protected.)

Or again: herewith, verbatim and in their entirety, the minutes of a special meeting of the executive committee of Derry Trades Council held on January 31st, 1972, the day after Bloody Sunday when thirteen people, seven of them trade union members, had been killed by British soldiers: "The purpose of the meeting was to consider the happenings of the previous day in our City. After lengthy discussion a vote of sympathy was passed to relatives of those who lost their lives. Hopes were expressed that those injured would soon be restored to health. This being all the business, the meeting closed."

It was readily explained to anyone who questioned whether such timidity was absolutely necessary that to have condemned the killings would have been . . . divisive.

And we could go on, incident by controversial incident down through the years to the present dreary day, the union leaderships advertising their non-sectarian credentials by steadfastly refusing to take a clear stand on anything directly relevant to sectarianism.

It could be different. The 200 delegates who gathered for the "youth conference" might usefully avert their eyes from the "official" campaign and consider instead the unofficial initiative taken by workers in the North's Department of Health and Social Services in 1986.

After an IRA death threat to anyone who worked for the security forces, the UVF announced its intention to kill Catholics working in the Lisburn DHSS office. The Lisburn workers promptly downed pens and came out on strike. They were joined by up to 4,000 other DHSS workers across the North. The response of trade union officialdom was acute embarrassment . . . quite unofficial, possible breach of Tory employment laws, politically-motivated etc., etc.

But that one-day strike did more within DHSS workplaces to create a sense of solidarity across the religious divide than all the poster campaigns and political pussy-footing of the official leadership in two decades.

What would happen if trade unionists in the North were to demand control of recruitment and promotion in industry and the public service with a view to ensuring that nobody was given an advantage, or put at a disadvantage, on account of religion?

It would not be impossible to win the support of a majority of workers of whatever religion for this most reasonable proposition.

It would, of course, be divisive. It would divide those in favour of the proposition from those against. Which is exactly what needs to be done.

11 February '88

07

The National Health Service And The Struggle For Civil Rights

WE CAME JAUNTILY PARADING UP Duke Street on the Monday before last, about a thousand of us or so, Derry's contribution to the "Save The National Health Service" day of action. The heavens were weeping in frustration at the obduracy of Mrs. Thatcher, which did nothing to dampen the determination of the hardy annuals among us.

I was ambling alongside Dermie McClenaghan, and we fell to reminiscing about the last time the long and winding road to socialism had taken this particular route. Almost twenty years ago in October '68, the civil rights march which began (and ended) in Duke St., detonated the troubles which still rumble on. As we reached the top of the street and swung right across Craigavon Bridge towards the west bank of the Foyle I remarked to Dermie that at least we were getting a bit farther today than we'd managed back then.

"Aye," he growled "and there's people say we've made no progress."

Times like this – you need optimism like that.

The demonstration around the North and all over Britain didn't deflect the Tories from disservice to national health in the following day's budget. But they did illustrate again what a remarkable institution the British National Health Service is, and what a warm, firm grip it has on the affections of millions of people.

The NHS is the biggest employer west of the Red Army, with around three quarters of a million on the pay-roll. About a million people a day make contact with the NHS. Every survey seems to show that the popularity of the NHS has gone up another notch.

The reason, I think, has less to do with the actual services that the NHS has offered ordinary people in the last 40 years than with the general sense of security it has provided, and with the notion it has propagated that all are entitled to the best health care medical science can give, no matter what their social status or ability to pay.

The NHS was never perfect, and it is very far from perfect now. But it remains true that a beggar who collapses with a heart attack and who is taken into the care of an NHS hospital will automatically be given exactly the same care and attention as a millionaire who arrives similarly afflicted in the next bed and neither will be presented with a bill upon discharge. This is a great thing, and worth fighting ferociously to preserve. It runs directly against the most fundamental idea of Thatcherite philosophy, which is that anything worth having in this life has to be paid for.

Thus the fight to save the National Health Service is not just a dispute over the allocation of resources. It is a struggle over what ideology is to dominate public life.

The great hero in the home I grew up in, in Rossville Street, in the Bogside, was not Wolfe Tone or Patrick Pearse or even James Connolly, but Aneurin Bevan. At the age of eight or nine I was stricken by some class of ailment connected with arthritis and was laid up in the front room for a couple of months. Every second day or so a doctor would come visiting to perform some jiggery-pokery or other. The mantelpiece was lined with a most impressive array of coloured bottles containing pills and potions which I was required to ingest, and the ingestion of which seems to have done the medical trick, in that I was eventually running the streets again and not a bother on me.

Quite frequently, after the doctor had gone, my father would remark with a certain almost jubilant satisfaction that "'Nye' Bevan is a great man!" I used to think that Nye Bevan was the man in charge of the doctors in Derry, which in a sense he was. Bevan was the Minister of Health who introduced the NHS in

1947.

Later this year there will be a gush of newspaper articles and television programmes about the beginnings of the civil rights movement 20 years ago, and I imagine that pictures of the October march up Duke St. in Derry will figure. Look out for the placards we were carrying so as to proclaim what we wanted and in what tradition we believed we were following.

On the night before the march we (that is, McClenaghan, myself and a couple of others) made a dozen placards. I know it was a dozen because I remember buying the sheets of cardboard. On six of the sheets we wrote: "'Tories are vermin' – Nye Bevan". Bevan had said that, while railing against Tories who had the same attitude to the health service then as Thatcher has to it now. We thought it summed up and caught the flavour of what we were saying, albeit in a somewhat different context. The march on Monday week ago wasn't a diversion away from the struggle launched along the same route in 1968. It was a diversion back towards it.

24 March '88

08

Memo From The Yanks To The Provos: Wholesale Slaughter Is Your Only Man

I MET A PROVIE LEADER in the pub the other night and told him straight. First Enniskillen, now Lisnaskea, people just won't stand for actions of that sort. Eleven punters gathered at a war memorial, then a bus-load of school-girls that it was only the mercy of fate weren't blown to bits . . .

The Provos should have bombed Enniskillen from the air and sent in fighters to machine-gun any survivors as they stumbled from the scene.

That way, you'd eliminate any family groups who happened to be present in job lots, and there wouldn't be any fathers of dead daughters left to make you look bad by expressing forgiveness. You could also rest content there'd be no horribly wounded young person making a slow, brave recovery which the media could keep tabs on and keep the human angle in the public eye.

But there you are. I've said it before and I'll say it again. The Provos don't think big enough. Not like the Yanks. The Yanks don't piss about bumping off people in batches of less than a dozen. 290 people, all the papers said, the Yanks offed in one go when they zapped that Iranian air-bus over the Gulf – a figure which is in fact selling the Yanks short. It was 290 passengers. There was the crew on top, which begrudgers in the media didn't mention.

Nor was there any great willingness to highlight the fact that among the 300-plus dead were no fewer than six dozen children!

Yes indeed. Wholesale slaughter is your only man if you want good write-ups in the papers. You read anybody bad-mouthing the Yanks for blasting the air-bus the way they bad-mouth the Provies for bumping people off in small groups? You read any newspaper with "BASTARDS" scrawled across its front page? You hear any ex-cabinet minister ask why Cardinal O'Connor hasn't made with the excommunication procedures? You hear anybody declare that decent people should shun the violent guys who did this foul deed and eschew all contact with their political associates? You see anybody ask what legal or moral right the armed forces of a country the width of a continent and the breadth of an ocean away have to be in the Persian Gulf bombing or shooting at the local population, military or civilian, in the first place? Nope.

Then there was the *Washington News*, which headlined the yarn, "Accident or Suicide?", offering as alternative explanations either that the innocent, life-affirming US forces "had been the victims" of an accident or that the Iranian air crew had performed a kamikaze stunt and taken the passengers with them so as to make the aforementioned life-affirming Americans look bad. Nice, that, the line that the Yanks were the "victims" of the incident.

Mind you, not everybody in the anti-men-of-violence camp has taken the same stance. Liberal, *Guardian*-reading elements have pointed out that Reagan, Thatcher *et al* might better have immediately conveyed regret and offered compensation . . .

"Dear Mr. Wilson, sorry about Marie, how much was she worth to you? Yours very sincerely, The Provos."

Would that have covered it, do you think?

* * * * *

Derry being a very friendly place, it's not surprising there's a Chinese family here called O'Doherty. One of the Chinese O'Dohertys drives a taxi.

Ming is quite a common name here, too. Charlie Ming used to be the supervisor at the William Street swimming baths.

One of the Mings hired a taxi the other week for a trip down to Donegal. A soldier at the Buncrana Road checkpoint demanded the names of driver and passenger.

"O'Doherty," said the Chinaman.

"Ming," said the Derryman.

They were let go after an hour.

14 July '88

09

Nationalist Or Unionist, Business Is Business

THE CHANCES ARE THERE'LL BE little change recorded in either of the local government elections in the North on May 17th.

I say "either of the elections" because for practical purposes there'll be two different polls taking place.

The Official Unionists will fight the Democratic Unionists and a scattering of smaller unionist parties for support within the Protestant community.

The SDLP, Sinn Féin and others will battle it out for the votes of the Catholics.

Analysts will afterwards analyse and commentators comment on the percentage-point shifts between the DUP and OUP, and between the SDLP and Sinn Féin. But nobody will look to see whether there's any shift of support from either of the first pair to either of the second. It's two separate contests in two separate, sealed-in communities.

Which is just another way of stating the dreary old truth that the line of political division in the North continues to run along the "interface" between the two religious communities, rather than, as socialists would prefer and insist would be more natural, along the divide between classes.

How pleasant it ought to be, then, to be able to point to an example of Catholics and Protestants here in Derry getting together in friendship and solidarity to further the interests of their class.

But I'm referring not to the working-class, but to what's commonly called the "business community". A united Derry business community has recently been speaking out in a single strong voice against an aspect of RUC policy.

There are Catholic members of the business community in Derry, who are 100% sound on the national question, perfectly at ease talking in terms of "we", "us" and "our side" in conversation with unemployed Catholic teenagers, great men altogether for cursing Free State governments for selling the Northern nationalists out.

Similarly, there are Protestant members of the business community who have never been known to breathe a bad word about the bigoted history of Unionist administrations in the area.

We are not dealing here with people who come together in a wishy-washy, easy-oozy, ecumenical sort of way, but with chaps who can be seen marching on Bloody Sunday commemorations and fellows who wouldn't miss for anything the annual Apprentice Boys' strut through the city.

They've come together without any of them having to ditch or deny their deeply-felt beliefs.

Let me explain. In recent times, the RUC, displaying its usual arrogance and casual contempt for the common citizenry, blocked off two of the busiest streets in town, Spencer Road in the Waterside and Strand Road on the City side.

The purpose of the exercise, explained a spokesperson for the cops, was to prevent Provie units making bombing runs past the Spencer Road and Strand Road RUC barracks. Some of us reckoned that another part of the reason was to delay, disrupt and generally drive people to distraction in the hope that they would, as a result, crave a return to "normality" even more.

One side-effect of this measure was that the trading turnover of shops in the two streets was hit hard.

Immediately, the Chamber of Commerce and the two relevant traders' associations erupted into action. Statements were issued, interviews given, warnings sounded. Delegations scurried hither and thither to meetings with police representatives, civil servants, even John Hume himself.

Throughout, the line of the business community was consistent and hard-held – that they totally accepted the RUC's right to take measures to protect itself but totally rejected the protective measure actually taken.

The half of them who were a hundred percent sound on the national question had no difficulty at all supporting the RUC's right in this instance to fend off the Provies, while the half with the sashes under their shirts had no problem opposing the way the RUC had chosen in this instance to do it.

Thus, cross-community agreement. Their common economic interest had overridden the ideological differences between them.

So why can't the working-class come together in the same way?

One of the difficulties was highlighted last month in the latest results from the "continuous household assessment" conducted by the research unit of the North's Department of Finance. This showed that the Catholic unemployment rate is still more than twice that of the Protestant rate, and that Catholics who do have jobs are more likely than Protestants to be in low-paid, unskilled positions.

The reasons behind this phenomenon are complex. What isn't complex is the observation that this – to coin a phrase as ugly as the reality it represents – differential deprivation operates to full effect only at working-class level. Catholic lawyers, doctors, etc. are no longer excluded from areas which were once Protestant preserves. Catholic traders, hoteliers and so on aren't compelled to work to a tighter profit-margin than their Protestant counter-parts.

Business people and "professionals" in the North find it relatively easy to come together. Their ideological disagreements don't reflect significant differences in their economic well-being.

But at working-class level the differences are real, and no amount of abstract analysis or moralistic demands for a "rejection of violence" can wish this hard fact away.

It is for this reason, and not for the reasons you will find cited in the mainstream media, that despite all, the Provos have – and will continue to have – solid support.

4 May '89

IO

Bullshit Liberals And The Broadcast Ban On Sinn Féin

THE MAN FROM THE BBC was jittery. He gripped me by the shoulder. "Eamonn, if you sit at the corner diagonally across from Conor Cruise O'Brien, I'll take the chair in the middle on that side, and that way you won't have to be near Peter Robinson at all."

I'd just arrived at a classy Edinburgh hotel to have lunch with the Cruiser; the deputy leader of the Democratic Unionist Party; and David Boulton, producer of Thames Television's Gibraltar programme, *Death On The Rock,* who were to make up a panel at one of the sessions of the Edinburgh International Festival, discussing the British Government's broadcasting ban on Sinn Féin.

This was the pre-gig nosh-up, and the Beeb biggie hosting the lunch was evidently twitchy lest Robbo and myself, maddened by the sight of one another, might indulge in savagery with the fish knives.

It struck me that here we had as neat an encapsulation as you could wish for, of the way well-meaning British broadcasters see their role in Northern Ireland.

Just to unsettle the lad, Robbo and myself took to discussion of the Great Bafflement of summer '89: why did David Gower keep waving his bat like a wand outside the off-stump in such a way as to ensure that the ball, if it made contact, was certain by all the laws of ballistics to loop gently, unerringly into the cupped hands of anybody standing at first slip?

The Beeb man rallied to say how important he thought it was that British broadcasters should do everything possible to "help Ireland", to which the Cruiser responded with the splendid story of how Lenin, when informed that the Red Cross was anxious to "help the Russians", enquired: "Which Russians?"

You may have gathered from the foregoing that I found myself more at ease with the Cruiser and Robinson than with the earnest folk from British television. And ever more so, as the evening wore on.

The gig itself was staged in the church of St. Andrew and St. George, beautifully-proportioned, austerely-ornamented Church of Scotland premises, dominated by a huge wooden cross and bathed in light tinged by the filtering of high stained-glass windows, with none of the oppressive religiosity which characterises Roman Catholic or "high" Anglican churches. The four of us and session chairman Barry Cowan were ceremonially arrayed at a table covered in white altar cloth, while the pews were occupied by producers, journalists, researchers, editors and so forth from programmes and companies involved in television current affairs.

It was a serious-minded audience, genuinely concerned about the implications of the ban for coverage of Ireland, and for television journalism generally. It included a number of heavyweight operators . . . John Birt, whom I remember as a petulant upsetter of applecarts at *Weekend World* in the early '70s, now deputy director general of the BBC; Gus MacDonald, '60s revolutionary, now boss of Scottish Television; Kate Adie, media heroine of Tiananmen Square; Rowan Hand, BBC Northern Ireland's acting Head of News; Liz Forgan, Channel 4 current affairs supremo, veteran of many a run-in with the establishment and ructions galore; and a couple of hundred others of the same ilk.

If British media personnel had some convincing strategy for defeating the Tory ban, to which they proclaim passionate opposition, it would certainly emerge from this gathering.

But it didn't, for the same reason as had led our lunch host to suppose himself a peace barrier between Peter Robinson and myself.

A BBC news reporter argued that appearances on television did not confer "legitimacy" on politicians and that the ban was therefore pointless.

A fellow who's just produced an ITV documentary on the North said the ban had prevented him putting Gerry Adams under pressure over IRA "mistakes".

A senior BBC man recalled an interview with the Sinn Féin chairman of Fermanagh County Council just after the Enniskillen bombing. That interview had done Sinn Féin enormous harm. But, under the ban, he wouldn't be able to transmit such material.

A programme presenter claimed that, in the year before the ban, interviews with Sinn Féin had occupied only six minutes of airtime on ITN: so it wasn't true that the media had been giving Sinn Féin open access.

And so on and on for 90 minutes, by the end of which O'Brien, Robinson and myself had formed a weird united front against them.

What we had in common was a willingness to recognise that the Tory ban, like Section 31 in the South, does do Sinn Féin great damage. That appearing on television does confer "legitimacy" on politicians, and banishment from television illegitimacy.

For this reason, Dr. O'Brien and Mr. Robinson were in favour of the ban and I was opposed to it.

Whereas the broadcasters wanted to present themselves as opponents both of the ban and of the people the ban keeps off the airways.

They wanted to come across as radical in their willingness to take on the government in defence of free speech, while simultaneously assuring anybody who'd listen that they didn't mean any harm. By the end of 90 minutes I understood anew why the Tory establishments here and in Britain, have nothing to fear from media "progressives". I'm pleased I went to Edinburgh. I'd almost forgotten how full of bullshit liberals are.

9 September '89

11

The Odd-Balls Of Kosovo And The North

I'M SITTING IN THE PUB as per usual, this being a night of the week, when Orchid McDermott hushes the clientele to be quiet and pay heed to images of the North that come flickering over the television. Wiry youths in denims with scarves around their faces flit across the screen, stalking police jeeps with petrol bombs. Only it turns out that this isn't us after all but youths of Albanian origin expressing truculence towards Serbian domination in Kosovo, Yugoslavia.

It was by no means the first time in recent weeks that the images and issues emerging from Eastern Europe have had an eerie resemblance to home.

Perversely, there's been something almost comforting about it – as if it's a relief to have it confirmed that we are not a uniquely crazy sort of people. We need reminding of this since it's suggested so often that there's madness in the air in these parts. If there is, it's a madness that can drift like chemical contamination in the breeze across the political and ideological barriers of Europe.

The notion that there's something funny-peculiar about Northern Ireland people has been around for a long time. That loathsome old warmonger Winston Churchill wrote of the tide of World War One receding from Europe to reveal a political land-scape utterly transformed – except for the North of Ireland, where the dreary steeples of Fermanagh and Tyrone still brooded over an ancient quarrel whose integrity had survived quite intact.

These are people bewildered by their own bigotry, ran the sub-text, unlike all other Europeans in the stubbornness of their irrationality.

This line continues to run through most commentary on the North. Editorials in the Dublin dailies repeatedly make the point – France and Germany are learning to live alongside one another in decent harmony after generations of suspicion and war; could not the Protestants and Catholics of Belfast learn likewise to share the patch of land they've been born onto?

The implication is that the problem lies in the minds of those involved, and not in the material circumstances which surround them.

The attraction of this "analysis" is obvious. If all that is necessary is for people Up There to begin to behave like everybody else, there's no need for anybody Down Here to disturb the tranquillity of their lives.

But now we know, do we not, that considered in the wider European context, the people of the North aren't odd-balls at all. Dozens of other examples of communal hatreds and fears, strikingly similar to those seething just beyond the Aughnacloy checkpoint, are paraded for our perusal on the news every night. And nobody that I've read has offered as an explanation that these people are just nuts.

It's taken for granted that the Armenians and Azeris have material reasons for being at odds with one another. Likewise, Kazakhs and Ukrainians, Georgians and Ossetians, Moldavans and Russians, etc., etc.

It's widely understood that cynical manipulation of these nationalities and ethnic minorities for more than half a century by Russian overlords inevitably resulted in the intensification of each community's consciousness of its separate self.

Anybody who rejected all this out of hand and suggested instead that the various groups and communities should close their eyes and concentrate, and renounce violence, and resolve to live together in peace within existing boundaries and constitutional arrangements, would be dismissed as foolish, ignorant and unhelpful.

And yet, when it comes to the North such stuff is trotted out, masquerading as wisdom.

* * * * *

John Peel on *Desert Island Discs* choosing 'Teenage Kicks' as his favourite single of all time reminded me of a problem of street etiquette recently encountered by the astonishingly youthful ex-Undertones bass-plucker Mickey Bradley.

The meteorically-rising Radio Foyle producer/presenter is dandering through Shantallow when a land-rover crammed with cops screeches and slows to a stop just ahead of him.

As the back door bursts open a member of the RUC, armed like he is *en route* from Armagh to Armageddon, leaps out and clatters towards the man who was once the cynosure of pre-pubescent eyes the pop-world over. Meanwhile, other cops scurry for covering positions.

The copper confronts our hero right frontally and fixes him with a trained laser glare. Local folk pause in their innocent perambulations, noting that there's no end to harassment in these parts.

Copper juts his jaw out, shifts his rifle position, scans the Bradley visage even closer. "You Mickey Bradley, hi?"

The local hero allows that indeed it is so. At which the copper instantly becomes covered in layers of smiles and makes with the hand-shakes and ultra-friendly body-language as he explains that he has all The Undertones' stuff, and never missed them at the Casbah, and never could understand how come 'Julie Ocean' wasn't a smash, and why did they break up . . . and the ashen-faced supremo of the afternoon Foyle schedules becomes increasingly aware of the aforementioned local folk now regarding this scene with more seriously quizzical intent than hitherto . . .

I couldn't help noticing, as Mickey recounted this tale of street trauma to me, that he's started to grow a beard.

22 February '90

12

You Don't Have To Be Irish To Be A Victim Of British Justice

THE BIRMINGHAM SIX CAMPAIGN HAS become the most popular cause in modern Irish politics. Church persons, politicians, newspaper editors and "personalities" from all arts and parts have joined in the demand that the six men be freed.

The sheer scale of the injustice is one reason for this remarkable unanimity. In less than a year, if the men aren't released, they'll have spent a hundred years in prison between them. More important is the fact that they are obviously innocent. There is no doubt that the confessions were beaten out of them and that the forensic evidence was fraudulent.

The real reason they are kept in prison is that letting them out would be tantamount to admitting that the West Midlands police and Home Office forensic scientists were guilty of torture, perjury and conspiracy to pervert the course of justice. And that high-ranking law officers, up to and including Lord Chief Justice Lane, had been so blinded by prejudice as not to notice that this was happening – or, worse, realised that it was happening and connived at it.

Anybody who has studied the case will know that there's no way this one can be put down to honest error or to the freelance machinations of a few bent coppers and their dodgy pals.

To concede that the Six are innocent is to concede that there is something fundamentally wrong with the system of justice in Britain. This is the "appalling vista" to which Lord Denning has referred, and which the British establishment is very reluctant to face.

And it is this aspect of the case which strikes such a loud chord with nationalist opinion in Ireland.

Of course this isn't untrue. But it's not the whole truth either.

Consider, for example, the matter of Detective Chief Superintendent Graham Melvin and the Broadwater Farm Three.

Earlier this month, Melvin was found guilty of a serious disciplinary offence over his interrogation of a 13-year-old boy, Jason Hill, who had been among 350 people from the Broadwater Farm estate in North London arrested for questioning after the murder of a policeman during a riot in 1985. Melvin headed the investigation into the killing.

Jason had been questioned over three days, during which he was denied access to his parents or to a solicitor. His clothes had been taken from him, leaving him dressed only in his underpants. He eventually confessed to stabbing the policeman, PC Keith Blakelock, in the legs and chest, and named a number of others as having joined in the killing.

At the trial, almost the entirety of Jason's evidence was shown to be sheer fantasy. PC Blakelock suffered no wounds in the leg or chest, for example. The trial judge, Justice Hodgeson, expressed "amazement" that Jason had been brought to trial and told Melvin from the bench that there had been "no justification whatsoever" for his conduct of the investigation.

As a result of Melvin's conviction on disciplinary breaches, solicitors for the three men convicted of the murder – Winston Silcott, Mark Braithwaite and Engin Raghip – are demanding that the cases be re-opened. Their local MP, Bernie Grant, raised the matter in the House Of Commons – coincidentally on the day the DPP conceded that the Maguire Seven had been wrongfully convicted.

Winston Silcott, for example, presently serving 30 years, was convicted on the basis of a statement which Melvin says he made but which Silcott denied having made. The statement was: "You ain't got enough evidence. Those kids won't give evidence in court. No-one else will talk to you. You can't keep me away from them".

That was all the evidence against Silcott. (Bizarre as it might seem, for reasons to do with the arcane procedures of the British courts, the jury was not aware of the judge's chastisement of Melvin over his evidence relating to Jason Hill when they came to consider his evidence relating to Silcott.)

One obvious point emerging from this is that you don't have to be Irish to have massive wrong inflicted on you by the British system of justice. At some times, in certain circumstances, it can help. But it's not necessary.

In other words, anti-Irishness can't be what's fundamentally wrong with the British system of justice. The British system is perfectly willing to grind down its "own" people, too.

And so is the Irish system.

A small dollop of credit is due to the *Sunday Tribune* for making this point forcefully on the weekend after the Maguire case announcement, at a time when self-righteous nationalist indignation had reached one of its periodic peaks. A *Trib* editorial (June 17th) recalled the case of the phoney fingerprint.

A very senior member of the fingerprint section of the garda technical bureau identified a finger-mark found at the scene of the assassination of the British ambassador in 1976 as the print of a prominent Republican. He and a colleague insisted on the identification long after other fingerprint experts had shown that they were certainly mistaken.

It was left to two relatively junior members of the bureau to expose what was happening. But far from receiving the thanks of a grateful establishment for averting what could have been a major miscarriage of justice, the two men were victimised.

To this day there has been no proper enquiry into the affair.

It might be objected that, after all, the possible injustice was averted in this instance. Nobody was wrongly imprisoned . . .

But around the same period some people were wrongly imprisoned. Nicky Kelly, for one.

Kelly's "confession" was extracted by the same sort of methods which cause Leinster House politicians to tremble with anger when they pledge support for the Birmingham Six. But not one of the "Heavy Gang" responsible for fitting Kelly up has ever been brought to book. Not one appears to have been in any way damaged in his career. On the contrary . . .

This is in contrast to, for example, the case of Chief Supt. Melvin. Almost certainly, Melvin will merely be rapped lightly on the wrist. But in Southern Ireland, he'd have been patted on the back.

And what of the courts which accepted Kelly's confession?

In 1985, after retiring from the Supreme Court to take up a post in Europe, Chief Justice Tom O'Higgins gave as justification for keeping Kelly in jail that: "He never once said he was innocent" – his point being that Kelly had exercised his right not to go into the witness box to give sworn evidence.

In fact, he would have had no right to draw any inference as to Kelly's guilt or innocence from his failure to give evidence. Not that that mattered, because Kelly in fact had gone into the witness box and proclaimed his innocence under oath. O'Higgins had presided over two of Kelly's appeals.

The relevant point here is that if any British judge directly involved in the Birmingham case had committed a public faux pas like that, it would be recalled over and over again in the Irish media and referred to frequently by the established team of politicians who "take an interest" in the Six's campaign. It would be as famous as Denning's "appalling vista" remark.

What's dispensed in Britain is not "British justice", in the sense of representing the British people. Nor do the wigged and warped people who sit in the Four Courts represent the Irish people.

In view of all of this, those who aren't willing to take on injustice in Ireland should be circumspect about how much anger they claim to feel about the Birmingham Six.

28 June '90

13

The Guildford Four, Sallins And The Judge Who Fell Asleep And Died

I focus the optics on the goggler and behold the Recorder of London, "Sir" James Miskin, holding forth on the nuances and niceties of how the justice system works.

The Miskin remark which subsequently attracted most attention was his suggestion that the Court Of Appeal had been "mad" to order the release of the Guildford Four. The IRA, he pointed out, could "easily" have bribed policemen to falsify documents to discredit the prosecution case.

He was not, he hurried to make clear, saying that this had happened. He had no evidence pointing in any such direction. And he realised that neither the police nor the prosecution nor anybody else had ever made any such claim.

Nevertheless it could have happened. And therefore, so the implication ran, it was "mad" not to assume that it had . . .

Since the publication of this piece of addle-brained fatuity, there has been much ho-ho-ho-ing and fruity waggery in the "quality" Brit press to the effect that Miskin is a rum old buffer, another of the colourful eccentrics who enliven the English courts, a "character" . . .

In fact, he was being interviewed – by BBC's Newsdesk South-East – upon his retirement after 15 years as London's Recorder: that is, the most senior judge at the Old Bailey, responsible both for presiding over cases and for allocating cases to other courts.

And, far from his being regarded as an eccentric of any sort, it was clear from the retirement tributes that he was seen as a perfectly regular, fit person to preside over and even to epitomise the British justice system.

"A fearless advocate, strong judge and delightful companion," ruled Mr. Justice Popplewell.

Popplewell was possibly basing his opinion on his knowledge of Miskin's ideas and observations on a wide variety of relevant topics.

For example, Miskin is on record as believing that everyone who comes before the court must be guilty. He's recently been quoted saying bluntly that "If people weren't guilty, they wouldn't have been brought to trial."

How come, then, that some defendants are found not guilty?

"The long period they spend on remand gives them time to make up excuses, and then they get off."

Miskin's view that all defendants are guilty was sometimes mitigated by consideration of particular circumstances. Take the case of Nicholas Boyce, who killed his wife and cut her body up into lumps which he boiled and then dumped in rubbish bins around London.

Boyce's case came before Miskin in 1985.

"You were simply unable to get on with your wife," the delightful old cove told the killer. "*(Any)* man of reasonable self-control . . . might have done what you did."

Boyce was sent down for six years.

Miskin has never hidden his belief that the right to silence should be abolished ("What innocent person would refuse to answer whichever questions he *(sic)* was asked by the police?"); "quality control" should be exercised in the selection of juries so as to eliminate anybody under 25 or lacking an unspecified "educational qualification", or ever convicted of "anything above a parking offence"; hanging should be brought back ("Why on earth have they killed the death penalty?"); also flogging ("undoubtedly had a deterrent effect"); and so on.

Surprisingly enough, given his belief that it would be "easy" to bribe a policeman to falsify documents, he has claimed (Observer, July 29th) that in all his years on the bench he never encountered an untruthful policeman. (Maybe there's no real contradiction. The police documents he believes might have been falsified pointed to the innocence of the Four; the police evidence he believes was all genuine will have pointed to the guilt of defendants. There's a consistency here if you can think it through, along the twists and coils of the reasoning).

Richard Ingrams has remarked that Miskin's views might be accepted "with tolerant amusement" if they were heard from "a semi-literate taxi-driver".

What Mr. Ingrams has against taxi-drivers, or semi-literate persons, I wouldn't know.

Miskin's views are those of a stupid, vicious-minded bigot. Despite this, he has been regarded as a suitable person to be senior Old Bailey judge over a period of 15 years.

I say "despite this". But, of course, it's just as likely it's been because these are his views that he's been regarded as a sound man for the position.

Either way, there can be no argument but that stupidity, viciousness of mind and openly-expressed bigotry don't disqualify when it comes to allocating high positions in the administration of justice in Britain.

The Southern Irish, of course, have no reason to feel uppity about this.

For all his manifold faults, Miskin has never, as far as I can discover, displayed such contempt for "due process" as to preside over a case while asleep. Perhaps justice would have been better served had he presided over his cases while asleep, but no matter.

A penchant for presiding over cases while slumped over the bench with closed eyes, snoring and snuffling and uttering the occasional dreamy grunt, may well be a specifically Southern Irish judicial characteristic.

Perhaps the practice depends on a certainty that fellow judges, including Supreme Court judges, if asked to pronounce on the condition of the cataleptic carcass draped over the bench, will chirrup that "our colleague is in particularly effervescent form today, alert and tingling . . . see how his eyes shine . . ."

This reference here is to three separate "findings of fact" by a total of nine judges, including five judges of the Supreme Court, that Judge William O'Connor was awake and fully alert during the hearing of the Sallins mail train robbery trial in 1978, when it was plain for all to see that the man was quite incapable of staying conscious for more than a few moments at a time: Judge O'Connor died on the 65th day of the trial which was then abandoned at a cost to the State of half a million pounds.

Whatever conclusion about British justice we draw from Miskin's remarks should be applied, doubled, to Irish justice.

9 September '90

14

John Hume - The Man Who Never Says No

WEE FRANKIE MILLAR – HE'S CALLED that in the North to distinguish him from his da, the voluble Belfast City Councillor, Big Frankie – was none too impressed by John Hume's leader's address to the SDLP annual conference in Derry the weekend before last.

Wee Frankie said so in his *Irish Times* column (November 20th), which was brash and brave enough of him, seeing as how John's something of a God down there in the South.

Indeed, there was a moment back during your presidential election, when it seemed that there was even three persons in the self-same God.

During *The Late Late Show* some subversive in the audience asked Mary Robinson whether she was a socialist. But after six months on the hustings, and with all that training by the image-enhancers under her exquisitely-chosen belt, Ms. Robinson wasn't about to be discommoded.

She replied that she believed in the sort of things John Hume believes in.

Quick as a flash-in-the-pan Austin Currie rushed in to remind us that he and John had been *that* close throughout the last 20 years of Northern Troubles: so he was the accredited Hume-person in this tussle.

After which it remained only for Brian Lenihan to blink at the cameras in a show of disbelief at his adversaries' brazen audacity: hadn't he only been Minister for Foreign Affairs and Tánaiste and whatnot in a whole series of governments which had accompanied John Hume every inch of the way along the path towards justice and peace?

And then the three surrogate johns sat back and smiled at themselves.

That, in its way, was a reflection of what had left Wee Frankie frustrated with John's Derry speech.

Here's John, for example, on the question of how to get talks between the SDLP and the Unionist parties under way.

"We have offered, and offer again, to the Unionists that we sit down, without pre-conditions, to discuss the problems that we face."

Any time, any place, no advance stipulations, he stressed.

Could anything be more reasonable?

Aren't the Unionists only revealing themselves as the intransigent lot when they turn down an invite as open as that?

Well, yes. And then again, no. Or to be absolutely precise about it, maybe.

Everybody agrees that the Dublin government will have to become involved in the talks at some stage. John says this should happen after a pre-fixed interval.

The Unionists disagree. They argue that Dublin should come in as soon as the SDLP and themselves reckon that "substantial progress" has been made on "internal" Northern matters.

John says that the Unionists are imposing a pre-condition. And maybe so. If it's lit from behind and you look at it sideways, it does sort of resemble a pre-condition alright . . .

But alter the angles and it's John who is putting down the pre-condition.

Now the question of who, if anybody, is right or wrong in this matter is not as important as the question of who's buying the next round. All that's important about the pre-condition issue is the underlying truth it reveals.

Wee Frankie accidentally stumbled on this when he remarked that: "The Unionist parties have not the faintest interest in negotiations about anything which might further weaken or diminish Northern Ireland's position within the United Kingdom."

Had he ventured a little further into the semantic undergrowth, he might have stubbed his toe on the rest of the truth: which is that the SDLP has not the slightest intention of negotiating about anything which might weaken the link with Dublin, forged in the Hillsborough Pact. In other words, the Unionists and the SDLP have nothing to talk about.

But since, as "constitutional politicians", they exist to solve problems by talk, they can hardly say this out loud.

The Unionists, being awkward, unsubtle sorts, sometimes come close to blurting the truth out. They use phrases like "Ulster Says No!", "Not An Inch" and so forth, and reinforce their image as intransigent assholes.

John never says No.

John sometimes means No. But John's a positive guy.

John never says anything about the North with which a reasonable person could possibly disagree, because John never actually says anything.

Which is why all the major parties down South endorse him.

30 November '90

15

John Bruton And His Plan To Commemorate Political Violence

FOR A MAN WHO'S NAMED AFTER 16 Popes, Gregory Campbell has some sensible ideas. Gregory is not only the leader of the Democratic Unionist Party on Derry City Council but is also head honcho of Dr. Paisley's councillors right across the North.

In addition, he is one sharp cookie and could teach Fine Gael leader John Bruton a thing or three.

Mr. Bruton recently suggested that any 1916 commemoration should include the men who fell at the Somme, as well as the lads and lassies who sallied out the same year behind Pearse and Connolly.

His idea was that a joint commemoration would help reconcile the Two Traditions on this Island; or at least wouldn't alienate one of the Two Traditions in the way a "straight" Easter Rising wing-ding would be likely to; and, most importantly, would prevent the commemoration being hi-jacked by outlaw elements of the Provo variety.

Mr. Bruton went on to muse on the further possibility of a "Commemoration of the Redmondites" being organised one day soon – the Redmondites being the followers of the constitutionalist John Redmond who, in 1916, was supporting Our Boys at the Front and denouncing the long-distance ruffians for stabbing them in the back from the GPO.

One interesting thing about the GPO/Somme joint commemoration idea is that it surfaced at Derry City Council some weeks before it occurred to Mr. Bruton. It was put forward by a councillor of independent persuasion as a way of avoiding unpleasantness arising out of a Sinn Féin proposal for official

Easter Rising celebrations. Gregory was on to it like, so to speak, a shot.

The people in contemporary Ireland who most closely resemble the men and women who rose up at Easter, he pointed out, are the Provos. This seemed to Gregory, as it seems to me, so self-evidently the case that it requires a particularly perverse exercise in illogicality to deny it.

How, he wanted to know, could the forerunners of today's IRA and the forerunners of today's British Army, be jointly honoured, even as outright war between them rages on?

It was not a question of the tradition rooted in Easter Week being hijacked by the Provos, but of the Provos having good title to the tradition. To attempt to obscure that plain fact by drafting in the ghosts of those who died at the Somme was both dishonest and deeply offensive.

I've phrased it more cryptically than Gregory, who makes a fair fist at the polysyllabic polemics when he gets going. But that was his general point, which I've suggested he might usefully convey to Mr. Bruton, when he has a moment to spare from defending us all from brass money, wooden shoes, knaves, slaves and Pope Gregories.

And there's something else Mr. Bruton needs telling, although in this instance Gregory is hardly the man for the job. Many, many more Irish people died while fighting for the British Army in World War One than died in the service of Republicanism in the same period. They died for a set of ideas: even, if you like, ideals.

Those who died were overwhelmingly from the working-class and peasantry of Europe, poor people recruited on the basis of carefully stimulated patriotic fervour, or conscripted on pain of imprisonment or worse.

They, and the communities they came from, stood to gain nothing from the conflict, whatever its outcome. It was unforgivable slaughter which in the end claimed as many as 20 million lives.

Mr. Bruton has reminded us just who it was in nationalist Ireland who whooped it up for war back then, and tramped the land urging young men to go kill in the service of colonialism.

It was the Home Rule Party, the Redmondites.

That is to say, the vast bulk of the political killing, and dying, done by Irish people in 1916 was done at the urging not of physical force Republicans but of constitutional nationalists, by the fore-runners of John Bruton, not of Gerry Adams.

Both Bruton and Adams are into commemorating political violence and honouring those who perpetrated it. The differences are these.

First, Bruton prefers to commemorate the greater violence, Adams the lesser.

Second, Bruton honours those who killed and died for colonialism, Adams those who killed and died against colonialism.

* * * * *

Nothing here is intended to convey admiration for the "75th Anniversary Committee", who are organising a "Reclaim The Spirit Of Easter 1916" festival.

I have to hand a newsletter issued by this outfit wherein I read that there is a "vacuum in the national psyche which is being gradually filled with non-national ingredients. The Irish sponge is soaking up all sorts of foreign dross". The end result of this process is envisaged as the Irish becoming a "mongrel community".

By and large, the people who fought in 1916 were pious Catholic nationalists, by modern standards conservative in outlook. But I suspect quite a proportion of them would have dropped the guns and skedaddled home if it had ever occurred to them that, 75 years later, they might be "commemorated" with that sort of shite.

21 March '91

16

Patrick McLaughlin - The Strangest INLA Bomber There Never Was

"THE THING IS," THE WOMAN said, "there's people will think you're pushing it."

She's probably right. Raise another case of an Irish person wrongfully in jail in England and some will say that you're pushing it.

The woman had phoned to ask if I'd help highlight the plight of Patrick McLaughlin, 31, married, from Derry, a father of four, doing life with a 20-year minimum, for conspiracy to cause explosions in London.

"There's a bit of a campaign being launched for him," she said.

He'll need it. The way I work it out, Patrick has a maximum of two things going for him.

He's got Gareth Pierce as his solicitor. And he's innocent.

Patrick arrived in London looking for work on November 8th, 1985, a Friday. He booked into an Irish hostel in Kilburn, then registered at the local social security office.

The following Sunday at lunchtime he was drinking in a local pub with other Derry people he'd met over the weekend. Come closing time, they piled into a van with a carry-out and headed for a flat in Harlesden where they joined in what appears to have been an alcoholic hooley. At some point Patrick fell asleep, drunk.

The next morning, November 11th, an unexploded bomb was found in the street outside Chelsea Barracks. It was "claimed" by the INLA next day.

The bomb was in a holdall, packed around with bits of clothing, a sleeping bag and a bin-liner. In the side pocket of the holdall, police found the birth certificate and national insurance card of one of the men who lived at the Harlesden flat.

The five occupants of the flat were speedily picked up, and provided the police with the names of the revellers from Sunday.

Patrick McLaughlin pottered around London from his base in the hostel for another week, then returned to Derry. He was arrested at his home on December 19th. The following day, Peter O'Loughlin, also from Derry, another of the Harlesden drinkers, having heard that he was "wanted" walked into a London police station with his solicitor.

The two men were jointly charged with conspiracy to cause explosion.

Some days later, on New Year's Eve, the police discovered a van which forensic evidence suggested had been used to transport explosives.

When the case came to court the Crown offered no evidence against Peter O'Loughlin, who was immediately released – "with reluctance", commented Judge Kenneth Jones, strangely.

Three pieces of evidence were offered against Patrick: a magazine on which he had written his name and address, found in the van; a single fingerprint on the bin-liner found in the holdall; and an alleged incriminating conversation with a police officer.

He didn't deny that the magazine was his, but suggested that it might have been planted in the van by the police. It was also possible that this was the van which had carried the party-goers to Harlesden, and that he had innocently left the magazine in it.

The police produced the bin-liner in court, but were unable to locate his fingerprint on it: the presence of the fingerprint would, anyway, have proven only that he had touched the bin-liner at some point, not that he had placed it, much less a bomb, in the holdall. There were other, unidentified fingerprints on the liner.

What turned out to be crucial was an account of a conversation between Patrick and a Detective Inspector Glass, in an interview room at Wormwood Scrubs on Xmas Eve, 1985.

Inspector Glass told the court that Patrick had told him that although he had been drunk at the Harlesden flat, he did remember that a couple of people had been up all night making the bomb. Patrick denied point-blank that he had said any such thing. This was the only item in Inspector Glass' lengthy account of the conversation which Patrick repudiated. Nothing in the rest of the conversation was incriminating.

Inspector Glass' colleague, Detective Constable Kemp, who had been present throughout, could not recall Patrick making the crucial admission.

Inspector Glass, a detective of 24 years standing, agreed under cross-examination that as far as he could recall he hadn't followed up on Patrick's alleged admission by enquiring as to the identities of the all-night bomb-makers.

Nor has Patrick ever been asked since for their names or descriptions or anything else whatsoever about them.

Campaigners for Patrick say that Judge Jones in his summing up gave the jury a wholly unbalanced résumé of the evidence.

They point to a series of confusions and contradictions – the judge thought that Patrick's mother was his mother-in-law, that the Creggan Estate is in Belfast not Derry, that explosive traces had been found at the Harlesden flat, etc., etc.

The judge also said: "He agreed later to stand on an identification parade and eventually he was, late on 21st December, charged with this offence and cautioned".

This formulation ran the risk, to put it mildly, of conveying the impression that Patrick had taken part in an identification parade and had been charged as a result.

In fact, he had agreed to take part in an identification parade. But the police had not organised an identification parade. There had been no identification parade.

In the course of an 11-hour retirement, the jury returned to the court four times seeking clarification and/or guidance. On the third occasion the judge issued a "Walhein Direction". Put simply, this is an instruction to get on with it. The procedure dates from the period when unanimous decisions were needed in all cases and one eccentric might hold up a verdict indefinitely.

Patrick was found guilty on a 10-2 vote. As Judge Jones pronounced sentence two of the jurors sat sobbing.

As INLA bombers go, Patrick cut a strange figure. On arrival in London, allegedly on a secret bombing mission, he had given his correct name and home address in Derry to both the hostel in Kilburn and the social security office, then introduced himself and chatted about his background, trying to identify mutual acquaintances among people he met in pubs.

He reacted to the news that the bomb had been found by hanging around the same pubs, still using his own name.

For what it's worth, people in what might be called 'INLA circles' in Derry scoff at the notion that he was ever a member.

His appeal was thrown out in May 1988, the three appeal court judges making a great deal of the fact that when originally picked up he had lied, denying that he'd been in London at all.

"Why did he lie?" the judges asked, as they thought, meaningfully.

The question shows only that working-class Catholics from Derry and appeal court judges in England live on different planets.

The "bit of a campaign" launched for Patrick in the wake of the Birmingham Six release hasn't exactly set the world alight. Indeed, it seems to be that, far from the Six case opening the way for other, similar injustices to be exposed and remedied, there's a feeling around that that's enough righting of judicial wrongs done to Irish people for the time being.

That it's pushing it a bit to raise cases like Patrick's.

He's been in for more than five years, which is a long time to wait for somebody to take notice.

He's a third of the way along a Birmingham Six stretch. And it looks like he may have a long way to go inside yet.

4 April '91

17

There'll Be No Justice Till We Get Rid Of The Judges

JUDGES IN THE SOUTH ARE attempting to thwart justice again.

Proposals for an independent review body which would look into cases of wrongful conviction are being blocked by unnamed "senior judges". The men in wigs would prefer innocent people to suffer rather than admit that the courts had done wrong.

This should come as no surprise to regular readers of this column. I have explained more than once that the main function of the law is not to provide justice for the people but to defend the privileges of the elite.

The new review body was suggested by a committee set up by former Justice Minister Ray Burke more than two years ago. Burke didn't make this move as a result of a fit of the head-staggers which caused him suddenly to become concerned about miscarriages of justice: he was under political pressure at the time, and reckoned the pressure would be eased by the establishment of yet another committee of inquiry.

The pressure had arisen from widespread enthusiasm for the release of the Guildford Four and the Birmingham Six. The Guildford defendants had just been freed and the Birmingham Six campaign was becoming something of a national crusade.

Political leaders in Dublin had good reason to feel uneasy. Under the Coalition Government of Garret FitzGerald Irish officials, most openly in the United States, had lobbied against the Six and the Four, pleading with commentators and political figures not to back campaigns for their release.

So the government in late 1989, while ostensibly joining in jubilation over the release of Paul Hill and his three friends, and adding its voice to the swelling chorus of demands for the release of the Six, was nevertheless nervous about the implications of the affair.

Specifically, it was uncomfortable when challenged to explain how come it was (belatedly) foul-mouthing British law as inadequate when its own legal system didn't provide even the mechanism for investigating miscarriages of justice which the Six and the Four had been able to avail of. That is to say, in southern Ireland there was no way of referring back a case which had exhausted all the usual means of appeal, even when grave doubt persisted and/or new evidence had emerged.

It was in these circumstances that Burke appointed a committee, under Judge Frank Martin, to determine whether and how a means to re-open troublesome cases might be found.

The committee unveiled its findings four months later, recommending that an independent body with statutory powers should be set up; appeals to the new body would be "filtered" through the Attorney General's office, to prevent every burglar who fancied he'd been framed pursuing his case all the way.

There was nothing particularly radical in this, and Burke immediately announced that the Government fully accepted the recommendation . . . "in principle".

And that's where things still stand.

In the *Irish Times* on February 17th, Niall Kiely explained why. Put simply, the legal establishment had refused to play ball. The Attorney General of the time, John Murray, had been "less than enthusiastic". The judges had been hostile. And that was that.

This sequence of events is important for what it tells us about the judiciary, and on account of its implications for individual cases, most notably the case of Nicky Kelly.

The judges didn't like the new scheme because, so they said, it compromised the "independence" of the judicial process.

This is possibly the most pervasive and certainly the most pernicious of modern myths — that the judicial process, and the judges, are "independent".

The judiciary is the most closed and secretive of all the major institutions of society. Despite the comical catch-phrase that

"Justice must not only be done but must be seen to be done", we never actually "see" the process by which justice – or, just as often, injustice – is brought about. Judges set their faces like flint against any suggestion that their activities should be open to scrutiny, or that they themselves should be held publicly accountable for their decisions.

The judiciary has no press or PR operation through which it might relate to the general public. The very idea is unthinkable.

Very rarely – nay, never that I can recall – are there leaks from within the judiciary, in the way that there might be from the police, the military, even the Roman Catholic hierarchy.

Judges never give interviews explaining their own political, religious or philosophical views. Indeed, they frown on any suggestion that they might individually have such views – despite the statistical fact that one of the main requirements for promotion to the most senior judicial positions in the Southern State appears to be prior, prominent involvement in either Fianna Fáil or Fine Gael.

Occasionally a middle-rank judge is allowed to break ranks and talk fairly freely – like the tabloid columnist Pickles in Britain, a clown to give the circus credibility. But that's all. Currently, there's no equivalent in Ireland anyway.

And of course the notion that a judge might be slammed – or sacked! – by an elected body causes them to foam with outrage.

This total insulation of the judiciary from democracy serves a vital purpose. It means that the judges can act as a check on democracy.

It was the British judiciary which, after Bloody Sunday in Derry, provided the mechanism which enabled the State to get away with murder. Had the process of inquiry been open at any point to democratic contestation, the British authorities would have been hard-pressed to avoid murder charges against the killers.

In the same way, it was the Southern judiciary which in the '70s enabled the State to ride rough-shod over the rights of citizens and to imprison individuals the authorities wanted out of the way. Had there been any democratic restraint on the rampage of the judiciary – even from a forum as fragile in its democratic commitment as the Dáil – it's hard to believe Nicky Kelly would still be seeking vindication.

This is what lies behind the determination of the judges that there will be no independent body to examine its decision. Any scrutiny of what it gets up to would compromise it in its role as unaccountable defender of the political and economic status quo.

Once in a long while, it should be said, a senior judge does let something slip . . .

In 1985, the former Fine Gael Cabinet Minister and two-time presidential candidate Tom O'Higgins retired from the Chief Justice's position he had been rewarded with, having been allocated an even more enviable judicial position in Europe. To mark this auspicious occasion, he gave a newspaper interview in which he looked back at the high points of his career. As has been noted previously in these columns, he had something to say about the Nicky Kelly case.

O'Higgins defended the courts' performance in the Kelly affair, offering as evidence that Kelly had "never once said he was innocent". And lest it be thought that this was a mere slip of the tongue, O'Higgins repeated the claim in an RTE radio interview shortly afterwards.

Now Nicky Kelly had been afforded the luxury of two trials; the first was aborted when one of the three judges, who had been sound asleep during much of the proceedings, died. Thus Kelly pleaded innocent not once but twice.

Of course, to give O'Higgins the benefit of the doubt, he may have meant that despite these formal pleas Kelly had not gone into the witness box and said straight: "I am innocent".

But in fact Kelly had gone into the witness box, taken the oath and said straight that he was innocent. O'Higgins' claim was simply wrong.

What is interesting about this is that O'Higgins had presided over two of Kelly's appeals. Which begs the question: at those times did O'Higgins believe that Kelly had "never once said that he was innocent"?

And, since he attributed some importance to this "fact" in his defence of the way the courts had handled the case, presumably it figured also in his own thinking as he decided to dismiss Kelly's appeals?

This is the sort of question an independent review body looking into Nicky Kelly's case might usefully raise.

It is, too, the sort of question the judges don't want mentioned at all.

There'll be no justice until we are rid of the judges.

16 May '91

18

Across The Great Divide - Let's Do The Mau Mau Together

CATHOLICS ARE MUCH BETTER THAN Protestants at Mau Mauing the flak-catchers. Or, as a speaker recently put it at a conference on Community Development In Protestant Areas: "If I am to be unemployed, then let it be in the Bogside rather than Ballinamallard".

The report on the conference, held in Fermanagh in April, has just been published. It is one of the more interesting documents about the North to have been released in recent years.

Ballinamallard is a tight wee town of the Protestant persuasion, the type of place where – so the conference speaker had it – "life very much revolves around work, hence the additional trauma of joblessness".

This "additional trauma" was cited as an example of how working-class Protestants are worse off than Catholics.

Which is, on the face of it, an eccentric way to look at things. Catholics, after all, are still more than twice as likely as Protestants to be unemployed. Thus, the "additional trauma" out-of-work Prods apparently experience is an indication of Protestant advantage. To cite it as an example of disadvantage seems positively perverse.

That, understandably, had been the reaction of a number of community activists in Catholic areas with whom I've discussed the report. (Actually, the reaction is better conveyed in a remark to the effect that "They can stick their additional trauma up their Orange arses" . . .)

But the conference speaker, Paul Sweeney of the Northern Ireland Voluntary Trust, had a point which everybody who wants to see an end to the sectarian stupidity would do well to think on.

On average, working-class Protestants are better off than Catholics. That's an outrage. Nobody should be disadvantaged in society on account of the religion they were "born into".

But averages are awkward things. The fact that working-class Protestants are better off than Catholics doesn't mean that they are well-off: generally speaking, they are not (and never have been) as well-off as their counterparts in Britain, for example – one of the reasons being the tendency to compare themselves with the Catholics around them rather than with people across the water.

Thus sectarianism has worked to the disadvantage of plain Protestants, too. And still does.

Paul Sweeney illustrated another aspect of this process with an anecdote about the mild Mau-Mauing in Newry of a flak-catcher from Stormont.

The guy was a civil servant involved in promoting the ACE scheme, or "Action For Community Employment", which is, roughly speaking, the Northern equivalent of the Social Employment Scheme down South. He'd visited community groups in Ballymena and Newry, explaining that if they came up with ideas for remedying disadvantage or generally improving life in the locality, the State, under ACE, would pay (underpay, actually) the wages of workers taken on for the purpose.

The Ballymena (Protestants) organisation telephoned back to say that they might be able to use one (part-time) person in a secretarial capacity; the Newry (Catholic) crowd came on the blower requiring sanction for a hundred workers immediately, with a view to expansion later on.

In a piece of roller-coaster rapportage describing the aftermath of riots in the late '60s in the black ghettos of Los Angeles, Tom Wolfe once offered a description of just such a civil servant, sent in by Washington to buy off the bother as cheaply as possible – to catch the flak.

The brothers off the block had him sussed straight off. No point being delicate or diplomatic in their approach. The point was to hit him hard and give him grief about the sore needs of the community and the ginormous sums which must be gushed in forthwith, else there was no telling what savagery might shortly erupt: they'd Mau-Mau the man.

The reason the Protestant community has been so pathetic at the Mau-Mauing of flak-catchers has to do with the old belief that the State belongs to the Protestant community. In sociology speak, this has been a thoroughly "disempowering" notion.

Jackie Redpath of the Greater Shankill Development Association referred at the conference to the way Protestants in real need still boast of not needing help.

"After all these years on the Shankill you still hear it. You hear it most of all from men, the very last to come to an advice centre about a problem. The first thing you will hear from them is, 'I've never asked nobody for nothing'."

In contrast, the Catholics' sense of being outsiders provided a rationale for self-organisation and struggle. "We quickly learned the language of the oppressed," one community worker recalled from his days in a Catholic area.

"Credit unions, housing associations, community arts, community education initiatives were common-place. A very important aspect to all of this was that we were never really held back by fear of failure. If your initiative failed to get off the ground or was not supported, you could always blame the State. What did you expect anyway?"

The result is that, in terms of community development, Protestants are worse off than Catholics. And this at a time when Protestant workers no longer have the compensating certainty of a job.

Said another speaker: "Proverbially, Protestant community leaders will point to the Falls Road with its semblance of animation, the obvious nationalism, the revival of the Gaelic language and culture, the articulate spokesperson being chased by the world's media . . ."

They'll point to all that and, reasonably, feel . . . under-privileged.

This is something new. And because it's new, there's no telling how it will work out.

It could result in continuing, maybe even stronger, support for those who give voice to sectarian resentment and hatred of uppity Taigs. But it could also result in a reappraisal of where the Protestant working-class interest now lies in relation to the State.

Most people I know reckon that the first of these options is short odds-on to win out. Maybe so. Then again, maybe not. The point is, we don't have to "just wait and see".

What we have to do – and what those who are most gung-ho for a "united Ireland" should be especially assiduous in doing – is to maximise the chances of a break to the Left rather than to the Right. That means making space for Protestant people in the politics of opposition to the State.

Which in turn means, as a bare minimum and very much just for starters, taking the notion of "additional trauma" seriously.

Let's do the Mau Mau together.

11 July '91

19

Open For The Provos

THE INTRODUCTION OF INTERNMENT without trial 20 years ago this week was one of the key events which transformed the struggle for reform of the Northern State into a war against the State.

340 men were seized by British soldiers and RUC men, who used sledgehammers to smash into homes in Catholic areas of the North at around four in the morning on August 9th, 1971.

Unionist prime minister Brian Faulkner explained that the operation had been intended to scoop the IRA up out of the community. In fact, the IRA had nowhere near 340 members that day. Potentially, though, it had 10 times that number the day after.

To thousands of young people, the notion of marching, picketing, being civilly disobedient, in an effort to win equality of treatment within the State, now made no sense at all. And that feeling hardened into solid certainty when word filtered out over the following few days of the systematic torture – "hooding", "white noise", sleep deprivation etc. – which the interned men were suffering.

The image and thought of British soldiers doing that to captured neighbours and friends on the say-so of a Unionist politician made the blood of people in places like the Bogside boil with anger.

So, in the aftermath of internment, maybe there was never any way of avoiding outright war. Certainly, that's become the settled belief of many nationalists in the North: that – whatever about the efficacy and/or morality of the armed struggle now – at the time, there was no real alternative.

It isn't what I believed then, and I don't believe it now. But browsing through newspapers of the period a while back, I was reminded of one of the reasons the alternatives on offer seemed unreal.

I was among those who'd argued from the outset of the civil rights campaign that we should base ourselves on the working-class, not the Catholic community. This wasn't an easy argument to put across: after all, the whole point and purpose of the civil rights movement was to remedy the grievances of the Catholic community.

And no doubt those of us advocating class politics multiplied the difficulties with our own special mixture of impatience and incompetence.

But even if the odds against us had been easier, and even if we had played our political cards better, there was one enormous obstacle in our way which almost certainly would have thwarted us anyway: this was that, judging by the behaviour of its official leaders, the working-class movement was, at best, ambivalent about opposing internment in the first place.

It was one news item in particular from 1971 which reminded me of this. Dated August 13th, the piece covered the agreed minutes of a meeting at Stormont between Brian Faulkner and a delegation representing the Northern Committee of the Irish Congress of Trade Unions.

It began with a statement by the delegation that "the committee reiterated its total opposition to all forms of violence as a means to political change but expressed the view that internment and other exceptional measures should be dispensed with as soon as possible".

The minutes recorded Faulkner's assurance to the delegation that "neither (internment) nor other exceptional measures would be maintained any longer than was absolutely necessary".

The delegation then declared that "every possible step must be taken to avoid the incarceration of innocent people".

Faulkner duly reassured them that "he fully shared the committee's desire that only those who presented a real threat should be interned".

The delegation next urged that a proposed "advisory committee on internment" should be headed "by a lawyer of international repute".

Faulkner readily responded that the chairman "would (be) of unquestionable integrity and standing".

And so on. There was no straightforward statement that the trade union movement was against internment. And no trace of even a half-hint that union leaders might sanction action to bring internment to an end.

In light of all that, the suggestion that the campaign against internment should be based on class rather than creed appeared abstract, even eccentric, to any who were anxious for action. And the Republican tradition, rapidly re-emerging at the time, was holding out the promise of action.

This is not to suggest that if union leaders had organised protest strikes against internment, the IRA would have remained marginal. It is to say that there was a battle for ideas under way at the time, and that the action of union leaders in deserting the field of battle strengthened the position of armed nationalism.

There'll be thousands out in Belfast this Sunday (August 11th) to mark the internment anniversary. To the vast majority of the marchers, the trade union movement will seem utterly irrelevant – an understandable attitude, given that union leaders at times of crisis prefer to exchange diplomatic niceties with Tory politicians than to involve themselves with the working-class people who invariably bear the brunt of the crises.

* * * * *

Not a lot has changed in this regard over the intervening 10 years. A few weeks back the ICTU annual conference at Killarney discussed a modest motion from Derry Trades Council calling for a trade union "day of action" across the North in protest against the harassment of union members. It was one of those determinedly fair motions, spelling out opposition to IRA harassment, British Army and RUC harassment, Loyalist para-military harassment.

But this was much too much for the ICTU bosses who success-fully urged delegates to maintain the tradition of doing nothing that might upset the Northern powers that be.

The same suited bureaucrats were next seen in public simpering in the background as a "peace train" set off on a silly journey to London.

8 August '91

20

Ulster Says No To Sex

BIGOTS UNITED WILL BE FIELDING a full-strength team in the battle against the establishment of a Brook Advisory Centre clinic in Belfast.

The SDLP had been rather slow to line out for the fixture, seeming to confirm rumours that the party was hesitant about plunging into this particular fray. But SDLP health spokesman and prospective candidate in West Belfast, Joe Hendron, has now issued a statement warning of "the dangers posed by the Brook organisation" and pledging that the SDLP will play a full part in the fight to prevent the clinic opening.

Those who have declared against the clinic now include: the Roman Catholic church, the Free Presbyterian church, the Society for the Protection of the Unborn Child, the Orange Order, the Democratic Unionist Party, the Knights of Columbanus, the Official Unionist Party and Opus Dei.

What they all find alarming about the Brook organisation – which already operates in 17 centres in Britain – is that its clinics offer free, confidential advice to young people on all aspects of sexuality. And if there's one thing Catholic and Protestant reactionaries in the North can unite on, it's that young people mustn't be allowed to enjoy sex.

Of course, that's not how they put it. They speak about their concern for young people, about the desperate dangers young folk face in this mad, modern world, and about the duty of older, wiser elements to shield the young from ever-threatening evil.

But really, what they are against is people – and, with emphasis, young people – enjoying sex.

It is interesting that although most of the anti-Brook propaganda has focused on the fact that the clinic will give young women with unwanted pregnancies advice on all the options – including the option of abortion – all of the attacks mention contraception, too, as an equal "danger" from which young people must be protected.

The Northern secretary of SPUC, Kathleen McQuaid, for example, refers to "the disastrous consequences of contraception and abortion". Another leading campaigner, Dr. Diane Cummings of Dungannon, tells readers of the *Irish News* of her "amazement" that anyone should propose to give young people advice on contraception. In the same newspaper, Joe Hendron's statement refers to the "dangers" of an organisation "which counsels teenagers on contraception and abortion".

There is an obvious sleight of hand involved in all of this. McQuaid, Cummings and Hendron – and others who make the same argument – know that many people in Ireland find the abortion issue difficult and deeply troubling.

But they are also aware that for a great majority of these same people contraception is not a difficult or a troubling issue. Reliable contraception has long been recognised as a great boon, particularly for women. No anti-contraception campaign would be taken seriously in Ireland, North or South. Younger people would treat any such effort with derision.

Because of this, the argument against contraception tends to be hooked onto some separate argument which does have a chance of being taken seriously. But this, in turn, raises an interesting question: why do the right-wing moralists insist on targeting contraception as well as abortion in campaigns such as the push to keep the Brook clinic out of Belfast?

In the *Irish News,* Dr. Cummings advances as an argument against the proposed clinic the fact that "Brook will not actively discourage adolescents from sexual activity". She goes on to refer to "the physical, emotional and social damage and pain which has already been done by encouraging a permissive attitude to sex and by promoting the idea that the short-term pleasure of sexual gratification as an animalistic desire is somehow whole-some and healthy".

The language of the passage suggests that Dr. Cummings may have been rather atremble as she wrote it. But its meaning is clear. She is saying that sex for pleasure is animalistic, unwhole-some, unhealthy: the corollary being that sex is only moral when undertaken for the purpose of pro-creation . . .

That – the belief that all sex is immoral which doesn't have pro-creation as its purpose – is why she, and others who think like her, regard contraception as a twin-evil with abortion, to be opposed by any means necessary.

Dr. Cummings and her co-thinkers are, of course, well aware too, that young people in droves are drifting away from the shadow of their sort of thinking. Hence the urgency of their efforts to keep the Brook Centre out of Belfast.

Hence the urgent need, too, of a counter-campaign to ensure that the Eastern Health Board, which has promised to part-fund the clinic, stands firm against them.

My own impression is that most young people in the North, Catholic and Protestant, don't differ much from their contempo-raries in the South or across the water in their attitude to sex. They want an active sex life, they want to enjoy it, they don't want to have to worry about pregnancy, VD or AIDS – a natural, healthy attitude.

At bottom, the argument has to do with democracy and free-dom, with the rights of the individual.

Mainstream political commentators both North and South prat-tle on endlessly about the need for "both sides" in the North to come together, by which they invariably mean that "the constitu-tional parties" should come to an agreement on how to run the place.

Well, the controversy over the Brook clinic gives us a glimpse of what sort of place this would be. The major constitutional parties are fully united on this one. No need for compromise or change of attitude or for talks of any kind.

They are all against young people enjoying their sexuality. Quite likely, they all suffer terrible headaches at the thought of teenagers giving and taking pleasure with people they care for. They are sour-minded, mean-spirited and frightened of the future.

What the North needs is a coming together *against* what these people represent.

5 September '91

21

Street Legal (Or How Henry Hugh-Smith Lost His Arm For England)

I'VE SPENT MOST OF THE last few months working on a book and a television documentary about Bloody Sunday – the day in Derry 20 years ago when 14 anti-internment marchers were shot dead by British paratroopers. It's been something of a bad trip, reliving it all over such a long period.

The most important thing I discovered didn't have to do with why the Paras opened fire, or exactly what orders had been given to them, but with the attitude which resulted in a massacre.

On March 18th, 1972, the day before the last sitting of the tribunal, in the course of after-dinner talk in the officers' mess at Ballykelly Barracks, where the Army lawyers had accommodation, members of the team remarked that although they'd been dealing with the streets of the Bogside at the Tribunal every day as if they had intimate knowledge of the area, none of them had ever actually been there.

This gave rise to a conversation which, fuelled by generous amounts of alcohol, ended in a suggestion from a Green Jacket officer that the party should set out for the Bogside there and then, for a "tour". And thus it was that a merry contingent of legal bods, dressed in borrowed combat gear, was dropped off at Stanley's Walk in the heart of the Bogside "no-go" area. The idea was that the party, accompanied by a Green Jacket patrol, would proceed through Stanley's Walk and then along Lecky Road and past the killing area in Rossville Street before being picked up again at William Street by the armoured transport in which they had travelled to Derry.

Within moments of being deposited in the area, the party became involved in an exchange of shots with the Provisional IRA. The circumstances of the encounter remain unclear, but I was able to establish that three of the British party, including one of the lawyers, were seriously injured.

Two Provos were killed by British gunfire the same night, although this may well have been in a related, later incident. What is certain is that at one point the British Army's solicitor, Henry Hugh-Smyth, found himself standing in the middle of the road firing a sterling sub-machine gun in a somewhat wild manner. He was hit in the wrist by a .45 bullet, probably fired from a Thompson. The bullet passed up through his lower arm to exit at the elbow.

The party was quickly evacuated from the area by armoured vehicles. Hugh-Smyth was taken to Altnagelvin Hospital and operated on immediately. His lower arm was amputated. Hugh-Smyth was later equerry (a form of high-class flunky) to the Duke of Edinburgh, and then military attaché at the British Embassy in Kenya, where he tended to respond vaguely to sympathetic enquiries about the missing arm.

A portrait of Hugh-Smyth sitting on the pavement against the wall of the gasyard on the Lecky Road in the Bogside waiting for evacuation, his sterling sub-machine gun resting against the wall beside him, hangs in the Green Jackets' regimental museum in Winchester.

Two other members of the British legal team visited Hugh-Smyth in Altnagelvin on the morning of the 14th, before rushing to Coleraine where, whey-faced and hungover, they managed to maintain a semblance of composure through the final day of the proceedings.

None of this has ever appeared in print before – in itself a tribute to the professionalism of the British military in managing the news. But it tells us a great deal about how the people of the Bogside were regarded by those who had come among us to represent the law.

One member of the jolly party is now a judge.

31 January '92

22

Kicking Against The Ticks

ALMOST CERTAINLY, THE BITTEREST battle in the UK general election a couple of weeks back was the contest between the SDLP and Sinn Féin for nationalist support in the North.

There were, of course, other areas of razor-edged rivalry. I'm told that in some constituencies the Labour versus Nationalist fight across in Scotland reminded the more grizzled class of commentator of the great days of the Glasgow razor-gangs.

But the encounter between the SDLP and Sinn Féin happened

for the most part within a community which already felt itself somewhat embattled. It was fought at close quarters, hand-to-hand stuff all the way, and there are still blotches of battle on the pavements and walls.

I say happened for the most part within the Catholic community: the anger of Sinn Féiners has focused particularly on the result in West Belfast, and on the fact that Joe Hendron found his majority outside the community, pulling in 3,000 votes from the Shankill to more than off-set Adams' lead on the Falls.

They "stole" the seat with the help of votes from the Shankill, claim Sinn Féin people. The nationalists of west Belfast have been "cheated" . . . I heard this over and over again, in the street or the pub, in the days after the election. And I understood what the Sinn Féiners meant.

My own political cradle was rocked by the late Eddie McAteer, for many years the leader of the Nationalist Party, and Stormont MP for Foyle. Eddie was a benign, silver-haired figure with a dry wit, a disarmingly droll turn of phrase and an invincible belief in the inevitability of a united Ireland, if only the nationalist people kept faith.

I remember sitting on a high stool (I was maybe ten, eleven years old) in a requisitioned billiards hall in Chamberlain Street, addressing envelopes for the dispatch of Mr. McAteer's election manifesto to voters. On the electoral register, every voter's name was marked with either a green tick or an orange tick. And it was terrific to turn over a page and find a preponderance of orange.

Such pages were easily completed. Orange ticks denoted Protestants, and Mr. McAteer didn't seek Protestant support.

It wasn't that he was a bigot, in the sense of consciously hating people. It was just that he accepted absolutely the identification of "Catholic" with "Nationalist" and "Protestant" with "Unionist", and saw no point in asking Protestants to vote, as it were, against themselves.

My father, who prided himself, rightly, on being a "Labour man", chastised me for colluding with Green Tories and told me that eventually I'd see sense. But it wasn't until too late, for that election anyway, that the light of political understanding broke through.

On polling day, loudspeaker cars advertising Mr. McAteer's wares patrolled Rosville Street where we lived, repeating a single phrase over and over again: "The Protestants in Belmont are all voting for McGonigle, the Protestants in Belmont are all voting for McGonigle".

The references were to a Protestant enclave in the overwhelmingly Catholic Foyle, and to Stephen McGonigle, the regular, lamb-to-the-slaughter Labour candidate in the constituency. The message was that if the Catholics of the Bogside didn't give McAteer a big enough majority to outweigh Protestant Belmont, the seat might be "stolen".

I still recall the simple thought that something didn't hang together here . . . how could we make a big deal of Protestants voting for the other guy when we had deliberately chosen not to ask them to vote for us? That thought marked the close of my nationalist career.

Joe Hendron isn't an exact equivalent of Stephen McGonigle. For all the weaknesses of Mr. McGonigle's style of socialism – he was a standard-issue trade union official propounding a moderate, Labourite message, about as left-wing, if the phrase has any meaning in this context, as Ruairi Quinn – he did at least talk of class, and of the stupidity of voting according to religious beliefs.

The SDLP is different. While pitching for Protestant votes in West Belfast, elsewhere the party ran as sectarian a campaign as we have witnessed anywhere in the North in the last 20 years. In Mid-Ulster, for example, a series of huge, and hugely expensive, newspaper adverts spelled out that 16,000 nationalists – i.e. Catholics – had failed to vote last time round. If half of these now turned out and supported SDLP man Denis Haughey, the seat could be won from the Democratic Unionist, William McCrea.

Here, as in South Down, Armagh and Fermanagh-South Tyrone, the SDLP's strategy was to mobilise the Catholics, not to put on offer a programme to attract voters from across the divide.

The pitch of SDLP canvassers in these constituencies scarcely overlapped at all with the arguments against Sinn Féin you hear from SDLPers on radio or television. There was little talk of the immorality of violence, or of the SDLP's wizardry in attracting "inward investment", or of the prospects for constitutional advance. The argument was that anyone who voted for Sinn Féin was "splitting the (Catholic) vote" and thereby risking a Unionist victory.

Sinn Féin, of course, where the figures gave them the opportunity, pitched their appeal along similar lines. In other words, the strategy of both parties was to mobilise the Catholics as a voting bloc. Just like Eddie McAteer all those years ago.

This is one of the reasons for the Sinn Féiners' chagrin. They know that Hendron's campaign was based on the same considerations of sectarian arithmetic which led the SDLP elsewhere to take a totally different tack. They know that the approach of the party was determined, constituency by constituency, by the numbers of green and orange ticks which might be marked on the register.

23 April '92

23

I Know It's Not Only Rock 'N' Roll - And I Like It

IN THE BEGINNING THERE WAS Jay Hawkins. At least that was its beginning for me, standing on a chair with my ear glued to the radio in the kitchen in Rossville Street between half-eight and nine on a Saturday night.

There had been shivery omens and intimations of magic for

some time: LaVern Baker with 'Tweedle Dee', Lloyd Price with 'Lawdy Miss Clawdy', and even, for one night only as I remember, S.G. Reeder's (Esquirita) 'Green Door', later ripped off and ruined by Jim Lowe (a disc jockey for chrissakes!), not to mention dickie-bowed boys' club cabaret-hero and bore Frankie Vaughan, and, eventually, Shakin' Stevens.

Anyway. There'd already been all these small detonations of delirium, seeming to suggest that something wicked was this way coming. I could hardly wait. And then, one night, it announced its arrival with Screaming Jay's 'I Put A Spell On You', which nobody since has ever had the nerve to try to emulate.

I positively guarantee that if 'I Put A Spell On You' by Screaming Jay Hawkins was re-released right now it would not only be a smash but would zap sudden light into the area of the psychic outback where rock's well-spring seethes and bubbles with new beginnings.

It was a screeching, snarling, grunting, groaning, panting, ranting, raving number, full of frantic threat and trembling danger, dripping with sweet and viscous sex, all swathed in an atmosphere of voodoo.

It came through on two oh eight metres on the medium waveband . . . "This is Alan Freed, America's King of Rock'n'Roll, bringing you the latest! and greatest! from stateside USA, on . . . ROCK'N'ROLL JAMBOREE!" I had to stand on the chair with my ear flat against the speaker because our radio was on a shelf maybe six feet up, and on a Saturday night the kitchen was always full of uncles and so forth who had called in to talk and none of them wanted to hear this stuff.

Later on, my father got tired of people asking whether there wasn't a wee want in the son on a chair in the kitchen cheek-to-cheek with the wireless, and him and Jim Sharkey from across the street rigged me up this contraption from a gramophone speaker and a roll of wire so I could listen to Luxembourg up in the attic, though the radio downstairs was turned off! This was amazing.

This was a secret world you could wire into, full of black people bawling out of them saying it was OK to feel free.

I think *Rock Around The Clock* happened around the same time. Alan Freed was in that too, playing himself, but mostly it was a Bill Haley movie. I saw it again a couple of years back and as movies go it's indisputably crap. But that didn't matter. It was the first-ever rock movie, and it was causing riots.

* * * * *

Word arrived long before the movie did, that across in England wherever it was shown, teenagers – now there's a word when you're 11, going on 12! – were ripping up the cinema seats and breaking shop windows. Driven mad by the beat, it was said. There was a very serious discussion in Derry, with the bigots of both council and Catholic Church involved, about whether it would be wise to let this intoxication loose, to rip through the younger local citizenry. Eventually it was decided to allow the movie in because at least it wasn't dirty.

It arrived in the City Cinema in William Street, where the first night passed off peacefully enough, although there were reports of girls screaming and yelling. But at about 10.30 on the following night, serious jiving began in the streets as soon as the crowds poured out. Some said sagely that the street-jivers couldn't have been driven mad by the beat because most of them hadn't actually been in to see the film at all, but had gathered outside in the hope of rascality.

The whole, heaving, jumping, jiving mob came round the corner of William Street and into our street, about a thousand in all and right in the middle of them Frankie Roddy and Teresa Shields, whom people kept a space clear for because they were the best dancers in Derry, probably in Ireland, maybe even on earth. Frankie was a champion Irish dancer, you understand, and today takes the ceol agus rince classes in the Pilot's Row Community Centre, which is built exactly opposite where our house used to be and where the *Rock Around The Clock* dance riot stopped for an exhibition, strobe-lit by the flickers of the street-lamp at Maggie Friel's chip shop.

The entire district assembled to spectate, frowning or frolick-

ing, tutt-tutting or tee-heeing according to taste, while close supporters of the participants clapped in wild unison and roared out
repeated choruses of the anthem, *"One, two, three o'clock, four
o'clock ROCK, five, six, seven o'clock, eight o'clock ROCK!"*.

Then the cops came to break it up, greeted by a flurry of brick-
bats and milk bottles, nothing vicious by the standards of later
years, and short-lived, but enough to establish that we, too, had
had a rock'n'roll riot. I must say I was very relieved. I'd been nervous we might let everybody down. A couple of years further
along there was a priest called Flanagan standing stiffly at the
altar in the chapel in St. Columb's telling us that Catholic boys
should steer clear of rock 'n' roll music and most especially of
Elvis Presley, who was evil. Elvis Presley, he went on, was singing
these songs for one reason only – to madden young women so he
might rape them. All his band and all others associated with him
were drug addicts and sexual degenerates.

I butted in from a back pew that he shouldn't be saying these
things about Elvis when Elvis wasn't present to defend himself.
What else could I do, with my sideburns nearly grown? They
turfed me out of the chapel and I've hardly been back since.

To be into rock, and especially to be a fan of Elvis', was to associate with a very bad element indeed. There was a couple of
boarders at St. Columb's who were heavy into Elvis and who'd
have been expelled – this is not a joke – if they'd been caught listening to him or reading about him. I used to bring in copies of
the *NME* – I had it on order with Melican's of Creggan Hill, 6d a
time, Keith Foydyce did the singles – and pass it on to them in
the bogs where one would shove it down the trousers while the
other kept lookout. We'd walk back to class, swaggering our
secret, agreeing with one another that Pat Boone was shite.

Rock 'n' roll was outlaw music. If it didn't help bind us together
in our outlawry, and put anger and fear into people who had
power over us, what was the point?

The conventional wisdom has it that this is entirely a genera-
tional thing, but it's not. Not entirely. There's a shimmer of
politics in it, too.

Who is there now to put the fear of no-god into the class which rules Ireland?

19 June '92

24

"I Was A Teenage Undertone." Mickey Bradley Lived To Tell The Tale

THE CURRENT AMERICAN EDITION OF *Spin* magazine carries a feature headed "WE WANT YOU BACK!", listing "10 bands that should reform". It's an idiosyncratic selection, including the naff (Haircut 100), the daft (The Bangles) and the suddenly chic (Abba), as well as the properly predictable, (The Jam, Madness, The Smiths, The Faces).

And then there's The Undertones. Mickey Bradley is chuffed to be told of his old bands inclusion. "That's kinda nice," he says.

Life itself is kinda nice for Mickey now. He's a BBC radio producer stationed at Foyle in Derry, which he agrees is an interesting job and middling well-paid, and he'd never have gotten it if he hadn't been an Undertone. "When I came back home Joe Mahon (then station manager) offered me a weekly programme, largely on the strength of having been in the band, and things went on from there."

It helps that Derry's a small place with a big opinion of itself. Joe, a former teacher, had known Mickey at school, and knew, too, that having an Undertone on the station's regular schedule would go down well with the local listenership.

Mickey's moved on since. "The first year I worked here people knew me as Mickey Bradley who used to be in the Undertones. But now people who know me think of me as Mickey Bradley from Radio Foyle. I like it like that." Still, he's perfectly at ease talking back over the band's glory days, no sighs of if-only or sour complaint. "It was great," he says. "I wouldn't have missed it for anything. And I got out in my mid-20s – just the right time."

The break-up of the band in 1983 was undramatic, apt for an outfit which had never made a big deal about delivering the sharpest songs, the sweetest sound to soar up from the North since Van Morrison.

"We had just finished a grumpy photo session with a photographer in Sweden when Feargal said, 'I don't want to do this anymore'. Straight off a couple of the others said, 'Neither do I'. And then we all said. 'We might as well call it a day, then'. And that was it really."

Feargal Sharkey, whose shimmering, artfully innocent voice had been the key to the band's exact expression of vulnerable, adolescent sophistication, thus became both the last to join and the first to leave.

"The rest of us never actually joined," says Mickey. "Like, I was the lead guitarist at one time. Then I was the rhythm guitarist. But that was all in the head, before we had any instruments or could play anything. I was just 'in the band'.

"I was in because I was a friend of Vincent O'Neill, a brother of John and Damien's. Vincent was in the band as well until his mother said he was to concentrate on his O-levels. Vincent was the Pete Best of The Undertones. There was a fellow called Dennis Boyle, too, and a few others. There must have been nine or 10 in the band at one time, sitting around in O'Neill's house listening to records and talking. We were the non-rioting youth of Derry, apart from Sharkey who used to riot the odd time. I believe the statute of limitations is up on that.

"Derry was a really grim place at the time. There wasn't even a pizza place to hang around in, and you couldn't get into the pubs at 15. Rioting or music was all there was. John dictated a lot of the taste because he was the oldest, plus he had an order for the

NME with Barr's shop on the Lone Moor Road.

"John was into The Beatles, the Stones, The Faces, Lindisfarne for some unknown reason, and bands like Little Feat and a lot of blues stuff. We were really just farting about, but we began to think of ourselves as fairly knowledgeable sort of people. We were in that period of saying that everything in the charts is crap."

In the middle of 1975 the O'Neills' father guaranteed the gang a Provident loan in his front room. They sped to a music shop in Raphoe in Donegal and came back with a drum-kit, guitars and amps and set about rehearsals in a shed behind a house in Creggan Street owned by Mrs. Simms who had coached new recruit Feargal to a number of triumphs in the boys' soprano class at the Derry Feis.

"There had been a wee dog living in the shed but we let it out and covered the walls with blankets to deaden the sound. It was great. We were there for two years, beginning to do Chuck Berry, Fleetwood Mac, Cream. We had five or six songs by the time we got the first gig, in a scout hall in the Creggan. I think Feargal was some sort of scout leader at the time. A couple of months after that we did our first 'big' gig, at St. Joseph's School, and then a couple of youth clubs. That brought us into the summer of '76."

Which was the summer when the Sex Pistols came with weeping pustules and snarling cysts to make people with pimples and sensitivity feel defiantly OK about themselves. In Derry, as every-where, teen groups gathered in soundproof huts to share the secrets of Sid, and of Iggy and the Stooges and Eddie And The Hot Rods and so forth.

"There was nothing for us to fit into in Derry," says Bradley. "When I read how other bands came together, they always seem to come out of a music scene, in Manchester, New York or wher-ever, which other bands were part of too. But there was nothing in Derry except heavy metal cover bands like King Rat and Toejam, plus a few people from pop bands who had a separate existence in rock.

"I remember Garvan O'Doherty who ran the music in five pubs

coming up to audition us in the shed, and we failed miserably. We were paying £3 a week each to be in the band and we needed the extra from pub gigs to help pay off the loan. But there was nowhere for us." However, the world, or at least the top of the Carlisle Road, beckoned at the beginning of 1977 when they discovered the only pub in town willing to give them house-room – The Casbah.

The Casbah had a reputation in Derry as a dive. It was said to be a haunt for prostitutes and drug-dealers, and many a parent would have balked at their adolescent offspring entering, much less frequenting it. But Bradley's father had worked in the Casbah during the war and reckoned, rightly, that it wasn't nearly as interestingly bad as it was painted. Not that it was painted.

The Casbah was a classic pub-rock venue where the walls wept more profusely than the fabled gable in Jerusalem and the bogs easily bested Jeyes Fluid to waft pungently through the premises. The Undertones played it every Friday or Saturday night through 1977 and into 1978.

"It was just wonderful," recalls Bradley. "We were beginning to write for ourselves. We could write a song and try it out there, change it or drop it, whatever. We had to battle other bands for the spot, Toejam, Jack Tar and so forth, civil enough people but rotten bands. We had a core of maybe 15 or 20 people, friends and fans, who were always there, and then the numbers who were always there began to build up. We were getting a sort of following, and became established in the venue."

Naturally, inevitably, in a grim and ground-down city, they attracted resentment.

"We had to pass the bottom of William Street with guitars and stuff on the way back from the Casbah, and you'd be taking your life in your hands. You'd get jumped. There were always a fair few of us together and we never came to serious harm. But there were fellows who used to hate Feargal. He was the singer and easily identified, but as well as that Feargal was never very subtle. He was arrogant about himself, about who he was. Fair play to him, but it wasn't appreciated by everybody. But mostly it was good being in a band. You knew that a lot of people would have liked to be in a band. And we had a regular gig every week."

Contrary to the standard account, The Undertones weren't discovered by some well-sussed individual happening upon them at the Casbah.

"Ah no, what happened was that one of the fellows Feargal was working with at Radio Rentals was a brother of a fellow called Bernard McAneaney, who knew Terri Hooley in Belfast. We went into a little four-track at Magee College and put down a couple of songs which Bernard then took up and gave to Terri. I don't think Terri was really into it, but we got Bernard to plague him until he put it out."

The songs included 'Teenage Kicks' and 'Get Over You', the first two singles. ('Teenage Kicks' was released on an EP. The Undertones thus became the first band ever to make their chart debut with an EP. This fact is enshrined in the Guinness Book Of Records and, Bradley is confident, will eventually figure in television pop quizzes).

"We re-recorded 'Teenage Kicks' for release by Terri on Good Vibrations, and that's what Sire picked up on. Feargal and myself went over to London to sign the contract and when we arrived back at the Waterside Station, Billy Doherty's parents were waiting for us and took us up to Feargal's parents. We hadn't exactly told them what we were up to."

Eventually, parental approval having been forthcoming, word got out that The Undertones from the Casbah had signed a record deal. In Derry in the late '70s this was an event.

"There was a certain amount of pride involved. I remember Arthur Duffy from the *Derry Journal* telling us, 'Sorry about the coverage', because he reckoned the *Journal* hadn't been giving enough space to a band that now had a record deal. Obviously, outside of our consciousness people in Derry were talking about us.

"And then we got onto *Top Of The Pops* with the first single. We played the Rocking Chair in Waterloo Street the night after that and the place was just incredibly packed. People began asking us to play benefits and telling us they were fans. But the best thing about it was that we were able to stop working. We put the money from Sire into the band and paid ourselves £30 a week. For Feargal, that was a wage-cut of £5 a week. Then we had to go on a tour supporting the Rezillos – this was November 1978 – which was the first time away for some of us and we fought all the time.

"We got a fellow from Derry with a Transit van to drive us. There were no seats or anything. It was terrible. Luckily, the Rezillos broke up after three dates and we were reprieved. The great thing was, we were back in Derry doing nothing and still getting paid! You could get up on a Monday morning with no work to go to and still get paid! We'd sit around in O'Neill's all day talking about songs and then go out for a dander around Derry.

"Of course, we had to get the songs together and so on. That was like doing homework. I remember sitting on the bed with an exercise book trying to write a verse I'd promised to come up with and thinking, 'Feargal has to sing this tomorrow. I'm never going to get it done'. I remember doing the second verse of 'My Perfect Cousin' like that." (Thus was produced the perfect – in a Derry accent – rhyme. *"My perfect cousin/Whatever I like he does-n't"*).

For the next few years, Bradley, Sharkey, John O'Neill (rhythm guitar), brother Damien (lead guitar) and Billy Doherty (drums) took off for tours, recording sessions, television shows and so forth but still based themselves in Derry.

"It wasn't 'We want to stay close to our roots' or any of that crap," Mickey explains. "It was just that Derry was where we lived and naturally we came back here when we didn't have to be away working. But it was unprofessional in terms of our careers. It definitely damaged us in that respect.

"I think Feargal and Damien really wanted to go for the big time, go on long tours, try to break America. I mean, we all liked being successful, but at the same time most of us knew it was all a bit of a cod. We used to buy the *NME* and scan the pages for the capital 'U' when we saw ourselves in there, we thought that was great. "Nowadays, a capital U means U2, but then it was The

Undertones. And the records were getting into the charts, which was great, and being played. My father was in his 50s, a ceili band man, but he started to listen to John Peel!

"At that stage we could have had a shot at it. I think if we'd really tried we could have cracked America. But we'd have had to cut the links here, and that would have been a terrible, self-destructive thing to do. The bottom line on it was that 60 percent of the band had no ambition.

"We knew that we weren't going to be The Beatles and get hugely rich. And there was always a barrier between us and the people we dealt with in the business. There were people working for us, going out and plugging our records, and we would hardly give them the time of day. We'd be nice to individuals but anybody with a silk bomber jacket, we'd laugh at them behind their backs. And there was a lot of permed hairstyles around too. It wasn't for us. We felt, 'Well, we've got the power to go back to Derry, so why not?'

"By this stage we were earning £100 a week – and we could still just get up and wander around Derry! And you'd notice people out of the corner of your eye recognising you. It was really great, absolutely brilliant. Our halcyon days."

When the band broke up Billy Doherty moved straight back to Derry. He now works at the United Technologies factory in the Bogside and plays with former HOT PRESS/Carling Band of the Year The Carrelines. They've just completed their own 16-track studio, aiming at the quality demo market.

Bradley and Damien O'Neill went to London and got together the short-lived, uncharismatically-named Eleven, which lasted a few gigs. "When you've been in a good band and then in a bad band, you know there's nothing great about just being in a band," muses Bradley now. He came back to Derry, gravitating towards Radio Foyle. Damien then joined John in That Petrol Emotion, who have a new album scheduled for release early next year. The Petrols' future depends on it. John left the Petrols and is now a key figure back in Derry in the North West Musicians Collective.

Feargal launched a solo career and brushed briefly against

super-stardom with a UK number one, 'A Good Heart'. But it hasn't worked out. He's now setting himself up in business in London.

"It's not too bad," says Bradley. "None of us had ended up an actual casualty. We didn't all end up in the Edgar Broughton Band. You don't read that the bass player was last heard of playing with Chris Rea.

"We have our recording contracts back from EMI, and Damien, John and myself have the song rights through West Bank Songs. I still get cheques for about £90 a quarter and occasional publishing money. And if they ever use one of our songs to sell Levis, the money will come to us directly.

"I was in America last year producing editions of the Gerry Anderson Show," (that's Gerry Anderson, bass player of Toejam) "and we called into Tower Records on Sunset Strip. So naturally I had to look under 'U', and sure enough, there was a CD of Peel Sessions by The Undertones. It's not great. I played it once. But I liked finding it there.

"It was great being in The Undertones. It was about the best thing that could have happened to us at that age.

"Mind you, it would have been better being in The Beatles."

2 July '92

25

The Violent Death Of Jimmy Browne

THE RECENT DEATH IN BELFAST of my friend Jimmy Browne set me thinking, again, about nationalism.

Jimmy would have been very quick to tell you that while he was a nationalist in the sense of having been born into the Lower Falls, he was in no sense a nationalist with regard to political ideas. I had an argument or two with him in my time about that.

You are a nationalist, Jimmy, I'd tell him. You are forever talking about "the nationalist people" and the need for "national independence" and all that sort of stuff. And he'd argue that, no, he was a socialist, a socialist Republican, following the political line of James Connolly.

The second-last time I saw him, in Dawson Street in Dublin a few months ago, I quoted a ballad of Connolly's to him, to make a point about socialism and nationalism being irreconcilably different. Jimmy responded that this hadn't kept Connolly out of the GPO.

The song was the one with a refrain running, *"Whoop it up for liberty/Shouts the patriot who can't stand socialism"* . . . (I may not have the words exact, but I have the rhythm of the sentiment right).

But Jimmy had a point about the GPO. Connolly hadn't been consistent in following the line of the lyric through. In 1916, isolated and under all sorts of pressure, he had joined up with just the sort of Patriots he had scorned in his song, to help launch the Rising.

It wasn't so much that he'd buckled under the pressures or trimmed his politics to slot into prevailing opinion. More important was the fact that, for the most part, the Patriots he made common cause with at Easter didn't slag off socialism at all, but argued rather that the time wasn't right to talk of such things.

Later, afterwards, they'd say, once freedom is won, then the question of how our Irish society is to be organised will come onto the agenda. The Irish people themselves, free of outside interference, will be in a position to make their own choices.

And then, the canny Patriots would proclaim, they themselves, bet your life on it, would be fiercely on the same side as the socialists. But . . .one step at a time.

The pertinent point was that the Patriots who couldn't stand socialism now, pledged themselves to stand up for socialism later. Which eased the way for socialists to accept that their differences with the Patriots could safely, for the time being, be put to one side.

This was the argument Jimmy had been referring to, which propelled Connolly into alliance with the Patriots and which has locked his legacy into the nationalist version of Irish history ever since.

No doubt it was an enticing argument at the time, when the prospects seemed dim for socialists operating on their own and nationalism seemed vibrant and in tune with the tenor of the times. It's an enticing argument still, in certain circumstances.

It occurs to me that few readers in the South are likely to see any of this as directly relevant to their own lives. Like, when's the last time you heard a heated discussion of whether the fight against unemployment, poverty and injustice must wait until Ireland is united?

Not yesterday, I'd risk a speculative pound sterling against a devalued punt, or the day before either.

But it's different up here, as so many things are. The question whether it's futile to fight for social justice while partition still exists is of obvious relevance to the view you might take of the Republican armed struggle.

If it is the case that there's no point trying to end injustice until the border has been erased, then there is a strong argument for the Republican campaign to speed the day when we can set

about the creation of a just and decent way of life; and for unit-
ing in the meantime with all and any who are willing to exert
themselves against partition, matteradamn what they think about
socialised medicine, a minimum wage, free education, Church-
State relations, whatever.

This perspective makes particular sense if you come from, say,
the Lower Falls and were 12 or 13 when the world around you
went clean mad in the late '60s. Against that dark background it
might seem blindingly obvious that the State itself, with all its
agents and institutions, was the main source of the ills which
crowded in on your community. It might seem clear and simple
that the only hope for a better future lay in mobilising the community against the State, and that the community, thus
embattled, was entitled to accept support from any quarter at all,
in the unequal conflict forced upon it.

You could be the sort of socialist who's able to argue the toss
about Stalin and Trotsky on the Chinese Revolution and to
juggle dialectics with the best of them and still believe it right to
line up with deep-green Fianna Fáilers and disgruntled Knights
of Columbanus to push forward the fight against partition . . . on
the principle that, until that fight is won, no other can sensibly
be waged. You could even cite Connolly's association with the
GPO Patriots in support of this proposition, as Jimmy did.

It is a perspective which assumes that at this stage the nationalist community is the subject of the revolutionary process – from
which it follows that the "other" community is best ignored, or
neutralised . . . or fought against.

This is the political context in which members of the IPLO, of
which Jimmy was a leading member, describing themselves as
socialist, believing themselves to be socialists, have carried out
sectarian attacks, most recently killing an elderly, inoffensive
Protestant man last May, as he sat drinking a quiet pint in a pub.

It is not a particularly bizarre or distorted context, as far as
Irish political history is concerned. It is an authentic, if extreme,
expression of mundane nationalist ideology, its extremity result-
ing naturally from the circumstances of the North over the last
25 years.

This, it's worth re-stressing, is not to say that nationalism tends inevitably towards sectarian violence. It's to say that there's nothing in or about nationalism to rule sectarian violence out, no necessary contradiction between the one and the other. And if socialist ideas are submerged within nationalism, then the contradiction which does exist between socialism and sectarian violence is hidden away, and ceases to matter.

This is important – at least it's important to me – because although Jimmy Browne was associated with and involved in atrocious things, and I knew him to be, I never thought him as an atrocious person. He was a bright, chirpy, amiable companion, with a sharp political intelligence and a genuine idealism in the sense that he sought little for himself from his pursuit of political objectives. And his political objectives, of and in themselves, were entirely decent and supportable.

But put at the service of a project which Jimmy believed had to be completed before they could ever be realised, they became their own negation, were transmuted into evil.

Nationalism, the political ideology which in one form or another is casually, unconsciously accepted by the great majority of the people on this island, and which, because of the continuing oppression of the Catholics, is to be found in its most intense form in the North, was the necessary catalyst for this terrible moral alchemy.

I saw Jimmy a couple of weeks back for what turned out to be the last time, in a pub in Derry. He was sitting near the door and we mumbled an awkward greeting to one another as I paused and then passed along the bar to join a mutual friend. "Did you see Jimmy, were you talking to him?" he asked, and I said, No, that I'd thought of sitting down with him, having a bit of a chat, but in the end had thought better of it.

I had in mind that the IPLO's sectarian pub killing in Belfast, the worst thing they'd ever done, had happened in the meantime, and any talk Jimmy and I would have had would have developed into the sort of political argument which it is better not to have in a pub in the North on a crowded Saturday night.

I know what you mean, said Dan. There's far too many people

want to blast Jimmy.

A while later Jimmy came by on his way to the toilet and we shared a bit of the banter people use to fill the space left when nobody wants to talk of the things on their minds.

We spoke last week about whether we should go up to Belfast for the funeral and decided against it, because your attendance could easily be misinterpreted, politically. I wasn't sure that this was the right thing to do. And I'm still not sure now.

10 September '92

26

It Started On The Hate Hate Show!

"I'VE GONE BEYOND HATE ALRIGHT," one of our more talented local cynics muttered behind me at the *Beyond Hate* conference in Derry a couple of weeks back. "I'm into loathing and detestation now."

He'd been sorely provoked. Ms Mairéad Maguire, formerly Corrigan, joint winner of a Nobel Prize in 1976 for her leadership of the Peace People, had just delivered herself of a long sing-song testimony featuring a mini-series of maxims ("There are no innocent victims, we are all guilty") which came close to accepting full, personal responsibility for all 3,000-plus deaths over the past 23 years.

Ms Maguire seemed to feel all the better for having rid herself of this awesome guilt, and glistened with goodness as she wafted her way out of the Guildhall.

I don't mean to sneer. Well, actually, I suppose I do, but not at

Mairéad Maguire personally. Her contribution harmonised well enough with the general theme of the conference.

The title Beyond Hate implies that the conflict in the North – and, by extension, presumably all communal or ethnic conflicts – is caused by hate; that those involved are morally or spiritually or psychologically damaged in such a way as to fill them with intense negative feelings for whatever group they are at daggers-drawn with.

The priority in the search for a solution, it follows, lies in finding a way of transcending or extirpating or somehow otherwise getting beyond this hatred, in reaching and changing the individuals involved in the conflict, rather than trying to change the social and political circumstances surrounding and underlying it.

This search for solutions through "saving" individuals tends to be conducted in a gossamer language of beautiful fragility which is pleasant and even pleasurable to contemplate but which, if prodded for meaning, tends to disintegrate delicately into a sad nothingness.

"People with power must redefine their dominance," a normally-sound, public-sector trade unionist summed up her contribution. "The tragedy of hatred is that it darkens the soul," observed a specialist in "cultural relations".

Delegates in public session thanked one another "for your wisdom" or "for your humility and humanity" or expressed a willingness to discuss disagreement not by offering to "take that up later", much less to "come outside and settle it", but rather by promising to "take further counsel on that with you".

It was in this context that a reference by Martin McGuinness to "the Christian way to proceed" – he was proposing that the conference express sympathy with the relatives of all the dead of the Troubles – while it may not have been the formulation which came to him most naturally, probably wasn't pure humbug either, but just the striking of a nicely-pitched political note. (For a number of foreign delegates their "discovery" of Martin McGuinness was among the high-points of their time in Derry).

The "religious" atmosphere was most striking at a widely-reported meeting where Brian Keenan, Terry Waite, Terry

Anderson and Fr. Lawrence Jenco recounted their most inward and intimate memories of being hostages in Beirut, and of finding a new sort of freedom by cleansing themselves of hatred for their captors. "That," said the local press corps' leading grouch, George Jackson, "was one of the greatest evenings of my life."

And quite likely so, poor chap. But the very uniqueness, the particularity and sheer intensity of the experience the hostages were drawing on, also emphasised the gap between the concerns of the conference and the day-to-day reality of conflict outside.

People in the North – or in South Africa, Palestine, Central America, Bosnia, wherever – do not experience oppression in conditions of total isolation but, on the contrary, as members of the group by which they define themselves.

Of course, they can, as individuals, cast off their oppression, but only by detaching themselves, either physically or emotionally, from the group and thereby leaving, not ending, the oppression. The oppression itself cannot be ended by individuals finding a means of transforming themselves.

All of this helps explain why the *Beyond Hate* conference was welcomed so heartily by the political and religious establishments – opened by Noddy Robinson, closed by John Hume, graced by "both bishops", addressed by British minister Richard Needham etc. It offered no challenge to any of the institutions these people represent. Its challenge was directed at people who, more or less by definition, are not represented by, or in, the mainstream institutions of society at all.

This isn't begrudgery from the margins. At the end of three days in the elegantly-dressed Guildhall, delegates with more direct experience of conflict than most were coming to the same conclusion.

Ivana Balen, an anti-war activist from Belgrade, conceded that the conference had been useful from the point of view of making contacts but regarded its central themes as "not directly relevant".

She complained, too, that "All these people would be willing to hug me to show that they have no hatred. But when many of them look at me they look right through me – because I am not important, I am not a man, I am not a Nobel Prize winner".

That, on its own, tells you more than all the rapportage, including my own, has been able to convey.

17 October '92

27

RTE - The Station That Likes To Be Bound And Gagged

Is RTE THE ONLY BROADCASTING organisation in the world which has ever gone to court to ask for stronger censorship?

Censorship controls on RTE were loosened on July 31st last when Justice Rory O'Hanlon declared in the High Court that there had been no need for the station to suppress a number of recorded interviews with Finglas man Larry O'Toole. The interviews, in the summer of 1990, had concerned a strike at the Gateaux bakery: as a member of the national executive of the Bakery Union and chairman of the Gateaux strike committee, Larry O'Toole had been the obvious man to go to, to get the workers' point of view.

But after transmitting one interview, RTE discovered that Mr. O'Toole was a member of Sinn Féin. So none of a number of subsequent interviews was transmitted.

Mr. O'Toole took a dim view of this, got himself a lawyer and headed for the courts. His argument was that RTE had no right to declare him a banned person since the relevant regulation (a Ministerial Order based on Section 31 of the Broadcasting Act) didn't say that members of Sinn Féin should be kept off the airwaves, only people acting as spokespersons or representatives of Sinn Féin.

He hadn't been speaking for Sinn Féin, but for his union and the Gateaux strike committee. There had been no mention whatever of Sinn Féin in any of the interviews. RTE had gone beyond what was required of it under law.

Justice O'Hanlon not only upheld this particular argument, but went on to find in favour of Mr. O'Toole on two other grounds as well.

He ruled that RTE's obligation under Section 18 of the Broadcasting Act – to observe rules of fairness and impartiality – was breached by the exclusion of members of a legal organisation.

Additionally, declared the Justice, to ban interviews with people on the grounds of their membership of an organisation which wasn't itself banned appeared to be in conflict with the guarantees of freedom of expression set out in Article 40 of the Constitution. That is, RTE's interpretation of Section 31 was not only plain wrong but quite likely unconstitutional as well.

Taken in its entirety, the judgement, while loosening the constraints of censorship, wasn't a ringing affirmation of radical values. It didn't come within shouting distance of the First Amendment to the US constitution, for instance. The ban on the direct expression of Sinn Féin views remains. But under the ruling people who are members of Sinn Féin can now be interviewed on air as long as they are not speaking for the Sinn Féin party.

Now since RTE management had been on record as opposing Section 31 censorship as a matter of general principle, a naive soul might have expected a statement from that quarter welcoming the judgement but pointing out that there was still some way to go before celebration was in order. But not a bit of it. Indeed, quite the contrary. What RTE management did was to announce that it would be appealing to the Supreme Court against Justice O'Hanlon's decision.

"No compromise! Restore full censorship!", lawyers "earning" a king's ransom of licence-payers' money will cry in the Supreme

Court . . .

The RTE argument is set out in the formal notice of appeal. It makes interesting reading for what it reveals about the political motivation of the supposedly non-partisan station management.

In essence, RTE argues that Sinn Féin does not exist other than as a front organisation for the IRA; moreover, that as a matter of party policy the activities of all Sinn Féin members on all issues are intended primarily to advance the cause of the IRA; that, therefore, Larry O'Toole's "involvement in the national executive of the bakery union and chairmanship of the strike committee of the Gateaux workers was (or could reasonably be construed to be) a practical articulation of such policy on behalf of Sinn Féin".

That is to say: given the alleged relationship between Sinn Féin and the IRA, Larry O'Toole, being a member of Sinn Féin, was acting for the IRA in explaining the case of Gateaux workers against the closure of their factory.

A "Staff Information Bulletin" issued at Montrose and designed to win the support of RTE Employees for the management position went further and, quoting inaccurately and out of context from a Supreme Court judgement in 1982, plainly implied that Larry O'Toole, in the course of the contentious interviews, was acting for "an evil and dangerous organisation whose object was to overthrow the State and its institutions".

RTE's "reasoning" here is not so much faulty as Fawlty: even if the characterisation of the relationship between Sinn Féin and the IRA were accurate, it does not follow that any individual member of Sinn Féin is necessarily speaking for Sinn Féin, much less for the IRA, when talking about an issue (redundancies in a north Dublin bakery) which has nothing to do with Sinn Féin and/or the IRA.

RTE adds that it "is committed to obedience to the law of the land". But right now the law of the land in relation to this matter is as the High Court has laid it down: the station may not exclude people from the airwaves solely on the grounds that they are members of Sinn Féin.

If RTE felt the slightest itch of discomfort at being subjected to political censorship, it would have welcomed the O'Hanlon judgement, as far as it went, and proceeded to use its small new measure of freedom to give its audience a fuller and fairer account of what's happening around them. But instead, RTE rushes in a state of some intellectual disarray back to the courts to plead for tighter restrictions to be re-imposed.

There can be no journalistic defence of the course RTE has embarked on. The station management has a clear political motivation for what it is doing. It has decided that there is no need for a pretence of impartiality when dealing with certain groups, or members of certain groups.

It is RTE – not the Government, not the courts – which, presuming somehow to act on behalf of "society", is now taking the initiative to decide which groups are to be regarded in this context as reprehensible and beyond the broadcasting pale.

A line has been crossed here over which no journalist should permit his or her management to go without making the most vigorous protest. It is disappointing then, although, sadly, not surprising, that by and large RTE journalists have accepted what's happening with a shrug of indifference.

21 Oct '92

28

Working For The Clampdown

RTE, ALREADY BELIEVED TO BE the only broadcasting organisation in the world to campaign for political censorship, is now asking the courts to extend censorship of the station into non-political areas.

This is clear from an affidavit sworn by the RTE sales and marketing director as part of the station's defence in a case arising out of the banning from the airwaves of an advert for a book of short stories by Sinn Féin president Gerry Adams.

The collection, *The Street And Other Stories,* was published by Brandon Books earlier this year. It marked an adequate if not an outstanding debut by Adams as a story-teller. It's in colloquial vein, lightly humorous, sentimental, full of standard-issue nostalgia. He's no Frank O'Connor, but he's not Jeffrey Archer either.

A commercial promoting the book, submitted to RTE by Brandon, was rejected on the ground that it contravened the Broadcasting Act. Brandon has appealed this decision to the courts: the sales and marketing man's affidavit contains the substance of the station's defence.

It says: "In the current context, the publication of a book of short stories can only have (or be reasonably be construed as having) the aim of portraying Mr Adams as an artist, as a man of culture and a man who writes stories which by their nature are intended to enable the reader to identify with both the story and, by inference, the writer and the message he conveys.

"The tenor of the advertising script proposed by the applicant further indicates the 'colloquial' nature of this attempt to promote Mr. Adams . . .

"It is RTE's view that any attempt by Mr. Adams or any person on his behalf to promote his own image in this way can only

have as its aim the advancement of the cause of Sinn Féin . . .
That organisation is committed to dismantling the organs of state
by violence and unconstitutional methods (and that) the broadcasting of any material of this nature emanating from Mr. Adams
(or any material whatsoever) must be reasonably regarded as
either likely to promote or to incite crime."

This seems to me an astonishing document to have been issued
in the name of the national broadcasting station. It suggests that
RTE has set its face against any depiction of Gerry Adams as anything other than a monster. This goes a long way beyond what
the existing censorship laws have been generally understood to
require of RTE: it indicates that RTE has formulated its own
political agenda with regard to the North and to Sinn Féin and is
operating according to this agenda.

Even if RTE is right about the nature of the Sinn Féin party –
which is not to concede that RTE has any right to make a judgement on such a matter in the first place – it is entering very
dangerous territory when it resolves to present Sinn Féin leaders
as having no existence other than in relation to their membership of the party.

* * * * *

In pursuit of its political agenda, the national broadcasting station is systematically depriving a category of people of their
humanity. It is saying not just that this category of people
behaves in a beastly way, but that people in this category are
themselves beasts and nothing other than beasts.

I do not believe that RTE can cite any other broadcasting organisation in the world – in the former Stalinist states of Eastern
Europe, in apartheid South Africa, in any Latin American military dictatorship: anywhere – which has publicly and explicitly
announced a policy devised by itself of demonising a group of
people in this manner.

The editor of the *Irish News,* Nick Garbutt, whose own relationship with Sinn Féin leaders is one of studied, mutual hostility,
was not, I believe, going too far when he accused RTE (*Irish*

News, October 26th) of "contributing to a climate of opinion whereby *(Gerry Adams')* murder would be welcomed".

Why have we heard nothing from RTE journalists about any of this?

18 November '92

29

The IRA Blow Jim Collet's Legs Away

AT THE TIME OF WRITING the word from Altnagelvin Hospital is that Jim Collet probably won't make it. He's classified as "critical" and on a life-support machine, and one of the medical staff says that they "don't anticipate any improvement".

Even if he were to defy the odds and come through, what sort of life would he have? Apart from both his legs having been amputated at the knee, he's suffering spasms strongly suggestive of brain damage.

Many say openly that they hope he dies, not out of compassion but because they want him dead.

Collet, 36, suffered his injuries in an IRA punishment shooting on December 8th. The IRA unit used a sledgehammer to smash into his home in Drumleck Drive in the Shantallow Estate at the northern edge of the city. He was seized and forced to lie on the ground. An IRA man then shot him at point-blank range in the back of both knees with a .38 Magnum.

It is not uncommon for the IRA to phone an ambulance to attend to the victim of a punishment shooting, the "sentence" having been carried out and deemed sufficient. But not in this case.

The bones, tendons, muscles and arteries of both legs shattered, he crawled to the front door, gushing blood and screaming and hammering for help. By the time neighbours were alerted and an ambulance summoned he was almost drained of blood. His heart stopped beating on the way to Altnagelvin. It was presumably at this point that lack of oxygen began killing his brain cells.

In a statement admitting the shooting, the IRA accused Collet of having sexually abused a large number of young children in the nearby Carnhill Estate. Investigation in the area confirms that this was true.

Almost all the children came from the square in Carnhill where the Collet children lived with their mother and her partner: she left Collet nine years ago after suffering numerous, serious physical assaults, as well as extreme mental pressure. However, Collet frequently visited his children in Carnhill.

Many of the families on the square are distraught and have asked the Housing Executive to transfer them to other areas. Others are demanding that Ms. Collet and her family move out, saying that their presence is a constant reminder of the damaging ordeal their children have been through.

Support for the IRA action is not restricted to the families affected, but is widespread in Catholic areas where Collet is spoken of as a sordid and malignant presence whose removal from the community, no matter by what means, is seen as wholly welcome. His involvement with the INLA in the '70s, when he served two and a half years on a conspiracy charge, and a suspended sentence for "flashing" at children in 1982, as well as various stories of casual street violence, are cited as examples of irreformable evil.

Collet's wife stood by him in 1982, when he agreed to undergo a programme of psychiatric treatment at Gransha mental hospital. He had begun beating her up within six months of their marriage. She hoped that medical treatment might "straighten him out". However, he dropped out of the hospital programme after a month. There appears to have been no monitoring of his progress, or lack of it, by any agency of the court.

The marital relationship effectively ended at that point, although the couple stayed together until late 1983 when, after a particularly savage beating which left Ms. Collet hospitalised with a fractured skull, she walked out, taking her three children.

She comes across now as a remarkable woman, forthright and articulate and handling her horrendous situation with courage and poise. She recognises that many of the families around her live in constant horror of what happened and that it is inevitable that their feelings are focused on her household. But the contentment of her family, too, has been shredded.

The story became public at the beginning of the month when – the local air already thick with rumour – local people approached the *Derry Journal,* which led its December 4th edition with the headline "RUC PROBE CARNHILL SEX ABUSE". At the same time, Sinn Féin's office on the nearby Racecourse Road was being "inundated" with demands that something direct and drastic be done.

The Republican Movement became central to the case because of the problem of policing areas like Carnhill and Shantallow. Voting figures suggest that the majority of people here are in the SDLP, not the Sinn Féin camp. But since there is, effectively, no support at all for the RUC, even SDLP supporters tend to look to the IRA when they want direct action against local criminality.

Given the fervour with which local people were demanding action against Collet, it is fair to say that the Republican Movement would likely have lost support in the area had its armed wing not exacted retribution.

Cases like Collet's are tailor-made for the Provos, horror and fear translating into acceptance of the IRA as enforcer of a communal morality – the targeting of drug dealers falls into the same category – and providing the organisation with a role which is separate from and largely independent of its armed struggle to force a British withdrawal. This has obvious attractions, particularly if the efficacy of the armed struggle as a means of advancing the nationalist cause generally is being called into question.

The IRA base of support is thus broadened, and the possibility opened up of a long-term role, irrespective of how it fares in its main task. Depending on outlook, the IRA's enthusiastic readiness to handle such morally-charged issues is either sordid opportunism or common political sense.

The vast majority of adults in Carnhill and Shantallow will have had friends, neighbours, relatives – people they knew well – killed in the Troubles, commonly by the security forces against whom there is no legal redress. The idea of responding with direct, extreme violence against anyone perceived as threatening the community has come to seem "natural", a first option rather than a last resort.

In a discussion of the story between journalists involved in its coverage, the opinion that "The IRA should have blown his brains out first day", while by no means unanimous, wasn't regarded as outrageous either. A respected woman trade union activist calmly declared that "I'd have had no problem if they'd tortured him first".

Nobody will ever know the exact process by which the demons came to scream in the darkness of his mind, but in some sense, to some extent, they must have derived from the society which surrounded him. He was one of 13 children, of whom two died in infancy, born in Springtown Camp, a scatter of corrugated tin huts on the outskirts of Derry which had been abandoned by US forces at the end of World War II, and then squatted by families from the Bogside who had been denied homes because they were Catholics.

He spent his formative years in deep poverty and in appallingly crowded conditions – the hut had two makeshift bedrooms – in a community over which a church which identified sexuality with sinfulness exercised ideological hegemony and in a wider society which every day, in a thousand subtle ways, invited even the most powerless of young males to believe that it was through sex that they could experience the feeling of power.

He was severely abused physically as a child and quite possibly – because it was a common occurrence – sexually as well.

It is fully understandable that those close to the children he devastated should feel neither pity nor regret nor any soft emotion at the fate which has befallen him.

But while the society which made him remains essentially intact, there will always be cruelty visited on the vulnerable. Incipient corruption will forever beleaguer the innocence of children.

As it is, the families face into Christmas living in a nightmare beyond their worst imagining, from which they fear they may never wake up. Many of the children, including Collet's own, have been damaged by adult evil for the rest of their days, even before some of them are of the age to stop believing in Santa.

If there is a fragment of hope gleaming anywhere amid the moral debris, it lies in those like Ms. Collet who manage somehow to transcend their own suffering, to feel for everybody and blame nobody, and to believe in a better day coming.

"Everybody in this story is a victim," she says.

December '92

30

Paddy Hill: The Cry Of The Innocent

"THAT," I SAID TO PADDY Hill of the Birmingham Six as he stepped down from the platform after the Bloody Sunday rally at Free Derry Corner on the Sunday before last, "was a bit of a performance".

"Ach," he replied, "I just thought I'd give them stick. I'm fucking fed up listening to the fucking bastards."

Paddy had just delivered a raging rodomontade against the British State and all its symbols and institutions. His furious philippic against the British Army in particular – "send them home in fucking boxes" – immediately sparked calls from predictable sources for him to be prosecuted for incitement to violence.

The way I see it, anybody who spends sixteen and a half years in prison for something he didn't do has a licence to say anything which comes into his head about the State which did it to him.

This is especially so when he didn't spend sixteen and a half years inside as a result of some terrible cock-up or series of mistakes but because representatives of the State beat the shit out of him to make him "confess", assembled fraudulent evidence to back the "confession" up, and then went into a witness box and solemnly took an oath to tell the truth and proceeded – 15 of them at an absolute minimum – to swear deliberate lies against him.

Different people handle these things differently. Some develop an indomitable serenity which seems to fireproof them against bitterness. Johnny Walker, another of the Birmingham Six, ambles around Derry now like he's the most contented man in town, which maybe he is. He has a smile more or less permanently draped over his face and he calls everybody even a couple of years younger than him "daughter" or "son".

"How about you, son?," he says to me when I bump into him in a pub, "C'mere and have a drink, and how's the work going, and the wain keeping?", and all that.

"I'm really worried about Paddy Hill," he confided a few months ago. "He's full of bitterness and it's not doing him any good. He'll have to find a way of getting rid of it."

In the Dungloe a few hours after the rally, Johnny told me he was headed for Finland during the week. "There's some human rights crowd invited me out last year and they're bringing me out again." He leaned forward. "Do you know about the saunas there? . . ."

Even as you read this it's even money Johnny is in a sauna in Finland, having a mighty time. I told him to have a swish of the pine twigs for me.

Judy Ward told me, as we had a cup of coffee before the march, that she still wakes up every morning and thinks, first thing: "Wow! This is great". Like Johnny, she seems ahead of the game.

"I enjoy everything I do," she says. "I was in Oxford Street before Christmas and everything I looked at, I thought, Oh, that's beautiful. People were looking at me and thinking I must be some sort of poor idiot. But I was just so happy. I'm a happy person."

Her happiness, and her apparent lack of rancour, is remarkable, near-enough miraculous. Any reading of her case leaves no room for even a faint shadow of doubt that the cops who charged her with the M62 coach bombing in 1974 knew at the time that she was innocent. They knew it to be a flat fact that she had been 200 miles away when the bomb was planted.

But they fitted her up anyway, concocted a "confession" (actually, three separate "confessions" each in stark contradiction of the others), manufactured evidence to confirm the "confession" and mounted a massive perjury operation to destroy her life at her trial.

She had a hard time in jail for a few years, but then somehow summoned up a calmness which sustained her.

Or maybe appearances are deceptive. Maybe deep down somewhere beneath the unruffled surface there's a rage boiling in her, and in Johnny. But I don't think so. I think that the two of them have beaten the bastards, that they've come out the other side in good shape, that they've won.

But for Paddy Hill it's still a struggle. The only way he was able to handle what happened to him was to fight every inch of the way. Johnny Walker has described to me the procedure Paddy adopted on each of his many transfers from prison to prison.

"He'd be taken before the governor or assistant governor as per usual and have the rules read out, and he'd interrupt. 'No, those rules don't apply to me, they are for people who are guilty of crimes, I'm an innocent man, I won't allow you to tell me what to do . . .' And he followed that through, implacable and recalcitrant, refusing for sixteen and a half years to do what he was told.

As a result, he spent a total of seven years in solitary. Seven years, like from here right into the next century, talking to the wall.

And he won't let go of the experience, because it won't let go of him. Not one of the State operators who did it to him has been made amenable for it. Not the cops, nor the lawyers, the judges or forensic scientists who fitted him up, treated him as rubbish to be got rid of in the interests of tidiness, as a person of no worth whatsoever, not one of them has been brought to book, required to shoulder any blame or show sign of remorse.

It's as if they've had in the end to admit that they were wrong but still aren't expected to feel bad on account of it, or to see it as a serious sort of thing.

They're still treating him like shit, and he's not the sort of fellow who can put something like that out of his mind. He's maybe the angriest man I've ever met.

I chaired a workshop he spoke at – on *The Corruption Of The British Judiciary* – at the Pilot's Row community centre on the day before the march, which wasn't easy. Three times I tried to bring proceedings to a close and three times Paddy remembered something else which he couldn't leave unsaid and snatched the mike.

"The three fellows in for the Carl Bridgewater murder, do something for them. Jimmy Robinson was in a cell beside me. And Vincent Hickey and Michael Hickey, totally innocent men. The bastard who turned down their appeal was one of the prosecutors at our trial . . .

"Winston Silcott, he's not Irish. Remember that, you don't have to be Irish, they do it to their own working-class people as well. The working-class people of England, they're the salt of the earth. And the Cardiff Three. It's all the same thing.

"There's hundreds of totally innocent people in jail, hundreds and hundreds who have nobody to fight for them. The slime, the fuckers, the rotten lousy bastards who run everything, they don't give a toss for anybody or anything, don't care a fuck who's innocent or guilty . . . you keep fighting, all of you, keep fighting . . ."

None of the reports of his speech at Free Derry Corner mentioned that he spoke twice. His second speech was a more or less exact repetition of the first. He grabbed the mike back and said it all again, as if uncertain that he'd gotten across what he felt, furiously determined to make sure. And thus it came out in the way that it did.

The DUP head honcho in these parts, Gregory Campbell, wondered aloud on Radio Foyle the following day whether, in view of his remarks about sending soldiers home in coffins, we could really be sure Paddy hadn't been a Birmingham bomber all along.

Shite, Gregory. The things that he said don't lead to doubt about Paddy Hill's innocence. Quite the opposite. It's his innocence he was screaming out.

10 February '93

31

The Provos And Peace: What Did Jimmy Die For Then?

COULD PEACE IN THE NORTH be delayed by somebody demanding to know why Jimmy had died? John Hume raised this moot point in the course of an interview in an American magazine a couple of months back.

Asked what he made of reports that the Provos were moving towards an end to their armed struggle, the ex-Maynooth man mused that if the Provo leaders ever gathered their people together and announced the terms of a peace pact, it's near certain somebody would immediately leap up at the back of the hall and yell: "What did Jimmy die for, then?"

Hume has a point here. At a gathering in Derry a couple of

weeks back I listened to a senior member of Sinn Féin giving a formal presentation of how his party saw peace coming about and my immediate thought was: "Well, what did Jimmy – and Paddy and Sheena and Mairead and Seamus and all the others on the long, ever-lengthening list – what did they die for, then?".

The Sinn Féin man wanted the Irish Government to become "pro-active" in pursuing an end to partition, and to pressurise the British Government to work toward the same end. He envisaged a role in this process for the European Community and for the United Nations and, possibly, for the "peace envoy" to the North promised by Bill Clinton during his presidential campaign.

The settlement which might emerge would acknowledge the separate identity of the Protestant Community in the North.

What struck me was how little the Provos are looking for. Reynolds, Major, Clinton, the president of the Bundesbank, the UN Security Council . . . the one thing we can say for certain about all and any of these is that they're not going to alter the balance of power, here, there or anywhere else, in favour of people at the bottom of the pile.

On the contrary, the record shows they stand firm on the side of privilege and power.

There is no mention any more in the rhetoric of the Provos of a transformation in society, or of the world, or this little patch of it, being turned upside-down, no suggestion of a different way of living for the mass of the people, no hint of – whisper it – revolution. What we heard in Derry, which Gerry Adams has since repeated, was eminently respectable, strictly constitutional, carefully deferential towards the existing order of things.

The message to the ruling classes of Britain, Southern Ireland, anywhere, was: we can be trusted, we mean you no harm, give us the chance and we'll become one of you . . .

In fairness, the Provos aren't alone among armed struggle groups in the rush for respectability. The spectacle of the much-diminished figure of Nelson Mandela pleading for support for a "power-sharing" arrangement with the racist de Klerk; the eagerness of Arafat to convince the American administration that

Western interests would be served by the creation of Palestinian "bantustans" on the West Bank and Gaza; the abject obeisance of the Sandinista leadership towards US power as they try to manoeuvre themselves back into office: all this, and more, tells us that the strategy of "national liberation" doesn't mean much any longer to anybody in Ireland apart from the poorer elements among the Catholics in the North. For practical purposes, militant Irish Republicanism is now a specifically Northern phenomenon, reflecting the experience of this one community – of oppression, humiliation and violence at the hands of the State.

As a result, the Provos are deeply rooted within the Catholic ghettos, but trapped too, unable to engender support from outside, with no hope of recruiting any section of the Protestant community or any substantial sector in the South. And the Northern Catholics – Sinn Féiners, SDLP supporters, high-rise flats, leafy suburbs, farmers, the lot – constitute less than 15% of the Irish population.

They can't win on their own. At this stage, all that the Provos can do on behalf of the Northern Catholics is to try to advance their interests in a way which doesn't contradict the interests of any powerful group or institution which might be persuaded to help. For as long as politics in the North are seen in terms of community – rather than, for example, class – there's no other way out.

It's of necessity, therefore, that demands are modified and moderated until, at last, armed anti-imperialists find themselves urging Bill Clinton to take time off from bombing Iraq to appoint a "peace envoy" to Ireland.

The settlement which might arise from all this would, obviously, be a modest affair. Capitalist property relations, it goes without saying, would be most tenderly preserved. The rich would stay rich, the poor poor.

British interests in Ireland wouldn't be trampled on; how could they be when it's envisaged the British Government would play a prominent part in brokering the deal?

There'd even be a continuing link with the UK in the Provos' perspective: acknowledging the separate identity of the

Protestant community can mean nothing else.

For this they've fought a war for more than 20 years, suffered 100,000 years in jail, seen ten men waste themselves away in the Long Kesh hunger strike, their own community brutalised, harassed, treated like dirt day in and day out, all that and much more?

They regard the settlement they are now outlining as a sufficient return on this massive investment of pain?

Even if they're successful in all that they now seek, somebody will want to know: "What did Jimmy die for, then?" And there'll be no adequate answer.

There's nothing to be won by nationalism now that's worth anybody's death.

Provo supporters who are out to win a world without ugliness and oppression should turn away from the problem of how to advance nationalist politics and ponder the possibility that it's precisely in the politics of nationalism that their problem resides.

25 Feb '93

32

There's A Soldier Looking At Me As I Write

On RTE's *Sunday Show* recently my occasional friend Jeananne Crowley told me that it was IRA violence which had led to peace campaigners at the rally outside the GPO last month spitting on pictures of children killed by British forces in the North.

Her argument was that the Provo campaign has angered and

alienated Southern people to such an extent that they loathe any-body and anything which, even by implication, might be taken as offering the Provos support.

This notion is sometimes taken farther, many commentators suggesting that the IRA has not only alienated Southerners from themselves and their Sinn Féin associates, but has also killed the South's ardour for a united Ireland. In a recent column Garret FitzGerald referred to "the alienating impact of [IRA] violence . . . upon the willingness of many people in this State to contem-plate any increased practical involvement with the people of Northern Ireland".

There may be truth in all this, but it's not the whole truth.

The reason the mass of people in the South have become iffy about the North is that they see no connection between what's happening in their own lives and what's happening up here.

If the IRA were to win and the British were to get out it's hard to see what benefits would shower down on the plain people of the 26 Counties.

Joblessness, poverty, poor housing, a ramshackle health service, lack of access to decent education – you name it, a British with-drawal from the North would do nothing to ease it.

Or, to come at the issue from another direction: when people in Southern Ireland band together to fight for a better life, it isn't the British presence in the North which they come up against. If the workers at Digital in Galway were to take my advice and occupy the factory to prevent machinery and jobs being shifted out, it would be the Irish courts and the forces of the Irish State which would confront them.

When Southern citizens organise against the oppression of women, demanding equal job opportunities, access to abortion or whatever, the British presence in the North doesn't stand in their way, but the Catholic Church and conservative nationalism.

In the South, for most people, on almost any issue you men-tion, the trajectory of any effort to make life a bit better doesn't lead towards confrontation with Britain.

If this were not so, if people in the South were to encounter the British presence in the North as an obstacle when they set about remedying practical problems, then even those appalled and sickened by IRA violence might nonetheless continue to associate themselves with the IRA's purpose. This is the way things work up here.

There's a British soldier looking at me as I write. Or at least there might well be. It makes sense for me to assume that there is. The window of the room that I work in is directly overlooked by a British Army "security observation tower", built high above the Bogside on Derry's Walls. The tower is packed with surveillance equipment, enabling British Army observers to watch and listen to as much of what happens in this area as state-of-the-art technology can contrive.

From the back of our house we can see an even more imposing surveillance tower, recently erected at the Rosemount RUC station. The two towers now dominate the district. Most of the time we don't think much about them.

When I drift down to the pub in an hour or two there's a chance I'll be stopped by some edgy lad with a Brummie or Cockney accent, made to produce proof of identity and to say where I'm coming from and going to, and perhaps turn out my pockets. And I'll do it in silence, without voicing any complaint, because that way I'll be delayed for only a couple of minutes, not hours.

It's no great hassle, but it makes me angry, every time.

Then there's the fact that one of the reasons for the mass unemployment in our area, with all its resultant poverty, sourness and frustration, is that the State which the British forces are in the area to uphold is based on discrimination against Catholics.

It doesn't do to exaggerate this either: nationalists who compare Northern Catholics to Palestinians or South African blacks only belittle the real cruelty of the oppressors of those people. And those who equate Protestants with Zionist settlers or South African whites are blinded by ignorance or bigotry or both.

Even so, Catholics are disadvantaged here on account of their religion, and this disadvantage is defended by the British military presence. So the trajectory of any effort to end religious discrimination does lead towards conflict with the British presence. As does an apolitical aspiration not to have spooks pointing their long-range lenses into your bedroom or to be forced to waste good drinking time teaching yet another selection of squaddies how to spell 'Eamonn'.

And thus it is that even people sickened by IRA violence can nonetheless feel an association with the IRA's presence.

This is the key difference between the North and the South reflected in different attitudes to the IRA, to the idea of Irish unity, to the calls and campaigns for "peace". It is not a matter of moral revulsion felt by sensitive Southerners, but not felt by hard-hearts from up here.

To suggest that it is, is to miss the point entirely.

5 May '93

33

Paras, Ears And Other Argentine Body Parts

THE CONFLICT IN THE NORTH is commonly analysed in terms of the kind of people involved in the violence. Paramilitaries, for example, are frequently explained, or explained away, as psychopaths or racketeers.

But recently, surrounding a book by Vincent Bramley throws light on the kind of people involved in military, as opposed to paramilitary, groups.

Bramley was a corporal in the Third Battalion of the Parachute Regiment. His book, *Excursion To Hell,* is about what happened to him in the Falklands War. It has sparked controversy in

Britain because of its account of how men of 3 Para shot and bayoneted unarmed prisoners to death and cut off their ears as trophies during the taking of Mount Longdon. *A World In Action* programme the week before last gave a graphic account of some of the incidents.

Detectives from Scotland Yard have travelled to the Falklands to investigate, and are to visit Argentina to talk to a number of men taken prisoner on the Islands, including one who says that two members of 3 Para botched an attempt to murder him at a time when he was unarmed and posed no threat to them.

The controversy in Britain centres on whether the investigation should be underway at all. Press commentators and MPs have argued that if some Paras lost the run of themselves in the after-glow of battle, so what? That's war. If a few did desperate things, they also did good soldiering. What's to be gained from digging up the entrails of small atrocities and raking them over for inspection?

Appalling things happen in war. I spent a couple of years trans-planting trees in London with a team of ex-squaddies who would occasionally while away wet-time (when a cloud the size of a man's hand passed across the face of the sun we'd implement a union agreement that we didn't have to work in the rain) recall-ing their service in the Malayan "Emergency" when they'd cut the heads or smaller bits off "Chinese communists". I remember one fellow passing round creased pictures of himself and his mates holding their prizes aloft.

These were conscript soldiers, the last intake of National Servicemen, not professionals. Generally speaking, when you pressed them, they'd admit to shame at what they'd gotten up to, but also to a certain fascination with the fact that they'd had it in them to do it.

And they'd all tell you that, hell, they'd been pussy-cats when compared to the prestige outfits, the crack troops, the corps d'élite of the military machine, the SAS, the Marines, the Paras.

The Paras are regarded by all other regiments, and especially by themselves, as not just the cream but the *crème de la crème*. This view is implicit in the length and legendary toughness of the regiment's selection procedure, which discards a large majority of them who aspire to the red beret.

Bramley's book, and a number of feature articles about the book published in the last few weeks, provide a detailed and devastating account of the qualities which go to make a Para, and of the culture which all-pervades the regiment.

Bramley admits to having been a "problem child" – and then a disturbed adolescent, into football hooliganism and generalised violence. By the age of 16 he had a conviction for causing actual bodily harm. It was during a period spent in a detention centre that he discovered that he liked this life of short hair, rigid discipline and hard physical fitness. On release he applied to become a Para, and felt immediately among his own.

"Remember where your average Para comes from," the *Independent On Sunday* quotes a corporal from Bramley's battalion. "In my section there was me – and I'd been a foster child – and 12 men under me . . . There wasn't a single one of them who came from a normal family, who hadn't been in council care, in foster homes and the rest of it . . . The Para Reg., with its rules and regulations and discipline, became our family".

And family solidarity was the order of the day. As Bramley describes it, the life of the Para during peacetime was filled with togetherness, extreme drunkenness and constant violence. Many looked forward to being able to kill.

On *World In Action,* one ex-Para recalled his response when the order to go into action on Mount Longdon was made: "To be given the order to fix bayonets, and just to fix my own bayonet, and to actually use it for the purpose it's designed for, to me it was a joy. It was a joy to fire a weapon for the first time, to kill someone, or do damage to someone".

Everyday violence was not just accepted, but celebrated. A sizeable number of Paras, regarding themselves as representative of the "true spirit" of the regiment, were devotees of tracts such as *Who's Who In Nazi Germany* and *Hitler's Teutonic Knights.*

They would end boozy, brawling evenings with heartfelt renditions of 'Lorelei', the Nazi song featured in the film *Cabaret,* which proclaims that *"Tomorrow belongs to me"* – or the SS marching song, 'When We March On England', or 'The Fallschirmiager Song', the anthem of the German airborne assault troops who spearheaded the blitzkrieg on the Western front in 1940. The Paras wanted to be seen as separate from, and threatening towards, the society around them.

They favoured rituals which celebrated their own relish of practices ordinary people would find disgusting. Consuming vomit, urine and excrement, for example.

Members of 3 Para found it irritating that it had been their colleagues of 1 Para who had shot dead 13 Derry neighbours of mine in January 1972. They resented the taunt that, "We shot one, we shot two, we shot 13 more than you". This appears to have been taken as a challenge to their honour.

In light of all this it's not surprising that members of 3 Para on Mount Longdon killed and mutilated prisoners. It was in character.

A former member of the battalion is quoted in the *Independent On Sunday:* "I remember one bloke, we'd overrun a bunker, and he bayoneted this Argy through the throat and as the guy fell back dead he grabbed him and sawed his ear off with the bayonet. 'Right,' he said, 'I'll be having that; and it went into his pouch". Another man from 3 Para, identified on *World In Action* as Stuart "Scouse" McLaughlin, was recommended for a posthumous decoration for bravery during the battle for Mount London, but was turned down when it was discovered that his ammunition pouch had been filled with ears and other Argentine body parts.

Some say that McLaughlin should have received his award anyway, despite his trophy-bag of body pieces. All who fought alongside him confirm that he displayed a reckless disregard for his own safety on the freezing slopes of Mount Longdon, and contributed mightily to victory in the battle.

It makes no sense to see the Paras' readiness to make rubbish of ordinary rules of human decency as a blemish on their behaviour in battle. On the contrary, it is surely the fact that they find viciousness congenial which makes them such exceptional warriors.

They are selected, trained and equipped for the precise purpose of inflicting the maximum physical damage on people identified as enemies by their political chiefs. How could they perform this function that they had been meticulously prepared for if they thought of the enemy as having rights, dignity, humanity of any sort?

Sawing the ears off an Argentine like he was an animal slaughtered in a bloodsport must make perfect sense to the Para-military mind.

It's understandable that British true-Tories like Nicholas Fairbairn are contemptuous of the investigation of what happened on Mount Longdon, that they long for the return of Mrs. Thatcher, under whom, so they say, such holy-joe moralising wouldn't be tolerated for a minute.

In the meantime, let us note that it was 3 Para which won that other victory in the pubs of Coalisland last year.

And let's keep Corporal Bramley's book in mind the next time some Fianna Fáiler, Fine Gaeler, Labourite, PD or Democratic Leftist starts wittering on about what sort of savages there must be in the North to have such a high tolerance-level for violence.

21 April '93

In August 1969 the Bogside erupted. (Above) the centre-spread from the September 1969 edition of *Nusight;* (left) the front-cover of an edition that contained almost 50 pages on the Northern crisis; (below) Eamonn McCann, pictured minutes after the first deployment of British soldiers in Derry at William St, August 14, with nationalist MP Eddie McAteer to the left.

Bloody Sunday, 30 January, 1972 was the day that the Republican armed struggle gained legitimacy for many. (Above) the dead and the wounded are carried away; (below) up against the wall, motherfuckers

(Above) McCann addressing a meeting in Carrickmore, Co. Tyrone, 1970 to protest at the imprisonment of Bernadette Devlin. Also on the platform Labhrás Ó Murchú, PJ Rafferty, Des Geraghty and Máirín de Búrca; (below) the years roll by and the death toll mounts – paramilitaries at a funeral in Belfast.

(Above) McCann selling copies of *Socialist Worker* outside Dunne's Stores during the strike there about the importation of fruit from apartheid South Africa; (below) Politics and religion make a lethal cocktail in West Belfast.

Peace can mean different things to different people. (Above) the U.S.S. John F. Kennedy came to Dublin weighed down with weapons of destruction; (below) Ulster Unionist leader David Trimble and Sinn Féin President Gerry Adams argue their cases as the Peace Process gains momentum.

(Above) Politics and religion IRA-style – the bedroom of the Shankill bomber Thomas Begley, who died himself in the blast; (below) the house in which the Quinn brothers, Richard, Mark and Jason, were murdered in a Loyalist arson attack, July 1998.

Some things haven't changed. (Above) Bonfires and facepaint to celebrate the 12th of July; (below) the Apprentice Boys of Derry doing their crazy thing, August 1998.

The moment the Republican armed struggle lost any residual vestige of legitimacy for Northern nationalists. (Above) surveying the devastation in the aftermath of the bombing of Omagh by the 'Real' IRA, 15 August,1998.

34

Conor Cruise O'Brien Is A Hypocrite

ON AUGUST 22ND THE *SUNDAY Independent* carried a number of articles attacking Michael D. Higgins for remarks he had made in an interview in HOT PRESS. One of these articles was by Conor Cruise O'Brien.

O'Brien wrote that "After reading (Higgins') HOT PRESS interview, I think he is temperamentally unfitted to be entrusted with responsibility for broadcasting, or anything to do with the media". He went on to accuse Higgins of "a crude abuse of power, and an attempted encroachment on the freedom of the press".

As evidence, O'Brien quoted what Higgins had said about articles which had previously appeared in the *Sunday Independent*.

Eamon Dunphy had written a piece referring to Higgins as "a national self-indulgence, a faintly ridiculous caricature of Ireland's vision of itself, the caring nation". Higgins commented in HOT PRESS: "That was a piece of personal abuse that was very offensive . . . when you read something like that, it's very hard to listen to Joe Hayes (the Independent group's chief executive) making the case for the high standards he and the NNI (National Newspapers of Ireland) are supposed to be about!"

In the HOT PRESS interview, Higgins gave other examples of what he regarded as low standards of journalism, and went on: "I have those articles on file and I would like when I get my next communication from the NNI for Joe Hayes to go back through all those things that were written and tell me how they fit with what they told me – and I accepted it at the time – about their interest in ensuring standards in the newspaper industry".

In his *Sunday Independent* piece O'Brien pointed out that, with one exception, "all those things that were written" consisted of references to Higgins himself. O'Brien went on: "I think the reader will agree that the passages I have quoted show that the Minister responsible for broadcasting is using his office to be revenged on journalists who have criticised him personally".

O'Brien quoted further from Higgins' HOT PRESS remarks: "The NNI pointed out to me that there is no Minister directly responsible for newspapers and I indicated that, should government decide they want me to deal with all aspects of communications, including the print media, I would be delighted to take on these additional responsibilities".

O'Brien expressed alarm at this. Higgins has threatened freedom of the press in pursuit of "personal vendettas", he argued. That threat would be all the greater were he to be given direct authority over the press. So, far from entrusting him additionally with responsibility for newspapers, the Government ought to remove from him the responsibility he already has for broadcasting.

The case for removing broadcasting from Higgins' ministerial brief was all the stronger, O'Brien argued, given that "Michael D. in this HOT PRESS interview, writes as if broadcasting were entirely his personal preserve".

O'Brien cited one example only of Higgins' alleged tendency to believe that broadcasting is "entirely his personal preserve". "He tells his interviewer: 'That soap is going to come back. I'm quite confident about that'."

Observed O'Brien: "A Minister who is quite confident about an item of programming, over which he has no statutory powers, ought not to have responsibility for broadcasting, or the vitally necessary democratic distance between Government and broadcasting will be eroded".

Before digging into the dirt-pile of dishonesty on which O'Brien built this case against Higgins, let's concede that some of the things Higgins said in the interview were ill-advised.

However: the suggestion by O'Brien (and a number of other *Independent* journalists) that Higgins' remarks amounted to "a crude abuse of power and an attempted encroachment on the freedom of the press" was stretching it, and then some. And even if this were not the case, even if Higgins' expression of confidence that a particular soap-opera would return to RTE for another series did indicate a desire to wield totalitarian power over broadcasting, Conor Cruise O'Brien has no right to make any negative comment.

Keeping files, threatening journalists, encroaching on freedom of the press . . . Let's look back to 1976, when O'Brien was a member of the Fine Gael-Labour coalition led by Liam Cosgrave, and held the ministerial office now occupied by Higgins. (The office was then known as "Posts And Telegraphs".)

In September 1976, the *New York Times* correspondent Bernard Nossiter visited Dublin to report on, among other things, a piece of "emergency" legislation which had been introduced in the Dáil by the Cosgrave Government following the assassination by the IRA of the British ambassador, Sir Christopher Ewart-Biggs. The proposed new law significantly increased the powers of the police and, to the same extent, diminished the rights of citizens.

Nossiter visited O'Brien in the expectation, as he explained later, that as "a distinguished writer" he would be the Government Minister least enthusiastic about the new measure, particularly about a provision which seemed to present grave danger to freedom of the press. In his *New York Times* piece, Nossiter quoted the relevant section.

"Any person who, expressly or by implication, directly or through another person or persons, or by advertisement, propaganda or by any other means, incites or invites another person (or persons generally) to join an unlawful organisation, or to take part in, support or assist its activities, shall be guilty of an offence and shall be liable on conviction or indictment to imprisonment for a term not exceeding ten years."

Civil liberties groups, newspaper editors, the National Union of Journalists and many other interested parties expressed alarm at the sweeping power this seemed to confer on the State to censor newspapers. Two Labour TDs, John O'Connell and David Thornley, defied the whip and refused to support the bill in the Dáil. In the Senate, Mary Robinson and Dr. Noel Browne voted against.

The *Irish Times* commented on the "lamentable absence of regret (by Ministers) for the reduction in civil liberties". The editor of the *Irish Press,* Tim Pat Coogan, told Nossiter: "We will have to trim our sails, tack and reef, and hope we don't go down". As it happened, Coogan in particular had good reason to worry.

Nossiter reported that far from O'Brien being perturbed, he was positively enthusiastic for curbs on freedom of speech. To make his point, Nossiter explained, O'Brien "pulled from his file letters to Coogan's *Irish Press",* which he offered as examples of the kind of material which the new measure might be used to suppress. A number of the letters – they had been clipped from the Letters to the Editor column – expressed opposition to a memorial fund which had been set up to commemorate the assassinated ambassador. Another had argued that "Britain maintained her grip on Ireland by violence".

Asked by Nossiter whether he seriously wanted to make the expression of these opinions illegal, O'Brien replied: "That is intended. We make no secret of it".

Asked whether he envisaged the writers of the letters being charged, O'Brien replied that he envisaged the charges being aimed at "the paper that gave them space".

Nossiter was so disturbed by what he'd heard that on his way to Dublin Airport he diverted by way of Burgh Quay, and warned Coogan in his office of what might lie in store.

This was an attack on freedom of the press of a very different character to the "threat" issued by Higgins in the HOT PRESS interview. At worst, Higgins was reacting petulantly to what he perceived as personal attacks on himself, and threatening to report the miscreant journalists to their boss. O'Brien, for political and not personal reasons, was threatening to have editors put in prison for up to ten years.

To his credit – and, as I understand it, against the strongly-expressed wishes of the owners of the Press group – Coogan used a full page of the *Press* a few days later to re-print eleven Letters to The Editor expressing exactly the opinions O'Brien had told Nossiter editors should be put in prison for publishing.

At the same time, pressure mounted on the Government from individuals and organisations who had been shocked by O'Brien's apparent eagerness to intimidate the press into line. A spokesperson for Amnesty International referred to the revelation that O'Brien had been keeping files of offending newspaper clippings as "one of the most disturbing aspects of the present situation . . . It reminds me of dossiers built up in countries where governments are suppressive of their people. There's a kind of implied threat in that thought-process which scares me".

The pressure worked. The measure was never used against journalists.

The relevant point here is that O'Brien wanted it used. O'Brien then, like Higgins now, had responsibility for broadcasting. But O'Brien's interventions in RTE went rather farther than seeming to bring "pressure" to bear to ensure that a favoured soap wasn't scrapped.

* * * * *

At the same time as O'Brien was looking forward to the opportunity to imprison print journalists, broadcast journalists were learning who was boss. It was suddenly announced that RTE TV's main current affairs programme, *Seven Days,* which had regularly earned the displeasure of the Coalition Government, was being cancelled. Its editor, Sean O Mórdha, resigned in protest. A former Coalition Government Press Secretary was put in overall control of the station's output.

An *Irish Press* editorial commented: "To a degree we must suspend judgement until the full story of what is happening at RTE unfolds. But it is peculiar, coincidental and disturbing to say the least of it that a shake-up – some might call it a purge – of the magnitude of this one . . . should occur just at the time when the Minister responsible for the television station, Dr. Conor Cruise O'Brien, should find himself in a controversy over his avowed intention in some way to censor press freedom . . ."

There is no need to labour the contrast between that set of circumstances and the circumstances which prompted O'Brien to claim that Higgins was unsuitable to have responsibility for broadcasting. Conor Cruise O'Brien is a hypocrite.

22 September '93

35

Why Hume And Adams Are Getting On Royally

THE USUAL PEOPLE HAVE BEEN spluttering the usual kind of outrage since the revelation in the *Sunday Tribune* (August 29th) that a former senior civil servant, Michael Lillis, met Gerry Adams on two occasions earlier this year to discuss peace in the North.

It's getting a bit repetitive, this passing cavalcade of controversy. Adams and Hume, Adams and Mary Robinson, Adams and Michael Lillis, and the same selection of sleek commentators complaining each time that the Provos have been presented with a propaganda bonanza.

So maybe, by way of variation, we could look at the issue from the opposite direction: why is Gerry Adams meeting with people who represent ideas and forces which Republicans claim to abhor?

The Republican Movement puts itself forward as something other than a traditional, conservative, Catholic-nationalist outfit. Its paper, *An Phoblacht,* as well as carrying approving accounts of the military and political activities of the Movement in the North, also features regular reports suggesting that this is, broadly speaking, a progressive publication, a paper of the Left.

The long struggle of women workers at Timex in Dundee was held up as the sort of action Republicans might support and associate themselves with. The fight for union recognition at Pat The Baker in Ballyfermot is reported regularly. Aer Lingus workers are urged to stand firm against the bullying and blackmail tactics of their management. The freedom struggles of Eastern Timor, El Salvador, Kurdistan and other oppressed areas are celebrated. The US role in the oil war against Iraq, the murder attacks on Libya, Western collusion in Zionist aggression, and so on, are exposed.

Generally speaking, the Republican Movement positions itself on the side of the oppressed and disadvantaged, and against the ruling élites, including the Southern Irish ruling élite. It is in the context of fighting for radical social and economic change that they locate their own efforts to end the predicament of Catholics in the North.

This raises interesting questions about Adams' meetings with establishment figures.

Michael Lillis was boss of the Anglo-Irish division of the Department of Foreign Affairs during the FitzGerald-led Coalition in the '80s. In this capacity he was one of the key figures in the negotiations which lead to the signing of the Anglo-Irish Agreement in 1985.

Lillis then became the first head of the Anglo-Irish Secretariat, the group of senior British and Irish officials based at Maryfield outside Belfast, which co-ordinates British and Irish Government activity regarding the North. He was later Southern Ireland's Permanent Representative at the United Nations in Geneva. More recently, he has hired his talents out to the private sector, and now heads Guinness Peat Aviation's aircraft leasing operation in Latin America.

Lillis is a prominent member of the ruling élite in Southern Ireland, with close ties to ruling-class elements in the UK and further afield. He represents no force for radical social or economic change. On the contrary, he has a clear and compelling interest in maintaining the existing order.

So what's with Gerry Adams holding secret meetings with him –

extended and "full" meetings, according to Lillis? And what are we to make of Lillis pronouncing himself "impressed" by the Sinn Féin president?

Of course, occasions arise in any conflict when discussions – "official" or "unofficial" – are in order between representatives of the opposing sides. And one side may well be "impressed" by a representative of the other without any principle being compromised. But that's not what was happening here.

Lillis explained in the *Tribune* that he had outlined the constitutional nationalist strategy embodied in the Anglo-Irish Agreement and had suggested to Adams that the Agreement could be more constructively used by the Reynolds government. He had argued that while the British had no strategic reason for staying in the North, their room for manoeuvre was limited by the certainty of Unionist resistance to a withdrawal, and that Adams and his colleagues should take this into account in framing demands to be put to the British side. He had suggested that, in this situation, the armed struggle had no useful role to play.

There was no hint in Lillis' detailed account that he and Adams had identified any contradictory views about the type of Ireland which might result from a cessation of violence, no suggestion that they represented or were speaking for different classes of people, no indication that the one had a vision of Ireland in the future which the other couldn't accept.

Evidently, there was no disagreement about where the two men wanted to go, only a difference of opinion about the best and most moral route to take.

The same is true of the Hume-Adams talks. The fact that Hume put his name to a "joint declaration" with Adams, and that the declaration included a reference to a right to "national self-determination", created such a furore among Unionists in the North and revisionists in the South that it has been very difficult to examine the development in any other perspective. But we should try.

What was missing from the Hume-Adams declaration was, again, any suggestion that the two men represented, or sought to represent, different sections of Irish society. In the text of the declaration, and in the many statements the two have since made about their talks, there has been no reference to differences of opinion on the social content of the Irelands they envisage. They, too, are discussing means, not ends.

Despite the excitement generated by this series of meetings, precedents of a sort are plentiful. Indeed, one of the most striking aspects of Republicanism in this century has to do with how naturally, easily, comfortably, successive waves of outlaw activists managed to integrate themselves into the mainstream once they decided to come in from the cold.

Cuman na nGael (now Fine Gael) in 1922, Fianna Fáil five years later, Clann na Phoblachta in 1948, Official Sinn Féin (now divided into the Workers' Party and Democratic Left) in the '70s, all peeled off from Sinn Féin/the IRA and, more or less immediately, became impeccably constitutionalist.

In each case, adherence to the tactic of armed struggle proved to be the only major factor dividing them from the respectable politics of their day. Once the armed struggle was abandoned, their innate conservatism was plain for all to see, and accept.

The same is true today. Take away the armed struggle and there is less between Sinn Féin on the one hand and mainstream nationalist parties on the other than is suggested by the ferocity with which Sinn Féin and its leaders are regularly denounced. Lillis and Hume have sussed this.

The IRA's armed struggle poses a threat to political stability. But the politics of the Republican Movement poses no threat to any fundamental establishment interest.

This is the most important conclusion to be drawn from Gerry Adams' meetings with Lillis and Hume. It is a conclusion which rank-and-file Republicans who do want to see radical change might usefully ponder.

8 October '93

36

What Do We Do With Taigs? We Spray Them

HARDLY ANYBODY TALKS ANYMORE about bringing the people together. All the talk is of policing us apart. And small wonder. On the face of it, people have never been more raw in their hostility and sense of distance from one another.

On the day after the Shankill bomb an acquaintance from Belfast told me heatedly: "I've worked on the Shankill, which is more than you've ever done, and I'm telling you some of those people are animals. Just animals".

The speaker is middling well-known in the North, would be considered a Left-wing and liberated fellow, uncontaminated by sectarian emotion.

Scores of others I've spoken with regret the way the Shankill bombing worked out but would have had no problem if the operation had gone according to plan: if the UDA leadership had been wiped out there'd have been rejoicing in Catholic working-class areas.

Not everybody would have joined in, maybe not even half. But there would have been a cock-a-hoop atmosphere in particular pubs, and scorn aimed at anyone who argued that this was a wrong, inappropriate response – this, despite the fact that even if everything had gone according to plan, innocent Protestants would still have been blasted to death.

One Belfast IRA statement said that it had been intended to issue a warning so that the area could be cleared, but this makes no sense. Any warning which would have cleared the area of innocent civilians would have cleared it also of the UDA targets. Nobody I know seriously believes that a warning had been included in the day's plan of action.

The IRA calculated that if they took out the UDA leadership, "collateral damage" of this sort would be acceptable to their supporters. And in this, as I say, they were probably right.

The reason Catholic working-class people have come to think like this is that Loyalist death-squads have been slaughtering Catholics in Belfast for months, without anybody in authority seeming to care tuppence.

In the three months leading up to the Shankill bomb,14 people were killed in the conflict. Two – both involved in contract work for the security forces – were killed by the IRA. The other 12 were killed by the UDA and UVF. One of these was a Protestant prison officer. The remaining eleven were Belfast Catholics. None of them was a member of any political or paramilitary organisation.

There have been scores, literally, of other attempts to kill Catholics. In some, people were wounded, in others guns jammed or the killers were off-target. People have been shot in taxis headed for Catholic areas, or shot through a door or window as they sat at home, or as they walked along a main road, or at work, or as they stood at one street corner or another. This has been a sustained, systematic murder assault on the Catholics of Belfast, and the thinking behind it is clear.

The UDA leader who was the main target of the Shankill bomb spoke to Maggie O'Kane in an interview published in *The Guardian* four days before the massacre. He said: "We are out to terrorise the terrorists, to get to the stage when old grannies up the Falls will call on the IRA to stop because it is ordinary Catholics who are getting hit, not the Provos behind steel security doors".

After a machine-gun attack on a taxi packed with six people en route to Ardoyne the previous week, the UDA had explained in a statement that "This was an attempt at mass murder".

The tactic of terrorising entire Catholic communities is not only openly admitted but asserted with gleeful enthusiasm. "Yeez deserve it, ye Fenian bastards," a Loyalist gunman shouted as he fled from the scene, having sprayed an east Belfast pub with bullets a few months ago. A while back, a UVF leader in the mid-Ulster area told me casually that he "loved going out hunting RCs."

Maggie O'Kane described an episode in Belfast involving the UDA chief she was interviewing. "A man sways gently across the road from the bar, he's one of us, says Mad Dog, ready to go at any time. The man with six pints in his eyes smiles in a friendly sort of way into the car. He strokes the lapel of his combat jacket. 'All ready to go?', he says. 'What do we do with Taigs?' Mad Dog asks. 'We spray them,' obliges the combat jacket with a friendly drunken grin."

In his introduction to Martin Dillon's pot-boiler *The Shankill Butchers,* Conor Cruise O'Brien expressed puzzlement about this sort of thing, about the Loyalist gangs' evident pleasure in inflicting suffering on its victims before killing them. This testified yet again to O'Brien's wilful refusal to face the realities of the North.

The psychopathology of Loyalist paramilitarism is readily explicable by reference to the nature of the Northern State, and is not otherwise explicable. The State was established to give expression to the identity of one community only, which is the same thing as saying that it was set up to deny the identity of the other community.

Loyalty to the State, more or less automatically, involved thinking of Catholics as lesser human beings. Catholics, when they got uppity, had to be put back in their place. This is what the campaign to terrorise the Catholics of Belfast has been about. There is no mystery about it, no need for puzzlement.

It's not surprising, bearing the nature of the State in mind, that some of the murder attacks on Catholics have taken place in circumstances which make it difficult to believe that the forces of the State put a high priority on stopping them. Many Catholics in Belfast, by no means all of them supporters of the IRA, or even Sinn Féin voters, are convinced that the RUC and British Army have, on occasion, given the Loyalist killers room in which to operate: because they, too, want the IRA – who might be defined in this context as the most uppity Catholics of all – pressurised into calling off the armed struggle.

At any rate, the fact that the IRA is anti-State and the Loyalists pro-State makes it reasonable to assume that the forces of the State view the activities of the two groups differently.

Elements of the security forces have certainly collaborated closely with Loyalist paramilitaries in the very recent past. The most relevant instance concerns high-level co-operation between the UDA and British military intelligence which was revealed in the trial last year of Brian Nelson.

Nelson was the UDA's Intelligence Officer, with responsibility for targeting Catholics for killing. He was also a military intelligence officer, and briefed a "Colonel J" about his activities every month. "Colonel J" told the court that he in turn briefed senior British Army officers, including the General Officer Commanding, Northern Ireland.

Among the Loyalist paramilitary activities which Nelson kept "Colonel J" informed about was the smuggling from South Africa in January 1988 of 200 AK47 automatic rifles, 90 Browning 9mm pistols, 500 fragmentation grenades, 30,000 rounds of ammunition and 12 RPG rocket launchers.

A third of this arsenal was quickly seized by other elements of the security forces and a number of men were jailed. Another quantity has been seized since. But more than a third of the consignment remains in Loyalist paramilitary hands, and has been put into service.

Between the arrival of the South African arms and the Shankill bombing 147 Catholics were killed by Loyalist paramilitaries. We know from evidence given at inquests and from the published results of forensic tests that at least 67 of these killings, and very likely many more, were carried out using weapons from the South African shipment.

All this is very widely known in the North. Stop anybody at random on the Falls or in the Bogside and ask about the "Nelson Affair" and there's a fair chance you will be told in detail about the UDA man Brian Nelson, "Colonel J", the killing of Catholics, the South African arms and so forth.

This is how large numbers of people in Catholic working-class areas, especially in Belfast, came to believe that the only way to stop the killing of Catholics week in and week out was for the IRA to take on and take out the Loyalist paramilitary leaders, and why some were willing to contemplate the killing of innocent Protestants in the process.

To say this is not to deny the ugliness of the hatred so generated, and it's certainly not to support the bombing of the Shankill. From the point of view of working-class Catholics, the main result of the Shankill bombing is that more, not fewer, have been killed since – which was always likely to be the outcome, no matter how the operation worked out.

So now, as I write, we are in the slough of despond, people on all sides more fearful than at any time in the past 20 years and seized with a vast apprehension of futility.

Janis Joplin said: "How come half the world is crying, when the other half of the world is crying too?"

We have to look hard for hope and, when we see a spark faintly glowing, blow gently upon it. In the week before the Shankill bomb about a thousand people, overwhelmingly Protestant, left their work at Shorts and stood in the rain in memory of Jody Reynolds, a Catholic painter gunned down by the UVF as he arrived at the complex for work. That's part of the reality of Belfast. There's still a fitful, faint sense of oneness across the barbed-wire barricades of the religious division.

What we have to do, as far as we can, is to boost and make predominant *that* sense of ourselves, rather than the sense of ourselves as separate and distant which we have come to accept most times as "normal". It can be done, because if it can't there's nothing left but desperation and nihilism and to be half in love with death.

It was interesting that Protestant workers came out from Shorts to protest against the killing of Jody Reynolds, because combustible material for sectarian trouble has been piling up at Shorts. The plant used to be a by-word for bigotry, with fewer than 5% of the workforce drawn from the Catholic community. That figure has increased to over 10% in recent years, on account of Fair Employment legislation and pressure from American interests. But now hundreds of redundancies are threatened.

If the old principle of Last In, First Out (LIFO) were to operate, a disproportionate number of Catholics, having been more recently recruited, would be sacked, and the religious imbalance would tilt back towards the past. The Fair Employment Commission is urging that LIFO be abandoned in these circumstances and redundancy programmes implemented in such a way as to preserve the existing composition of the workforce.

Danger crowds in on this proposition. It opens up the possibility of Protestant workers of some years' standing being given their cards so that new-comer Catholics can hold onto their jobs. You wouldn't have to be much of a Protestant bigot to be outraged at that.

At the same time, 11% isn't a fair proportion of Catholics. You wouldn't have to be a particularly ferocious nationalist, either, to be outraged at the suggestion that the figure should be allowed to fall back.

There's one way only out of this which could ignite into a real flame of hope: what if workers at Shorts said, No Redundancies, full stop?

What if union officials went around section by section saying, "We won't let them divide us on this, we'll defend every job, we'll insist at least on no compulsory redundancies, if they try to force one person out the gate we'll bring everybody out"?

That sort of approach, which can be generalised into other areas and issues across the communities, giving people on both sides a common cause to fight for, would do more to marginalise sectarianism and nurture a feeling of oneness than all the prayer meetings and moralistic pleadings of the massed ranks of moderates.

We will either fight one another – or find something to fight together for.

That's what's missing from all the mainstream proposals and initiatives, the Hume-Adams process and so forth – a vision which might bring us together, rather than police us apart.

3 November '93

37

After The Shankill Bombing And The Greysteel Massacre, There Is Sadness Overlaid Upon Sadness Overlaid Upon Sadness . . .

IT HASN'T BEEN AN EASY time to raise political arguments. I was on UTV's *Counterpoint* programme the Thursday after the Greysteel massacre and had sharpened my thoughts in advance for cut-and-thrust interplay with ex-UDA chief Glen Barr, Gregory Campbell of the Democratic Unionists and Mark Durkan of the SDLP.

But then Michelle and Ian Williamson and Mena Donnelly spoke and I knew that I couldn't slice into anybody else's argument just then. It wouldn't have been appropriate, and I wasn't able to anyway.

Michelle and Ian's mother and father had been killed in the Shankill bomb, Mena's father-in-law at Greysteel, and all three of them spoke with that astonishing, quiet decency that we have come almost to expect from people whose happiness has been suddenly shattered in the violence here.

It has sometimes seemed to me when people have said those noble, forgiving things – that they don't feel bitter and want to appeal for no retaliation – that they have been speaking from a standard approved script, that it's become a sort of television ritual after each atrocity, this recital of saintly forgiveness, because who knows what to say in the middle of such hitherto unimaginable grief, but even so you have to be saying something, and it's easiest to repeat what you remember others in the same situation saying to general approbation.

I'd seen Michelle on television immediately after the Shankill bomb and she had said that of course she was bitter against the people who had done it, and it struck me at the time that it would have been eerie if she'd said anything else. But now she said, on the programme and off-air, that she wasn't bitter any more, that she'd used all her bitterness up, she had none left in her. She looked across at Mena and said, "The men who did that to your family weren't acting for us". I was sitting just behind and between the two of them and there was no doubting she didn't speak from any internalised script but from the sweetness of her heart.

She was petite, as they say, with sallow skin and a mass of dark curls, and smiled apologetically and complied when the floor-manager asked if she'd take off a bright sweater which was too "hot" for the cameras. She was only about 20. She explained that her mother and father had gone out on the day of the bomb in great form because they were about to move into a new house. Their mission up the Shankill was to buy curtains.

I stopped to talk with her after we finished transmission but couldn't think of anything and just clumsily gave her a hug and said, 'You know . . .', and she said, 'Yes, I know. Thank you very much'. Imagine that. She said, 'Thank you very much'.

I headed off straight after that because I felt too inadequate to remain in her company because I was crying and I definitely wasn't going to stay like that in the presence of Campbell, Durkan and Barr. Gregory, true to form, had harped on a bit during the programme about Protestants being done down in Derry over the past 20 years, but nobody took him on.

I headed up the Strand Road toward Peadar O'Donnell's and then the Dungloe Bar, telling myself to wise up about these fits of weeping and wondering if I'd take a bit of stick for not taking a tougher political line. But everybody in the Dungloe, where they'd been watching, said there was nothing you could say.

On the following Sunday I walked down from Creggan to the Guildhall Square with a march organised by Sinn Féin to draw attention to collusion between the British security services and loyalist paramilitaries and in solidarity with the beleaguered

Catholic communities in west and north Belfast. It was one of those days of thick freezing-damp air when you'd far rather have been indoors watching United versus City live from Maine Road, which probably helped account for the middling-at-best turn-out of maybe 500.

Joe Austin, a Sinn Féin councillor from North Belfast, was the main speaker, gaunt and tense and raising the only laugh of the day, or the week even, when he referred to, John Adams . . . I mean Gerry, and somebody shouted, Aye, Gerry Hume, which could all be taken as a Freudian slip if you were searching hard for something unconsciously significant.

On the way down I'd lost step with the Socialist Workers' Movement comrades I'd been walking with and fell in with my friend Daisy Mules, who is a member of Sinn Féin and also trea- surer of Derry Trades Council. She introduced me to Bobby Lavery alongside her. He's another Sinn Féin councillor from north Belfast. Earlier this year, Loyalist paramilitaries had come to kill him, and when he wasn't in, shot his son dead instead.

I know who you are, he said. I know some of your aunts on the New Lodge Road.

I know you, too. I responded. I'm sorry about . . . He cut me short, not in any unfriendly way, nodding, Aye, Aye.

It was the only Sinn Féin march I can remember which didn't have a tricolour on it and didn't finish with 'The Soldier's Song'. There was no mention from the platform of a united Ireland or Brits Out. Joe Austin said that what we wanted was an end to unfairness, in employment and everything else, and recognition of the nationalist identity.

After the meeting I drifted part of the way back up to the Bogside with Tony Doherty, who asked me what I'd thought about the *Counterpoint* programme. Tony's father was Paddy Doherty, one of the 14 men gunned down in Rossville Street by the Paras on Bloody Sunday. I mumbled that I hadn't felt able to say much.

You couldn't have said anything, he agreed. It was just very sad listening to that young couple from the Shankill. Just very, very sad.

That's mainly the way it was. Sadness overlaid with sadness overlaid with sadness until everything else in us was smothered. I'd been out at Greysteel doing a piece for the *Sunday Tribune* on the Friday night, hanging around outside the Rising Sun with my tape-recorder and interrupting the quiet reveries of the queue which was constantly replenished with people coming to contemplate the banks of flowers and the wall festooned with condolence cards and mass cards and messages of sympathy. Nobody refused to talk with me, which was amazing enough in itself, although this didn't yield a piece of contrasting colours since everybody had more or less the same expected things to say.

I presumed to knock on the door of the house which was nearest to the Rising Sun and had a light on, and was welcomed in to tea and slices of cake. The man of the house had been in the pub when the killers struck, had come face to face with them. His wife was a Protestant. His children were Catholics. His eldest had the date set for marrying her Protestant fella.

I thought, as I left, that the right journalistic thing to do would be to do a piece about them. They'd have made a brilliant story, especially with a picture, if I'd be able to coax them that far.

It wasn't delicate sensitivity or any consideration of ethics which dissuaded me from pursuing this, but a feeling which was beginning to weigh heavy that this theme of people intermingling easily with one another and of shared sorrow triumphing over hatred and division, although in harmony with the immediate, emotional facts of the matter, was operating as something of a lullaby, too, soothing us towards a dreamy, devoutly-wished disregard for the ugliness which still outcropped all around.

One of the reasons for the intensity of the emotional expressions of togetherness has been precisely that there are no structures for expressing togetherness in any more practical way. People do not weep together as a prelude to coming together politically but because they cannot come together politically.

There are no structural links or ideological channels connecting the shared emotion of the past month with the political system here. The political system cannot provide a means of bringing

Michelle and Mena together. They can only come together and share in a sense of themselves outside the political system.

We need politics which enable people to identify themselves other than by reference to the community they come from. This is by no means impossible.

Every poll, survey and piece of academic research into attitudes here tells me that a majority of Catholics and a majority of Protestants would prefer to live in mixed estates, send their children to mixed schools, have jobs in mixed workplaces – if this were possible.

The deeper down you are plunged into poverty in either community, the more segregated you are likely to be. If you leave your local school and can't get a job, or can only get a "job" on one of the myriad make-work schemes which are almost invariably community-based, you can slouch your way through life hemmed inside your own community. The people with most reason and right to be angry at the way the system has treated them are the least likely to have clear sight of a non-sectarian way to remedy the reasons for their anger.

There's nothing wrong with people being angry. What's wrong is that the anger is too often directed against one another.

We don't need a new, more subtle and sophisticated, fairer way to manager our sectarian society. We need a great, angry crusade against the causes of sectarianism. Against poverty, and the powerless and unfairness which goes with it, and the new measures devised almost every week now to drive working-class people even deeper into poverty.

Any such crusade is certain – sooner or later – to come into conflict with the State. It is at that point that it will become possible for us together to resolve the problem of the association of one community with loyalty to the State and of the other with hostility to the State.

Many Republicans know that it is not possible for them within the parameters of their own politics to carry their project much further forward. That's the main reason the politics of their parade in Derry were so subdued. And many Protestants know that the game's up too for the Ulster-is-British brigade.

We need an alternative axis for political organisation. We will stop fighting one another not when we stop fighting but when we start fighting together against the State and the disturbed and divided society from which all this insane evil emanates.

18 November '93

38

Please Forgive Us - We Have A Sectarian Murderer In The Family

DAVY CAME OVER TO ME as I stepped down from the platform after speaking at one of the huge trade union rallies against sectarianism a fortnight ago. He looked like a cool sort of dude, 20ish, with a good-humoured face, the right jeans and long blond hair, styled just-so. He said that I'd once promised to come and see the band that he played in and then hadn't turned up.

I agreed that this was perfectly possible, what with all the various commitments I had, and one thing and another, and any of the other excuses that came to mind that I use in these circumstances. We stood talking slightly awkwardly for a couple of minutes not quite knowing how to break off the encounter, before settling on an agreement that we could both do with a pint and dandering up the hill and into the pub.

It turned out that it wasn't the band he wanted to talk to me about at all, but the suffering his family was going through as a result of the killings, and his aunt and uncle and their family too.

He was a cousin of Robbie's, one of the men charged with one

of the incidents of sectarian slaughter which had been instru-
mental in bringing so many people onto the streets. He had the
same surname as Robbie, and they lived about 50 yards apart on
the same street. "My father and mother, my aunt and uncle, all of
us, our lives are just ruined," he said.

None of them could believe it when word came that Robbie had
been picked up and was being questioned about murders. They
hithered and thithered up and down into one another's houses,
full of agitation, boiling with anger. They contacted councillors
and clergymen asking them to intervene, to have the young
fellow released. They were outraged that his arrest might be seen
as associating them with the unspeakable violence which had
unnerved the whole community.

Robbie's father was well-known locally for his deep religious
convictions and abhorrence of violence. They didn't just want
the youngster released, they were determined that the RUC
would explain publicly that it had all been a mistake, that they'd
picked up an innocent person.

Then the phone calls started. They'd lift the phone and somebody would start attacking and abusing them, calling them
Orange bastards and Loyalist murderers. Because they had the
same name and came from the same street, there were as many
calls to Davy's home as to the uncle and aunt's.

To begin with they answered back, shouting, Our young fellow
is innocent, how dare you say such things to us – and they
would slam the phone down then and rail against the injustice
and vindictiveness of it all, and try again to have someone intervene and right the mistake and clear their family of this stain.

As the days passed they allowed themselves to relax a little,
seeing an end to their ordeal in sight. The police could only hold
people for seven days without charging them. Neighbours were
saying that everybody arrested was being held for the full seven
days because of the anger over the spate of killings, and the need
to reassure people that something was being done. They could
understand that, recalled atrocities from the past when they had
looked at the papers themselves to check if there'd been any
arrest yet. But it still wasn't right that their whole family, espe-

cially Robbie, who was hardly out of his teens, was being put through this torment.

They weren't able to get in to see Robbie while he was being questioned and they didn't ask themselves, didn't allow the thought to surface fully, whether there was any chance he might actually have been involved, because that was too terrible a possibility to contemplate, and anyway they knew him, better than anybody, knew it wasn't the type of him. So they waited for the days to pass and release to come.

When a solicitor called to say Robbie was being charged and would be up before the court the next morning, accused of murdering all those people, machine-gunning them, they were struck dumb with horror. They pulled the blinds in their houses. There was hardly a word spoken between them for hours through the evening. They all cried and caressed one another and knelt down and asked God please not to let this happen, to lift this darkness from their lives and let them see the brightness of joy again.

Afterwards, somebody mentioned that it must have been like this for the relatives of the UDR Four and the Birmingham Six and they said in whispers to one another that sometimes these things can take ten, 15 years before the mistake is admitted. It was worse, said Davy, far worse than having a death in the family. When there's a death it's over, you can only look back in sadness. This was like looking forward to death every day, forever.

It was when Robbie and the others who had been charged with him appeared in court that the true depth of the horror opened up before them. It was his attitude, the angle of him, the way he walked, the way he looked, his expression. And when he shouted and ranted UFF slogans in defiance, the truth showed itself to them with a devastating suddenness, like a dark thunderclap of the soul.

Now they had to admit the thought that they'd been pushing away from them since the moment they'd heard of the arrest. They had never really managed to get rid of it, they could acknowledge that, now it didn't matter. Some of Robbie's family felt that they could never speak with him again, never look into his eyes, never see him as one of theirs. None of them could fit it together in any way that made sense, put the Robbie they knew and had been tender with, alongside the person who was being accused of erupting into savagery and a maelstrom of death. Like everybody else they had pictured the scene when they'd first heard. Now they had to picture Robbie in it, and they couldn't, but they did because they had to.

It was all out now, the name and the face, and the phone calls came incessantly. Fucking murdering Orange bigot scum bastards, the 'Ra should fucking torture you, burn you out, you'll fucking die in agony. Davy's father who had been the strongest of them all in the beginning and arguing back was now weeping and apologising. I'm sorry, I'm sorry, please forgive us. I'm sorry. I'm sorry.

Davy didn't go back to work for four days. He's a construction worker, on a site with a majority-Catholic workforce, and he felt he couldn't face them. He remembered when he would hear of somebody charged with an IRA offence that he'd think, if he knew somebody from the same family, that, Jesus, I never knew they were like that, assuming that they must all be of the same way of thinking, or at least that they must have known.

He knew quite a lot of Catholics, mainly through work. His best pal, a workmate, was a Catholic from the Lecky Road in the middle of the Bogside. Now, he thought, they all must be thinking that about me. Eventually, he phoned a shop-steward and asked what would the score be about coming back in and was told, for fuck's sake, Davy, wise up. And it had worked out OK. His best friend was with us as we talked. They had left work and gone to the rally together.

He said that he did get the impression some of the people he worked with were different with him now, more reserved. He'd thought once or twice they were looking at him and talking about him, but he couldn't be sure. Maybe he was only imagining it. His pal said that to be frank there were people like that alright, but then there were ignorant fuckers everywhere.

We sat drinking and talking about the ignorance of all manner of fuckers until the three of us were the worse for wear and then we went to another pub and, as far as I remember, took to shorts and became paralytic. Then, five days later, on Tuesday of last week, there was a statement in the local paper from a former mayor, a member of the Democratic Unionists, complaining that two families were on the brink of having to move from their homes because of the deluge of hatred descending upon them. It seemed that after they had had the phone taken out, the hate started coming by the bundle in letters every day.

I phoned Davy's pal and asked if there was anything I could do, maybe make a public statement, or talk to somebody on the Catholic side who might have some influence on the people concerned. But he said, no, you might just make things worse, they're just victims of the situation now, that's all there is to it. And for the moment I couldn't think of anything else to say. There's thousands like them.

1 December '93

39

The Greatest Barrier To Peace Is Catholic Nationalism (Or There'll Be Peace In The Valley . . . Some Day)

WE KNOW NOW THAT THERE won't be peace by Xmas. In my own estimation, there won't be peace by Xmas next year either. Maybe there won't ever be peace, this side of outright revolution. That's what it feels like anyway, in this strange time we are living through. Those of us who are managing to live through it.

We are told on the one hand that the prospects for peace have never been brighter. And on the other hand we are warned that civil war is imminent. At first sight there's a bewildering contradiction here. But maybe it's just the weary old business of things looking different according to what side of the divide you are viewing them from.

The optimism about peace has been, largely, a Catholic-nationalist phenomenon. The Hume-Adams talks did not produce, but have rather been a product of, this phenomenon.

The real phenomenon consists of a major change in the attitude of the Catholic nationalists of the North to partition. Although a united Ireland has been the defining aspiration of Catholic nationalism since the Northern State was set up (if pursued for only one brief period with real intensity) a consensus has now developed among Catholic nationalists here that a united Ireland isn't on. Not now, or in the foreseeable future. This change, if sustained and established, is of profound historical significance.

Of course, there are those who say that they can see a united Ireland clearly up ahead. They calculate that Catholic nationalism will be the majority ideology within the State in thirty years, or fifty years, or whenever. But a lot of other people contest the figures involved in this calculation.

One of the reasons – not the only one – that Catholic nationalists are coming round to this way of thinking lies in a growing acceptance that Protestants aren't going to allow a united Ireland, now or in the foreseeable future. And that it would be unreasonable in all the circumstances to expect them to take any other attitude.

Thus, the optimism about peace in Catholic nationalist areas is experienced as being of an entirely non-sectarian character. And it is this, in turn, which makes the reaction to it of mainstream unionist politicians seem at best mischievous, at worst motivated by bigotry.

We have been here before, sort of. The civil rights movement arose in the late '60s because Catholic nationalists, particularly of the working class, had come to the conclusion that a united Ireland wasn't on, and that it therefore made sense to seek instead for full citizenship within the North.

That notion was beaten out of people's heads by the cops and their semi-official auxiliaries, in Duke Street in Derry in October '68, at Burntollet and then Bombay Street in 1969, on the Falls in 1970, with internment in 1971, Bloody Sunday in 1972. The cumulative result was the rise of the Provos.

People who suffer murderous repression by the State when they ask for full citizenship are likely to conclude that full citizenship isn't available within the confines of the State: some will proceed then to make war on the State. The unionist insistence that the civil rights movement contained within it the seeds of another IRA campaign was, in the event, self-validating.

Now we have come full circle. The elemental upsurge of Republican militancy which followed the suppression of the civil rights movement and which was expressed in the '70s slogan "It's a united Ireland or nothing" may well be seen by history as an atypical spasm which has now subsided.

The question being posed now, again, is whether arrangements can be made within the Northern State to acknowledge Catholic nationalists as first-class citizens. In response, Unionist leaders issue the same, stern answer as before.

Every morning for a number of weeks now a flotilla of Unionist politicians has sailed into media view, loudly proclaiming that Protestants shouldn't listen to this palaver about peace, that the Protestant people are being duped. Some of them seem sometimes to be saying that it makes sense for Protestants to believe they're being duped whether or not there's reason to. Just to be on the safe side.

One question which arises is whether, and in what numbers, those Protestant proletarians to whom politicians have allocated the roles of killers and cannon fodder in the predicted civil war are going to accept the role – or whether some movement is going to emerge with a sense of history, and of class interest, to seize the time and the possibility of reasonable peace.

There are great problems in the way of such a movement. The political uselessness of the bureaucrat drones at the top of the trade union movement, the only institution which can lay immediate claim to represent the specific class interests of either section of the North's workers; the insulting secrecy surrounding Hume-Adams; Catholic nationalism itself. The greatest of these problems is the last.

The predicted civil war will come about unless the balance of opinion within the Protestant working class tilts towards rejection of the policies and perspectives of the unionist leaders. But Catholic nationalism cannot help in that process. On the contrary, Catholic nationalism of its nature seeks to bind Catholics of all classes together, excluding the Protestant working class.

It is for this reason that – despite the obvious democratic credentials of the demand of Catholic nationalists for full citizenship within the State – no process or initiative grounded in Catholic nationalism can bring an enduring peace. Just because something is democratic, in the ordinary bourgeois sense of the word, doesn't mean that it will work. If it were otherwise, we'd have had democracy and peace here since the '60s.

For the Shankill to break with unionism, the Falls must go beyond nationalism.

15 December '93

40

The Ruling Class Is Guilty Of Fraud

THE CHAIRMAN OF THE IRISH Council for Civil Liberties, Michael Farrell, has drawn attention to the ominous and unexplained behaviour of the courts in handling the case of the former footballer Stephen "Rossi" Walsh, sentenced last year to 15 years for an arson offence. A further cause for serious concern has been highlighted by Garda handling of the investigation into the murder of Philomena Gillane, the Caltra, Galway woman found shot and stabbed in the boot of a car at the railway station in Athlone.

Last October, Mr. Walsh was convicted and sentenced by the no-jury Special Criminal Court (SCC). The SCC had been set up in the '70s to deal with "subversive" crime: an alleged threat to the State by paramilitary organisations at the time was used to justify the abolition of jury trials in this specific category of cases.

However, there was no suggestion of paramilitary involvement or "subversive" motive in the arson offence Mr. Walsh was charged with. So how come he was denied his right to trial by jury?

This question formed the basis of Mr. Walsh's appeal to the Supreme Court, heard on April 25th. The appeal was rejected – on what grounds we must wait for the written judgement to discover. However, many may agree that the court's *bona fides* have already been called into question by its decision to hear the appeal at the Green Street Courthouse.

The Green Street Courthouse is the home of the SCC and is closely identified in the public mind with the SCC. The Supreme Court hadn't sat there before, ever. It chose to move to the SCC courthouse for the first time in an appeal which turned precisely on the appropriateness of the SCC for handling the case . . . In the absence of any other explanation, and there has been none, it is difficult to avoid the conclusion that the judges wanted to create an atmosphere of dangerous subversion around the case so as to make their eventual rejection of the appeal seem "natural".

Vincent Browne has noted in the *Irish Times* how another piece of legislation enacted to deal with "subversion" was brought into play in the Gillane case. Three people, a man and a woman arrested at Caltra and a man detained at Gort, were held for questioning about the killing under Section 30 of the Offences Against The State Act. Section 30 allows gardaí to detain and question people for a specified period without bringing charges –

but only when they have reason to believe that the offence under investigation is of a "subversive" nature.

Again, there has been no suggestion of any "subversive" aspect to the appalling murder of Mrs. Gillane. So who decided, and why, that Section 30 should be brought into play?

In both these cases vital civil rights – the right to trial by jury and the right not to be detained without charge – have been denied to citizens through the invocation of an entirely fraudulent "security" consideration.

The cases would appear to have been carefully chosen. "Rossi" Walsh has for years been a, well, colourful and controversial character around the Four Courts. It might have been calculated that there would be little enthusiasm for upholding his civil rights. Equally, it may have been anticipated that nobody would be overly concerned about what procedures were used, or even mis-used, in the hunt for the savage killer or killers of Mrs. Gillane. Thus, without public outcry, repressive measures intended for use against "subversives" are imported into ordinary law.

The price of liberty, they say, is eternal vigilance. The people we should be keeping a vigilant eye on include policemen and judges.

Meanwhile, back in the North, there was jubilation in many parts on the night the Chinook helicopter clattered into a hillside on the Mull of Kintyre, killing all 29 people on board. I don't suppose you knew that.

Jubilation? The crash happened shortly after six o'clock and was flashed on Channel 4 News an hour later. By nine o'clock the jokes were flying. ("Chinooky ár lá".) By closing time, at least two new versions of Paul McCartney's dirge 'Mull Of Kintyre' were on offer. And that's just in one pub.

None of the reality reflected in this burst of creativity figured in the extensive coverage of reaction to the crash. Instead, statements from bishops and suchlike suggesting that the entire North had been plunged into mourning were relayed by journalists who must have known that they were conveying, at best, an incomplete account.

The crash victim who received most media attention was Brian

Fitzsimmons, head of the RUC Special Branch. He was presented in a number of soft-focus features as a decent man, who had dedicated his life to ending the cruelty of terrorism. I don't doubt that that's the way many people saw him. But it's not the way everybody saw him, nor the way everybody experienced him.

Similarly, the British Military Intelligence agents and MI5 spooks who were on the Chinook may well have been loved by their families and friends. And I imagine that the work they were engaged in will have been seen by their colleagues and by people of particular political persuasions as essential for the good of society. But, again, others took, and had reason to take, a different view.

The picture of reaction in the North presented to people in both Britain and Ireland was in all senses of the word, partial. Once again, the political needs and sensitivities of the ruling class triumphed over the truth.

It happens all the time, and on both sides of the Border. At least, we have that much in common.

15 January '94

41

You Are Now Re-Entering Free Derry

WE AREN'T PAINTING THE TOWN red to mark the 25th anniversary of British soldiers coming onto the streets of the North, but Colin Darke is doing it to Free Derry Wall. I passed by the Wall last weekend and there he was with his ladder and brushes and

buckets of red paint, coating the edifice in the scarlet of socialism.

Colin had explained to the *Derry Journal* that he wanted to pro-
voke questions about what the Wall means now, to incite
discussion of how its significance has shifted and adapted down
through the years, as politics and warfare swirled around.
Naturally, I paid attention. After all, it's my Wall.

You've probably seen a picture of Free Derry Wall, or at least a
picture with the Wall in the background. It's a gable-end on the
Lecky Road in the Bogside which was left free-standing when the
terrace of houses it used to be part of was demolished in the
early '70s, Even then, it had come to be seen as a local-historical
monument, the inscription on it, "YOU ARE NOW ENTERING
FREE DERRY", understood as a statement of community defiance.

Nowadays you can buy souvenir badges in the shape of the
Wall, and t-shirts, mugs, dishcloths and all manner of paddy-
whack nick-knacks with the Wall as a logo. On any summer's
day there's tourists taking turns being photographed against it,
even squaddies in groups as they come to the end of their stint
here. I never begrudge them.

It's the usual site for Republican rallies in these parts. It was
where thousands gathered to welcome our neighbour Johnnie
Walker home after his release with the rest of the Birmingham
Six. And it's the end-point of the annual Bloody Sunday march,
as it had been for the demonstration on the day in 1972 which
was destined to become Bloody Sunday.

The Wall has sometimes been paint-bombed and vandalised,
and cops or soldiers in an armoured car once rammed it in the
dead of night in an effort to tumble it down. It's always been
repaired and repainted and the lettering ever-more neatly, too-
neatly, touched up. And there it still is, now in vibrant red, and
the inscription in yellow.

I thought the colours were familiar when I caught sight of the
finished work. Something about the combination stirred an eddy
of remembrance. It was obvious enough really, after a moment:
the Wall is now in the colours of the Viet Cong, which back in

1969 would have been obvious immediately. Flags in exactly that shade of red, with a star in the middle in that shade of yellow, decorated a zillion student bedrooms then, and swayed in forests along heaving revolutionary marches as young people seemingly everywhere shouted out their opposition to US imperialism and declared their solidarity with the resistance of the Vietnamese people.

The Wall, at last, has been colour-coded correctly.

I came up with the slogan "You are now entering Free Derry" in the middle of a night in January 1969 as a group of us sat around a fire on a piece of wasteland in the Bogside waiting for the rioting to resume. It was in the immediate aftermath of a student civil rights march from Belfast to Derry, and then a police attack on the Bogside which had been beaten off in hours of riot and resistance.

The slogan wasn't original. I took it from a picture of a protest at Berkeley College in California, one of scores, maybe hundreds, of universities and colleges in the US, Europe, Australia, wherever, disrupted around that time by demonstrations, mainly against the Vietnam War but also focusing on the other great issues and oppressions of the age. It was the style of the most militant of the student demonstrations to expel the university authorities from campuses and to erect barricades and declare "Free" universities. Within these, in theory, all power relations were abolished, and formal classes replaced by "teach-ins" about how oppression might be ended and liberation won.

The reality didn't always match the rhetoric. I recall speaking on a "liberated" campus in New York State during the period, and becoming aware in the course of a very long evening meeting of an atmosphere of unmistakable intimidation, with student leaders aggressively silencing anyone who dared show opposition to their "line". In contrast, some occupations in Britain had no sense of seriousness at all.

Still, the occupations were part of a process in which many millions of young people felt a sense of togetherness across great distances and cultural barriers, of involvement in a vaguely apprehended but nonetheless real common purpose, to do with changing the world for the better, and people beginning to make themselves free. Everywhere you looked you could see it.

Africa was in the throes of de-colonisation, and buoyant with optimism for the future. The political agenda in Latin America was dominated by discourse about reform-or-revolution. In Asia, particularly in Indo-China, huge anti-imperialist struggles were being fought. In the United States, black people in the deep South and the inner cities were rising in open revolt. Europe was in a ferment of opposition to the Cold War and nuclear weapons. The gay liberation movement was readying itself for eruption. Some of the key texts on women's liberation were already being published.

It made sense then to see what was happening in the North as an element in a great global upsurge, part of a struggle for freedom involving vast numbers of people and challenging an array of oppressions of different kinds and contexts. We weren't looking into ourselves or backwards through history for inspiration, but out across the world and on towards the future. It was natural enough in the Bogside to recall a picture of an occupied college in California and the slogan "You are now entering free Berkeley", and to have a local adaptation inscribed on the handiest gable-wall.

If the exact reference to a particular place wasn't obvious to all at the time – there was no particular reason it should have been – there was a good enough understanding of what the words were generally getting at. Free Derry was a fragment of a liberation going on everywhere.

That's not what the words are taken to refer to any longer. I have watched racist bigots from the Ancient Order of Hibernians in the United States posture with local liberators for pictures at the Wall, all untroubled by any awareness of contradiction. The freedom the Wall proclaims now is Irish Freedom, as this has traditionally been conceived. The inscription no longer contains a socialist libertarian, but a standard nationalist, sentiment.

I don't say this by way of complaint. Whatever about the broad context, the precise inspiration for the slogan had been in the physical surroundings and the immediate events. "Free" in the first instance had meant freedom from the RUC and the oppressive State whose authority it enforced. And you didn't have to be a political or historical analyst to draw a connection with the old notion of "Irish Freedom". The meaning which attaches to it now came naturally, as it were.

And anyway, if the vast majority of those a slogan or a symbol purports to speak for understand it to mean a particular thing, then that's what it does mean.

But, as Colin's coat of paint strikingly reminds us, it's not the only thing it can mean. There are other possibilities which we have glimpsed before and which we will eventually have to grapple with again at closer quarters. Not least because it is only in the process of striving towards that brightness that the Bogside might achieve an Irish liberation worth the price paid in suffering around Free Derry Wall.

Strange the things that come into your mind, staring at walls.

28 July '94

42

Two Cheers For The Ceasefire

AT THE MIDNIGHT HOUR, AS the Provo ceasefire came into force, I didn't go up to the Rosemount Barracks to cheer and jeer and bang on the security fence. Instead, I headed up to the Dungloe to listen to Martin Hayes on fiddle and Steve Cooney on guitar. I thought I'd feel better in that atmosphere. I was iffy about the unrestrained air of celebration which the Republicans were insisting was the proper response to the "dawn of a new era" (*Irish News*), although I hadn't yet worked out why.

But I had a vague sense that there was something false about the air of triumph and it's come more into focus since. The scenes on the Falls as Adams cradled bouquets of flowers and buideals of champagne, besieged by adulation, betokened genuine jubilation, but there was, I think, something else too; a sense of relief, or more accurately of release, from a burden which people had found harder to bear than they'd been able to acknowledge, perhaps even to themselves. Some may have been celebrating a measure of freedom *from* the armed struggle.

The anti-Provo propaganda which has passed for news coverage in much of the media for much of the past 20 years, and more, had involved the demonisation not just of IRA activists but of the communities the IRA was rooted in. "IRA supporters" have been presented as having minds of dark malice which come to light only when filled with glee at somebody on the other side suffering, which is far from the truth.

Of course, there are vicious little bastards everywhere and no shortage of people on the Falls or in the Bogside who in their own minds have reduced Protestants to an abstraction. (And not just in the Falls and the Bogside: some of the worst sectarians in Ireland are to be found among the hush-puppy patriots of the South.) But for much of the time, many of the people here who have supported the IRA have had a struggle within themselves too.

In our pub, on the morning of the Enniskillen atrocity the most representative thing said was that "They [the IRA] are asking too much of us."

There was the same feeling after the Shankill bomb and, regularly in the wake of individual killings – which almost unnoticed, or at least unremembered – have punctuated recent past history, of Protestants with some unremarkable association with the RUC or British Army. Many who hate this pitiless infliction of grief nevertheless couldn't bring themselves to join in the instant denunciations engaged in by the type of media moralists who had, or have, no problem with killings in other contexts. The IRA was, and is, "part of what we are"; generated from within the community precisely by the pressures under which the community was put, and consisting in the main of the sons and daughters, friends and neighbours of ourselves and the people of the same street. There was a sort of duty placed upon people by that consideration which has now been lifted, and they walk with a lighter step.

Had there been any strong feeling that the armed struggle was useful, there wouldn't have been so widespread a welcome for its ending. There are some who have doubts about what's on offer in return, but no powerful faction has emerged to argue that continuation of armed action is the best way to win more. That reflects another emerging element in Catholic working-class attitudes, to do not with morality but with utility – the feeling that the armed struggle, whatever argument there might be about its role in the past, has become counter-productive to the interests of the community in whose name it was being waged.

That, too, is one of the reasons – likely the main reason – for the cessation; the IRA was reacting to the wishes of its "own" people. It's of passing interest that this went unmentioned in many commentaries. A big part of my iffyness has to do with the alternative strategy that Republicans are offering, of an alliance with the SDLP, the Dublin Government and the Irish-American lobby around Clinton to which Sinn Féin has been promised direct access. This is an impressive line-up in terms of general political clout but as a coalition, it can only hold together within the confines of a conservative agenda. It may be able to deliver some advance to the Catholic community in the North *vis-a-vis* the Protestants, but it will not deliver radical social change to anyone. And it certainly won't sanction any tactic or campaign which might upset the economic applecart. A number of commentators have wondered about the wisdom of Albert Reynolds associating himself so closely with Gerry Adams. I wonder about it the other way round.

There'll most likely be pressure towards a deal which, in substance, will amount to joint British-Irish authority. In one perspective, that would represent progress for the Catholics who for the first time could feel that their sense of identity was reflected and respected in the institutions of the State. But this would be achieved at the expense of Protestants feeling that they had lost further ground. And it would leave neither Catholics nor Protestants of the working-class better off.

Class has always been a major factor in the Northern situation and still is. Class is the main determinant of how Catholics vote. Broadly speaking, the poorer a Catholic you are, the more likely it is you'll vote for Sinn Féin; the better off, the more likely to support the SDLP. And if you are seriously rich, there's a chance you contribute to Alliance. It's always been the working-class doing the bulk of the killing and the dying, and the long years in jail. People who claim that class has no relevance are wrong.

Looked at in terms of class, Albert Reynolds is as alien to the Falls as to the Shankill. Any deal he will push for might make the Falls feel a bit better about itself, but it won't meaningfully lessen the level of exploitation on either road. What's more likely to emerge is an intensification of economic competition between the two.

There'll be demands that every low-paid job that US investment creates on the Falls is balanced by one on the Shankill, that every penny of "aid" on one side is matched on the other. By the same token, politicians on each side will squabble about fair shares of suffering as cut-backs and redundancies continue in existing employments and services.

All of this could happen "peacefully", of course, but not only would it be a poor sort of peace for us to stumble into at last, it would have the potential, when we rubbed up against one another too abrasively, to flare up into fighting again.

There's need for sharp debate in the Bogside and the Falls about what an "unarmed strategy" means, about what demands or campaigns it should encompass, on which section of society it should be based, to whom it should reach out and try to embrace – and who should be allowed to set limits to its ambition. Can the Falls reach out to the Shankill and yet keep faith with Reynolds? And if it cannot, which road should we now take? This is the key question which those who want to see the struggle through have to answer. First, though, it has to be asked. And an atmosphere of unquestioning and somewhat artificial euphoria isn't conducive to sharp questioning.

Two cheers for the ceasefire.

7 Sept '94

43

Is Gerry Adams Really The New Eamon de Valera?

THERE WAS GREAT CONSTERNATION AT government buildings on the day, a few weeks back, when Albert Reynolds, as he saw it, welcomed Gerry Adams into the constitutional fold as the de Valera of the 1990s.

That wacky woman who chirrups and trills about religion in O'Connell Street on Saturday afternoons and never misses a public meeting or mixum-gatherum in Dublin had smuggled herself into the middle of the media pack and was all set to erupt out onto the steps and into the camera-shots, even as Albert and Gerry and John clasped hands in tripartite pan-nationalist harmony – which, had she succeeded, would have detracted disastrously from the dignity of the occasion and, worse, given the world a chance to smile in wry amusement at the way quaint and colourful religiosity still intrudes into Irish affairs, even at the most inappropriate moments. But the wraith with the rosary beads was shooed swiftly away.

Then again, maybe it wouldn't have been entirely inappropriate if the lilting ecstatic had managed to insert herself into the picture and blessed the occasion with a verse of an oul' hymn or a decade of the rosary *as gaeilge*. De Valera himself, when it suited him, made no sharp distinction between the political and the religious in the public life of the land.

De Valera. Now there was a man with a will o' the wisp way with words. Nobody ever asked him for clarification of his pronouncements, possibly because they didn't want to be confused any further. De Valera was both excruciatingly articulate and precisely vague. Not that he was subtle when he saw no need. He once announced that he would wade knee-deep through Irish blood before he would accept the Treaty which established the 26-County State. Following which, he waded knee-deep through Irish blood, and then he accepted the Treaty and the 26-county State.

Many Republicans will have shuffled uneasily from one metaphorical foot to the other when Reynolds, speaking on the Sunday after the Handshake, at the annual Liam Lynch commemoration, made explicit his view that Adams was indeed following directly in de Valera's footsteps. The Long Fellow ranks high among hate-figures in Republican eyes, precisely on account of his acceptance of the 26-County State and the subsequent cold determination with which he put down old comrades who had held onto their arms and tried to stay straight on the Republican road.

The de Valera path may not be the route Republicans want to take, or believe they are taking, but it is the path Reynolds thinks he has enticed them along, and he is determined they won't stray off easily into the outback again.

This is what Reynolds will have meant when he said that the Republican ceasefire and the political realignment it prompted was "the pinnacle of my career". He was likely referring not to the achievement of "peace" but to his success – where de Valera, Lemass, Lynch and Haughey had all failed – in bringing Sinn Féin and the IRA to an acceptance of the legitimacy of the Southern State, and of the consequent right of the government of the State to be seen as the legitimate leader of all Irish nationalists. In historical terms this is a real gain for the Southern State and its government. So far, it's the biggest gain anyone has made from the Northern Troubles.

Commentators who have argued that Reynolds was moving dangerously fast in inviting Adams to meet him within a week of the ceasefire and then authorising a meeting between government officials and a Sinn Féin delegation are missing the point or contriving to confuse it. Reynolds wanted Adams into Government Buildings without any delay so as to have it publicly made clear that Sinn Féin now accepts the authority of the Dublin government. He knows, or at least his advisers do, what an enormous move away from Republican orthodoxy this is.

It was because Adams was wary of how this would be received in his own ranks that he insisted on Hume being present as well. Had he gone in to see Reynolds alone, and emerged for the photo-call with Reynolds alone, the occasion might too easily have been seen as the Republican leadership formally relinquishing something which the Movement had always regarded as a core belief. The inclusion of Hume made the picture presentable as three nationalist leaders conferring together, rather than one conceding legitimacy of leadership to another.

It is worth mentioning, too, that – whether or not this was made explicit during the talks in Belfast last month between Sinn Féin and the US delegation led by former Congressman Bruce Morrison – the goodwill of what we might call "official Irish America" towards the Republican Movement is now effectively conditional on the Republicans staying on-side with Reynolds.

US visas for Republicans, and access to centres of power in the US, are essentially in the gift of the Reynolds Government. The Provos have been put on their best behaviour and Albert Reynolds is to be judge of their behaviour.

He could snatch away from them, in an instant, all that they have gained in terms of political standing and international credibility. The suggestion, on offer in the *Irish Independent* from Conor Cruise O'Brien's grand car-boot sale of shop-soiled notions, that the Republicans have Reynolds on the run and are in the process of pushing the Southern State towards military conflict with Britain, is all the more ludicrous for its mis-handling of history.

Reynolds would turn on the Provos with implacable viciousness rather than let an open conflict between his State and the British State come about, and he'd have the support of the entire Southern establishment in doing it. He would, in a twinkling, don the mantle, not of de Valera *circa* 1923 whom he held up to Adams as a role model, but of de Valera *circa* 1943. The barbed wire would be up around the internment camp on the Curragh before sunrise.

In the euphoric aftermath of the ceasefire announcement it was hard to find an audience in Catholic areas for advocacy of any alternative to what the nationalist alliance had put on offer. But we live in fast-changing times, and there's an undertow of uneasiness, too, about where we are headed and a dawning realisation that the prizes which were promised if "the violence" was called off may be longer in coming than was anticipated, and may glitter less brightly than the PR sheen initially led many to believe.

I wrote in the last issue that I hold to the belief that working-class unity is the way forward. An old feminist friend asked me how on earth (actually, "How the fuck" was her formulation) I had arrived at that conclusion. But it's not my conclusion. It's my starting-point.

As little as ten years ago, virtually everyone who wanted an end to the sectarian State up here was at pains to explain that they were not out to extend the remit of the South across the whole island, that, on the contrary, what was wanted was a New Ireland altogether, fundamentally different from society as it stood on the other side of the border. Even "pure" Republicans who had no time for quaint notions like class struggle pitched their appeals to Fianna Fail at the "grass roots" of the party, and implicitly urged revolt against a leadership perceived as being class-biased against the poor and having sold out.

That pitch may have cut little ice with most Protestants, but at least it focused attention on the social content of the society which was envisaged as emerging from the Troubles. It put the Falls in a position, potentially at least, to discuss with the Shankill what sort of society might suit both. But that's off the agenda now. It's taken for granted that what suits one community will discommode the other.

Any advance which the Catholics make in the North will be measured against the position of the Protestants.

The rioting on Protestant working-class streets in Belfast reveals that Protestants see it this way. There have been loyalist paramilitaries stirring the violence up, motivated by murderous hatred of Catholics. But there's also the fact that the Protestant working-class has been deserted by Britain, and has been told, almost in so many words, that things will likely get worse for them now, not better, especially as compared with the Catholics.

There are big problems in all this which cannot be addressed within the framework of an alliance led by forces characterised by social conservatism and belief in a free market economy.

The heartfelt welcome rightly given to the IRA ceasefire should not prevent critical analysis of the strategy of the Republican leadership. Taking the de Valera road leads nowhere except up Albert Reynolds' garden path.

5 October '94

44

A Dedicated Follower Of Fascism

RICHARD LYNN IS THE UNIVERSITY of Ulster's dirty secret. He is Professor of Psychology at the university's Coleraine campus. The authorities there hope that he will go away quietly when his tenure ends next year. But members of the Anti-Nazi League are determined to drag the questions raised by his activities out into the open.

Lynn is involved in a network of academics on both sides of the

Atlantic who supply racist organisations with "respectable" arguments for campaigns of hate. The network is subsidised by a New York-based foundation, the Pioneer Fund, which was founded in the '30s to promote "eugenics" – the project for producing a "master race" which reached its highest expression in Germany under Hitler. Lynn has received vast sums from the Pioneer Fund towards his "research" at Coleraine.

Lynn is no closet academic remote from the practical implications of his work. He eagerly seeks mainstream outlets for his views, and appears to have little difficulty finding takers. His most recent broadside appeared in the *Irish Independent* on November 1st, reprinted from the *London Times*.

In an extended review of *The Bell Curve,* a book by two of his US co-thinkers, Lynn declared that "two percent of the population fall in the IQ range of 0-70 and constitute the mentally retarded, while a further two percent fall in the range 130-170 and constitute the intellectual elite.

"Virtually all the readers of this article," he assured his *Indo* readers, strangely, "will belong to this intellectual elite, or be close to it."

He then got down to cases: "The average IQ of mothers of illegitimate children is 88; of chronic welfare recipients, 85; of recidivist criminals, 80; of the long-term unemployed, 77. Collectively, these social problem groups are known as the underclass, and the bottom line is that the underclass has an intelligence deficit."

Now even if the IQ scores were accurate – which they are not: test results vary far too widely to admit of such exact figures for particular groups – it wouldn't matter much. Nobody can say for certain what IQ tests measure, apart from the ability to do IQ tests. Lynn simply defines intelligence to mean the ability to do IQ tests and then proceeds blithely down his chosen path towards race hatred and totalitarianism.

Moreover, the fact that the ability to do IQ tests might very roughly correlate with the position of different groups in society tells us nothing about how this correlation comes about. The long-term unemployed tend, for example, to have a lower body weight and a shorter life-expectancy than the generality of the population.

Few sensible people would conclude that the unemployed are out of work because of low body weight and short life-expectancy. They would see the relationship the other way round and take it as accentuating the urgency of fighting long-term unemployment. But that's not how Lynn and his network handle their evidence, such as it is.

"Intelligence is largely under genetic control," the Coleraine professor proclaims. "This means that the underclass is, to a significant extent, a genetic problem and will not be readily cured by the kinds of solutions advocated by economists and politicians . . .

"With an average IQ of 77, the chronic unemployed are not much above the level of mental retardation and many of them are below it. The brutal truth is that many of the chronic unemployed are mentally incapable of learning the skills increasingly required in advanced economies. All they are capable of is the unskilled work which is less and less in demand."

Lynn, like the authors of *The Bell Curve,* Richard Herrnstein and Charles Murray, moves unerringly from this "perception" towards the conclusion that they very likely had in mind from the outset.

The low-IQ underclass, they note, is not evenly distributed among the races. "In the United States," writes the University of Ulster man, "the average IQ of blacks is 15 points below that of whites, and 16 percent of blacks have an IQ of below 70 and are mentally retarded, as compared with only two percent of whites . . .

"Furthermore, the black underclass is growing in numbers . . . There is one thing the underclass is good at and that is producing children. These children tend to inherit their parents' poor intelligence and adopt their sociopathic lifestyle."

It is at this point that Lynn's activities at the Coleraine campus overlap with the overt racist campaigning of far-Right groups in both Europe and the US and, at the edge, touch on outright Nazism.

Four years ago the *Independent On Sunday* traced Lynn's connection with the US-published magazine *Mankind Quarterly,* which also enjoys the financial support of the Pioneer Fund, and has links with former Nazi geneticists. The UU academic confirmed that he was an "honorary associate editor" of the magazine, and that the ancient Baron Otmar von Verschuer was an editorial adviser – although Lynn insisted he didn't know Verschuer personally. Verschuer had been director of genetics and eugenics at the Kaiser Wilhelm Institute during World War Two and had recommended his pupil Josef Mengele for the position of camp doctor at Auschwitz.

Mankind Quarterly is edited by an expatriate British academic, Roger Pearson – another Pioneer Fund recipient – whose views on the necessity of racial purity were quoted last month in *Rolling Stone:* "If a nation with a more advanced, more specialised or in any way superior set of genes mingles with, instead of exterminating, an inferior tribe, then it commits racial suicide."

Words like "Nazi" are nowadays flung around far too frequently, used as generalised political insults until they have lost all precision. But in Pearson's case the term can be properly deployed: that is the statement of a Nazi. And Professor Lynn of the University of Ulster openly, readily announces his association with him.

Lower-level Nazis appear to have picked up on the association, too. A few months ago the Anti-Nazi League organised a march in Coleraine protesting against the university providing Lynn with a base for his 'research'. As the 100 or so marchers, mainly teenagers, walked along the main shopping street, a score or so of extremely angry men burst out from a pub screaming slogans and holding aloft the Ulster flag and copies of the National Front paper, *Bulldog,* and attacked the march with fists and boots. In the ensuing fracas, a number of people on both sides took blows before the attackers withdrew.

It was a minor incident which as far as I know was reported only in the *Belfast Telegraph* and in the local *Coleraine Chronicle.* What struck me most at the time was one of the slogans of the attackers, "White Rights! White Rights!", and the "insult" they chose to direct at their targets: not, as the display of the Ulster flag might have suggested – "Fenians" or "Provos", but "Red scum", "nigger-lovers" and so forth.

If the University of Ulster can't make the political connections, clearly there are others around Coleraine who can.

Members of the university's academic staff tell me that the college authorities anticipate Lynn retiring next year, and hope that the issue will disappear quietly with him. In the meantime, the official university line is that Lynn's racist activities and associations are none of their concern, since the work financed by the Pioneer Fund is conducted not by the Psychology Department but by an outfit run independently by Lynn himself.

This organisation is styled "The Ulster Institute For Social Research". However, no such title is listed in the North's telephone directory, nor is directory enquiries aware of its existence. Pioneer Fund documents obtained by anti-racist researchers in New York give the "institute's" address as 276 Drumcroon Road, Coleraine, BT 51 3QT. This is Lynn's home.

The New York researchers have been able to fax to me details of one Pioneer Fund grant supplied to Lynn, of $50,000 forwarded on February 12th 1992 for a study of "the effect of nutrition on intelligence and male-female differences in ability and motivations." (Lynn is also on record as believing that women are inherently less intelligent than men.)

This wasn't Lynn's first Pioneer Fund bonanza. *Rolling Stone* says that between 1971 and 1992 he received grants from the fund totalling $325,000 – and *RS* locates the beneficiary not at Drumcroon Road but in "Univ. of Ulster."

The Pioneer Fund was set up in 1937 by one Wickliffe Draper, a multi-millionaire who had made his money from the labour of textile workers in New England. Its first president was Harry Laughlin, one of the best-known US promoters of "master race" theory at that time. In the '20s Laughlin had played a key role in pushing through legislation to keep Jews, fleeing from persecution in Europe, out of the US, testifying to Congress that IQ scores showed that 83 percent of Jewish immigrants were feeble-minded and likely to dilute the quality of the nation's gene-pool.

Laughlin had also been the author of the Model Eugenical Sterilisation Law, which he circulated and campaigned for across the US. Adopted in various forms by 30 states, it resulted in the forced sterilisation of tens of thousands of "retarded" people, mainly blacks, the unemployed, 'immoral' women etc. It was used as the basis of the Nazi eugenics programme under which at least two million people in Germany were forcibly sterilised.

The Pioneer Fund organised "Draper Committees" which lobbied for restrictions on immigration and, for example, for the segregation of white and black blood in blood-banks. In the '50s, it was heavily involved in court actions to halt integration in schools, restaurants etc.

Rolling Stone lists more recent recipients of Pioneer Fund largesse. These include: University of Northern Iowa educational psychologist and vice-chairman of the pro-Nazi German-American National Congress Ralph Scott, financed to tour the US in the '70s, arguing that school integration would reduce academic standards; University of Southern Mississippi anthropologist Donald Swan, assisted to continue "research" to show that blacks were of a different, lower *species* than whites; William Shockley, a Stanford University mathematical-science professor, financed to develop a plan to offer social welfare recipients of low IQ incentives to be sterilised – $1,000 for every IQ point below 100; John Hopkins University sociology professor Robert Gordon, who has a "softer" scheme for convincing people of low IQ to agree not to have children; Lina Gottfredson, an educational studies professor at the University of Delaware and heroine of leading white supremacist David Duke, a campaigner against affirmative action to reverse racial discrimination in education and jobs . . . And so on.

The Fund distributes around a million dollars to about 20 recipients every year. The emphasis is strongly on academic projects located in respectable universities. The pre-determined racist results can then be presented as objective and even authoritative. This is what Lynn is at.

The fact that drunk thugs flaunting a Fascist party's paper wade in with boots and fists to defend him is appropriate.

Rolling Stone reckons Lynn is currently the fifth-largest recipient of Pioneer Fund money in the world.

Meanwhile, the university bosses ring-fence their racist with hypocrisy and cant about his "independent" research projects. But it is his position in the university which confers spurious respectability on him. In both the *Times* and the *Irish Independent* he was identified as "Professor of Psychology at the University of Ulster, Coleraine".

* * * * *

Rita O'Hare sounds very uncomfortable in that new trouser suit. The flame-haired Sinn Féin press officer was interviewed in the *Observer* two Sundays ago by John Waters.

"The 's'-word' is not, it seems, a problem for Sinn Féin," observed the Castlerea man, and went on: "'Our socialism is an Irish socialism,' stressed Ms. O'Hare. 'It is based on the ideas of people like James Connolly and Fintan Lawlor (*sic*) and was never based on anything outside Ireland'." The fella that put the cool into culchie was mightily impressed with that.

That's the way forward into the new Irish millennium, alright. We wouldn't want a sort of socialism that was contaminated with them dirty, foreign ideas. Sinn Féin's socialism has the Guaranteed Irish tag dangling from the hand-stitched buttonhole on its lapel. No need for anybody to worry on that score.

Marx, Engels, Lenin, Trotsky, Luxemburg, Kollontai, Gramsci, Maclean . . . dirty foreign divils every last one of them, out for some exotic sinful class of socialism:

"In Ireland it is an English importation, in England they are convinced it was made in Germany, in Germany it is a scheme of traitors in alliance with the French, in France it is an accursed conspiracy to discredit the army . . . in Russia it is an English plot to prevent Russian extension towards Asia, in Asia it is known to have been set on foot by American enemies of Chinese and Japanese industrial progress, and in America it is one of the baneful fruits of unrestricted pauper and criminal immigration."

That's the opening passage in Connolly's *Workshop Talks*. I half-remember that the most glamorous granny ever to come out of Belfast used to know it off by heart. But then, as I say, she doesn't sound entirely comfortable these times.

It's probably the trouser suit.

30 November '94

45

Patrick Mayhew And The Illegal Use Of Arms

SHOULD THE ILLEGAL ARMS BE handed over? The Northern Ireland Secretary, Sir Patrick Mayhew, was, understandably, very anxious about the answer to that question. And he's probably even more anxious now, as he awaits publication of the report of the Scott Inquiry into arms-related sales to Iraq.

Sir Patrick has been prowling the high moral ground recently, arching his aristo eyebrows and tilting his noble head just so, as he pronounces in orotund tones on the necessity for the IRA to hand over its weapons before their Sinn Féin associates can be fully accepted into the "democratic process". Can't have fellows toting guns and such-like outside the law, and then ambling into the conference room pretending to be proper politicians . . .

Then again: if the illegal use of arms was an impediment to inclusion in the "democratic process", would Sir Patrick himself be let in? Not that he has ever lain in wait in a ditch with an AK47 at the ready for a Para to pass by. Nothing as trivial.

Sir Patrick was Attorney General under Mrs. Thatcher in June

1990 when her Government was shaken by news that customs officials had descended on the Department of Trade and Industry (DTI), with what the department's head of export control described at the time as a "whopping great pile of blueprints". The customs officials claimed that the blueprints suggested that a Midlands firm, Matrix Churchill, had been illegally exporting machine tools to the Iraqi regime of Saddam Hussein for use in the manufacture of munitions.

The purpose of the customs team's visit was to alert the DTI to the fact that they intended to raid the offices of Matrix Churchill with a warrant for the seizure of documents, and to ask for any relevant papers about exports to Iraq which the department itself might hold. This was a key moment in the sequence of events which led to the establishment of the Scott Inquiry and which may yet see the end of a number of British Ministerial careers.

The inquiry under Lord Justice Scott has been a mammoth affair. It was set up in November 1992, held public hearings from May 1993 to July 1994, and is expected to produce its report in the spring of next year. Small, delicate beads of sweat may well form on Sir Patrick's stiffly elegant upper lip when his thoughts turn, as they occasionally must, to that certain eventuality.

When DTI officials called up files in 1990 on exports to Iraq they discovered to their consternation not only that Matrix Churchill had indeed been flouting export controls on Iraq, but that their own Minister, Nicholas Ridley, and quite possibly other Ministers, had known all about it all along, and had done nothing to stop or discourage it. This was all the more devastating given that the department was already in difficulties trying to explain its role in the "supergun" affair: the DTI had known about the export to Iraq of huge tubes, ostensibly for use as chemical pipelines but in fact components in the construction of the biggest gun in all history.

To make matters worse, it was only a few months since British public opinion had been outraged at the execution by the Iraqis of *Observer* journalist Farzad Bazoft, convicted of spying after being arrested in Baghdad while investigating a story to do with Saddam's military build-up.

If prosecutions went ahead against the directors of Matrix Churchill, or of Walter Somers, the main firm involved in the supergun affair, the defendants might well argue that they had had government approval for what they'd done. Faced with these unfortunate circumstances, the DTI swallowed hard and then passed on all the relevant information to the customs team and wished them well in their doughty efforts to unmask the merchants of death who had been supplying the monster Hussein with the means of murdering millions. You might think.

What they actually did was to hightail it round to the office of the Attorney General and to ask Sir Patrick if he could think of a wheeze to get them out of this one. And no better man.

After hugger-mugger discussions between high officials of the DTI, the Ministry of Defence and the AG's office, a confrontation took place on November 9th, 1990 between Sir Patrick and a number of his officials on the one hand, and a team of customs investigators on the other. By this stage the issue had become even more explosive: on August 1st, Saddam had inconveniently ordered his army into Kuwait and was now effectively at war with the West.

In the face of angry and bitter opposition from the customs investigators, Sir Patrick argued that the evidence in respect of the supergun affair was inconclusive, and "advised" that intended prosecutions be dropped. He didn't reveal anything of Ministers' complicity in the matter, but did indicate that if the case were to come to trial, the line the defence was likely to take could give rise to embarrassing suspicions which the country didn't need at this time of national trial. He reminded the customs team that even if they insisted on pressing ahead he, Sir Patrick, would have authority to enter a *nolle prosequi* when the case opened – i.e. to instruct prosecuting counsel to offer no evidence.

And so it was that on November 15th, 1990, at Sheffield Magistrates' Court, the supergun case was abandoned without any evidence being called and two defendants walked free. A number of Labour MPs and papers like the *Guardian* tried to stir up concern about the murkiness of the business. But since the defendants, naturally, weren't complaining, and there was no evidence on the record to be parsed and analysed, it was hard to take the story any further.

The customs officials, outraged and frustrated in equal measure, were now more determined than ever at least to pin Matrix Churchill. Their chief, Sir Brian Unwin, wrote to the Cabinet in February 1991 warning that three directors of the firm, Paul Henderson, Trevor Abraham and Peter Allen, were imminently to be charged.

The Government was in a tricky position. The Gulf War was now in full spate, with Allied planes pounding Iraq and ministers and the media hammering out the message that Saddam was the "new Hitler", who had to be stopped at all costs. Men who had broken the law to help arm the "new Hitler" could expect little sympathy from the public or leniency from the courts. This time, the customs team looked forward to a successful and popular prosecution.

On the other hand, Ministers knew what the customs men didn't: that the defendants had been told by nods and winks – and even discreet handy hints about how to disguise destinations on consignment documents – that everything they were doing was hunky-dory by the government. The customs investigators had, of course, looked into this claim – it was the basis of the defence case – but had been assured, and had accepted, that there wasn't an iota of truth in the bizarre allegation. The case opened in October 1992.

Sure enough, the three men in the dock pleaded that they had had government approval for the illegal exports and demanded that documents from a number of departments, which they said would prove their claim, be produced. For a time it seemed very unlikely that this would be done. The prosecution argued that there was no evidence that any such documents existed and that a futile trawl through government papers touching on such sensitive issues would be contrary to "the national interest".

However, the leading defence barrister, a suave fellow called Geoffrey Robertson, refused to let go of the issue, successively demanding the production of lists of exports, records of meetings at the DTI or between DTI officials and diplomats dealing with the Middle East, minutes of meeting of MoD officials, reports to the cabinet office, special branch reports etc. etc. But it all seemed a wasted effort. No fewer than six government ministers signed "Public Interest Immunity Certificates" (PIICs) testifying that it would be contrary to "the national interest" to release the classes of documents Robertson was asking to see.

And then something very strange happened. The judge, Mr. Justice Smedley, called for the documents Robertson had cited so as to determine for himself whether their release would in fact damage the "national interest". He eventually concluded that a sizeable proportion of the documents did support the defendants' story, and either didn't compromise the "national interest" at all, or didn't to an extent which would justify their being withheld at the risk of denying the defendants a fair trial. In effect, he ruled that the references to the "national interest" had been no more than a ploy. The Matrix Churchill case, too, instantly collapsed.

Over the following days, even the most rabid of Tory newspapers expressed editorial anger that ministers had tried to withhold vital defence evidence from people charged with offences which, it was now clear, the same ministers had actually sanctioned. It was to still this furore that the Scott Inquiry was established.

There was a government reshuffle during the period we have been considering. Two Attorneys General were involved at various stages in offering legal advice to the ministers concerned. One was Sir Nicholas Lyall, the other the current resident of Stormont Castle, Sir Patrick.

All of this information has emerged at the public sessions of the Scott Inquiry.

What it shows beyond a glimmer of doubt is that British ministers secretly conspired to facilitate the export of lethal equipment to a vicious dictatorship, breaking their own laws, regulations and policy commitments in the process; that they desisted only when the regime in question attacked another dictatorship deemed more important to British interests; and that they then conspired to withhold information from the courts in an effort to ensure that people down the line took the rap.

Sir Patrick Mayhew, the highest legal officer in the land, was up to his neck in this filthy business.

How Lord Justice Scott estimates his role remains to be seen. We have learned from as far back as Widgery on Bloody Sunday, to the May report on the Guildford Four and Maguire cases, to Hamilton at the Beef Tribunal, that the most compelling evidence, publicly given, of serious wrong-doing by senior politicians, does not necessarily lead eminent judges to the obvious conclusions. That said, Scott has conducted his inquiry so far with a rigour which the regime that appointed him will not have anticipated. We must wait and see.

In the meantime, would Sir Patrick not be wise to observe a discreet silence on other politicians' alleged knowledge of or complicity in the illegal use of arms?

30 November '94

46

Humans, Ants And Worse . . . Richard Lynn

MY CONTINUING INVESTIGATION INTO the rancid lunacy of Richard Lynn, Professor of Psychology at the University of Ulster, unearths an article published by the London *Times* during the Gulf War.

Why are there wars?, the learned professor ponders. And answers thus: "Over millions of years of evolution the genes predisposing people to war have become universal in the human species. Any peoples in which they were not present have long ago become extinct . . .

"Imagine two adjacent tribes. One is peaceable and has no liking for war . . . its neighbour, however, is highly warlike. Sooner or later the warlike tribe picks a quarrel with its peaceable neighbour. It starts a war which it is bound to win. The warlike tribe then takes over the territory of the peaceful tribe. It kills the men and impregnates the women. The genes for warfare have spread and the genes for peacefulness have been extinguished."

Mind you, it's not just humans. Take ants . . . "the species that most closely resembles our own in organised warfare between populations numbering millions. Like us, ants fight for the same objective, to gain territory from their neighbours, or to defend their territories from take-over."

I thrust from my mind the possibility of advancing this as a defence should I ever be charged with doing Richard Lynn a terrible injury – "Couldn't help myself, your honour, biologically predisposed after the manner of ants to hit him a blatter on the bake as soon as I saw him" – and continue to the bit where Lynn considers the awesome implications of his thesis.

If we are biologically programmed for war, are wars not always inevitable? And in the era of weapons of mass destruction, does this not mean that our species is programmed for extinction?

Well, no. Y'see, "Biologically programmed propensities can be held in check. For many centuries in Christendom, the sexual drive was kept so well under control by social constraints that many people were celibate until they married in their late twenties. It is equally possible to curtail the biological propensity to warfare."

That's a relief, eh?

But how do we set about curtailing this propensity to wipe out our neighbours?

"For this purpose we need international agreement to prevent the absurdity of the technologically advanced nations selling sophisticated weapons to countries such as Iraq. It will also be necessary for the United Nations to act decisively where and whenever an aggressor nation attacks a neighbour. The near unanimity with which the UN has acted in the Gulf is an encouraging sign that the biological propensity for war may yet be held in check."

Got that? Saddam Hussein invading Kuwait and killing hundreds of innocent people – that's the biological propensity for war. Western forces frying and shredding 200,000 Arab people, the vast majority of them civilian men, women and children – that's curtailing the biological propensity for war.

Did I mention that this fucking lunatic is Professor of Psychology at one of our Irish universities?

3 May '95

47

The Making Of Seamus Heaney

THERE WILL BE AN "EXPLOSION of joy" at St Columb's College in Derry next week when the Nobel Prize for Literature is presented to Seamus Heaney.

Heaney's bauble has already made St Columb's dizzy with delight. Senior staff at the school, and the Derry Catholic establishment generally, are only half-recovered from their celebration in September of the announcement that the prize had gone to an Old Boy. The formal conferral in Stockholm will be marked by such delirium that I fear for the safety of a few clerics with bad hearts.

The prize has shed a brilliant light on the school. We have already had a spate of articles wondering what it was about St

Columb's that it should turn out such distinguished men. Heaney, Hume, Deane, Friel, Coulter . . . there'll be more of this in the next fortnight. Camera crews have already trawled through the grounds to prepare feature-pieces. An entirely positive picture of St Columb's is being projected.

I went to St Columb's from 1954 to 1960. I had some good times there, as almost all of us did in our schooldays. And like many another, I tend to concentrate on the good days when I hark back. But I also remember oppression, perversion and fear. Most mornings, I hated going in.

I do not believe that St Columb's can claim credit for "producing" Seamus Heaney. St Columb's conscious raison d'être had nothing to do with producing poets or peacemakers or encouraging imaginative engagement of any kind with the outside world. It was a Catholic diocesan secondary school for boys. Its specific purpose was to maintain a flow of recruits into the priesthood, while constantly reproducing a conservative, middle-class leadership for the Catholic community as a whole.

It was natural enough, in light of this mandate, that little emphasis was placed on the opening of minds. We had a history teacher who at the beginning of the school year might instruct us to rip out, from a set textbook, pages containing "English lies" such as that Charles Stuart Parnell and Ms Kitty O'Shea had been more than good friends.

Of course we were led to believe that sex was dirty and disagreeable. Pop was denounced as – they used the exact phrase – "the devil's music". The school president once walked onto the school stage at a concert by our French class to stop Derek McMenamin (later Derek Dean of The Freshmen) singing 'C'est Ci Bon' and to deliver a rant against "le jazz Americane". Those involved in the production were hauled up the next day and left in no doubt of the gravity of our offence.

Insofar as it could be contrived, nothing alien was permitted to penetrate the school walls. This cannot simply be put down to the suspicious conservatism of the age. It was a conscious effort by the school and the Catholic diocesan authorities to discharge a "duty" to protect us potential recruits to the priesthood "from the contagion of the world", as Fr John Blowick, founder of the Maynooth Mission to China, put it in his influential *Priestly Vocation*.

This regime was imposed by force. Some of St Columb's teachers were savages. A few gave every appearance of getting their rocks off by beating up small boys.

Fr A: "Kearney, think of a number."

Kearney: "Two, Father."

Fr A, counting from the top of the class: "Porter one, McLucas two. Come out here, McLucas."

McLucas was then battered around the classroom before being sent back cringing and crumpled to his seat with the injunction, "Don't blame me, blame Kearney, he picked your number." My, how they must have cackled into their cassocks in the staff room about that one.

Or Fr B might beat a boy unconscious with his fists for not knowing an Irish translation, then tell his classmates, "Cart him outside, I'm not having him lying about in my classroom."

Fr C's favourite technique for encouraging greater efforts at mastery of the third declension was to instruct a boy to kneel on a platform at the front of the class holding his hands straight out in front and with his feet behind raised off the ground. He would then be made to open his mouth wide so that Fr C could insert a wooden-handled felt chalk duster into it. Fall forward onto your hands or tilt backwards so that your feet touched the floor and you would be battered around the head. Thus, balanced precariously on the fulcrum of his knees and emitting animal grunts, the student was invited to agree by a nodding of the head that he was a useless ignoramus who would never be fitted for anything better than digging ditches and had no place here in St Columb's, wasting teachers' time.

It strikes me now that some of these galoots may have been clinically insane.

Not all were like this, of course. There were decent men there too. But the guys who were sick in the head were a well-integrated element.

A few years ago, a St Columb's teacher was removed from his

post after complaints that he had been fondling boys' thighs and buttocks. He had been at it in my day too. A couple of teachers were known to every boy in the school as fondlers. Staying out of their reach at particular times was regarded as almost a game. I find it difficult to estimate how deeply we were damaged by this. Most of my contemporaries, when we talk about it now, say, "Ah, sure it did us no harm, old X was a pathetic sort of figure really." And maybe so. But the agony of embarrassment that burned inside me for days afterwards at getting an erection visible under short trousers at the front of the class as a teacher caressed my thigh and cooed in Irish still remains as my most vivid single memory of six years at St Columb's. It can't have done us any good. And everybody knew they were at it.

It is commonly said that "in those days" pupils rarely complained to parents about abuse in schools, or that if they did they weren't listened to. This is true, but, again, it's not the whole of it.

With regard to the college's primary role, parents had no rights. More accurately, children were deemed under Church law to be exempted from parental control while in "junior seminaries" like St Columb's. Parents had a right to interfere in the process of channelling recruits towards the religious life only when there was a demonstrable "grave need" so serious as to override the Church's own needs. As Blowick scornfully puts it: "Against what is the boy to be protected in the alleged interests of his parents? Against his own higher good? Against the interests of the Church, which is in grave need of priests?"

So it wasn't only the temper of the times which discouraged protest. It was also the specific Catholic nature of the institution.

The class bias of the school flowed from its secondary role in the replenishment of the layer of conservative middle-class laymen tasked to police the lower orders.

The Church in Ireland has never sought total control of the education of all Catholics. Although the key encyclical – *Divinis Illius Magistri* of 1929 – forbade "Catholic children on any pretext whatsoever to attend neutral or "mixed" schools," the hierarchy took the view that Catholic children could study "crafts and agriculture . . . but not general education" in the same room as Protestants. (It was on this basis that the Cosgrave government in the South was granted permission in 1930 to establish Vocational Education Colleges). In other words, the Church took a fairly relaxed attitude to the context in which proletarians learned to work with their hands. But when it came to shaping the minds of the intended social élite, rigid control was the order of the day.

Thus, in the '50s, there was no problem about young Bogsiders of both sexes attending the integrated State sector "Strand Tech", while up in Bishop Street St. Columb's strove hard to preserve its exclusive, monochrome ethos. But of course it was fighting a losing battle.

Almost every article on Heaney's Nobel Prize has alluded to the fact that the Bellaghy man was among the wave of Catholics who were eventually to swamp Third Level education in the North as a result of the passage of the "11-plus Act", providing scholarships to secondary school and then university for anyone who passed the none-too-difficult exams. The shuddering impact of this wave of bright and belligerent Catholic youngsters on bowler-hatted Ulster Unionism has frequently been chronicled. Less well-covered has been the way it initially unnerved the conservative Catholic establishment.

I have written elsewhere of my first exchange with a clerical teacher on my first day in St Columb's.

"Where do you come from?"

"Rossville Street, Father."

"Ah yes. That's where they wash once a month."

Again, this wasn't just the snobbery of a rural oaf, but the expression of something central to Catholic education. As the secretary of the Catholic Headmasters' Association had once warned: "The majority must be engaged in unskilled work, for which, whatever doctrinaires may say, overmuch education totally unfits them, if only by making them discontented."

Heaney's poetic pulse didn't quicken until long after he'd left St Columb's. In the nature of things it's impossible to quantify how important his time there was for the honing of his talent and the shaping of his imagination. My own guess is that it wasn't important at all. But whatever the extent of its influence, it's a nonsense to suggest that St Columb's "produced" Heaney, other than in the sense that the medieval papacy could be said to have "produced" the great works of the Renaissance.

It was in the ideological collision between the sense of wonderment of young people deemed unfitted for "overmuch education" and the stale assumptions of a repressive Church that sparks flew, and some caught fire.

It isn't in St Columb's, as much as in the working out of discontent within it, that we might look for the reason why some fashioned from their time there an experience to prize.

30 November '95

48

Bill Clinton: The Executioner's Song

THE FIANNA FÁIL TD JIM McDaid said on *Questions And Answers,* on RTE television that not even Jesus Christ could have matched Bill Clinton's miraculous performance at Mackies in Belfast. Mr McDaid quickly corrected himself. He hadn't meant to go that far. What he'd intended was that only Jesus Christ could have bettered Bill Clinton.

It was interesting that nobody on the *Q&A* panel or in the studio audience erupted into laughter. This, I imagine, was because it wasn't outrageously extravagant in the context of the general coverage of the Clinton visit. Never in the field of Irish journalism has so much goo gushed from so many.

I have read and heard it said that the Clinton visit was a "defining moment" for Ireland. Who's to say? We may well look back in a year or two or three and see that, the flood of euphoria having receded, little is changed in the political landscape. Or maybe, again, the Clinton visit will be recognised as a significant plot-point in the broad narrative of our history.

Quite likely it will be regarded as a defining moment in one particular sense anyway: that it drew the definitive line between, on the one hand, those who believe that the world is divided along the horizontal line of class, and, on the other, those who have either never held or have given up on such notions.

The sheer shamelessness of Inez McCormack's and Nóirín Byrne's intros to Hillary Clinton certainly defined the trade union and feminist bureaucracies for the foreseeable future.

Michael D. Higgins capering around Clinton like a bit player from *Darby O'Gill And The Little People* accurately summed up what that particular strand of soft-Left moralism is worth in these days of political discount. And then there were Provos frantically waving US flags . . .

Twenty-five years of anti-imperialist struggle and it's come to this.

About 20 of us turned out on Clinton Day in Derry, mostly from Amnesty and the SWP, with placards calling attention to Cuba, arms sales and the death penalty in the US. As far as I know, there was no mention of this demo in any media outlet. Which was fair enough in a way. If there's 20,000 out to bid Clinton welcome and only 20 with a bad word to say, the 20 can't expect splash headlines. Especially when the journalists covering the event are apparently to be included in the 20,000.

I was one of half a dozen who spent the 10 minutes or so of Clinton's piss-poor speech – it didn't compare with Dana's address when she came home from winning the Eurovision – holding aloft a placard saying, "Remember Rickey Ray Rector – murdered by Bill Clinton". Others handed out copies of a four-page Amnesty tabloid publication detailing the use and abuse of the death penalty in the US, and sketching Clinton's record on the issue.

Rickey Ray Rector, who was black, was killed by lethal injection at the Cummins Unit of Arkansas State Penitentiary on January 25th, 1992. He had been convicted of the murder of a white police officer, Bob Martin. After shooting Officer Martin, Rector had tried to kill himself by putting the gun to his temple and firing.

Rector survived. But the wound, and even more so the surgery to remove the bullet lodged in his brain, resulted in a frontal lobotomy – the loss of a square three-inch section of his brain. He was left with acute memory loss and serious mental impairment and wholly unable to assist his attorneys at his trial. A doctor who appeared for the defence testified that he was "like a child" and estimated his mental age at six.

The date set for Rector's execution fell at a key moment in the last US presidential campaign. Clinton was emerging as the front runner for the Democrats as they bid to end 12 years of Republican domination. Democratic Party strategists had locked their focus onto the mistakes made four years earlier by Michael Dukakis, who had lost out to George Bush. In their analysis, the Willie Horton issue had cost Dukakis dear.

Horton was a black man who had been allowed remission and released from a rape sentence in Massachusetts, and who had gone on to kill a white woman. The Bush camp used this to denounce Dukakis, the Governor of Massachusetts, as "soft on crime". The image of the black rapist and killer was used on billboards and TV ads to stir up the half-suppressed fears of uneasy white electors. Dukakis presented an undignified spectacle as he ran scared from the issue, and probably deserved to lose as badly as he did.

Clinton was determined that he wouldn't be tripped up by any "Horton factor". As his biographer John Brummett makes clear, he welcomed the Rector case arising, just as voters prepared to go to the polls in the first and crucial primary in New Hampshire in January 1992.

Clinton's press people distributed copies of the letter he had signed telling Rickey Ray there'd be no reprieve, he was to be killed.

Clinton took time off from the campaign and flew back to the Governor's Mansion in Little Rock so that he could be there as the sentence was carried out. There was no necessity for this, no law or protocol demanding the Governor's presence in the State at the time of an execution.

But on reflection, he wasn't taking time off at all. The trip home to Arkansas was on the campaign trail. He wanted to be seen to be associated with the killing.

Amnesty says: "The execution itself was carried out in an extremely disturbing manner. Witnesses to the execution reported hearing moans or outbursts coming from the execution chamber as technicians searched for almost an hour to find suitable veins in which to inject the chemicals. Rickey Ray Rector was apparently aware of the problem and helped the execution team in their task. In a newspaper article on January 26th, 1992, the administrator of dental and medical services for the Arkansas Department of Correction said: 'We weren't just sticking him every minute. We were looking for a new vein. We kept thinking the next one would be it. We thought we had it but we didn't. That's unusual, but it happens. He had spindly veins that collapsed easily. We searched. We were lucky to find a vein at all'."

Once Rickey Ray had died, Clinton, contented, returned to the hustings in New Hampshire. What a nasty piece of work Clinton is beneath all that pudgy *bonhomie*.

And she's no better.

19 December '95

49

The Worm At The Heart Of Direct Action Against Drugs

"HE GOT WHAT HE DESERVED. Anyone that entices children to take drugs . . . drugs are disgusting. I'd have shot him myself if I'd been asked." Thus one woman from the Norglen Parade area of west Belfast quoted by Susan McKay in the *Tribune* (December 31st) reacting to the killing of Martin McCrory on December 27th. The killing had been claimed under the covername "Direct Action Against Drugs".

There had been acerbic comment in some quarters on the cool nerve of the IRA in operating under such a see-through cover. It's a flimsy device, so it's said, intended merely to give Sinn Féin leaders space in which to prevaricate publicly, while the military wing continues to let everyone in "our" areas know who's boss. And maybe so.

But the title "Direct Action Against Drugs" fulfils another purpose. Any claim of responsibility under this name for a killing or beating carries an in-built suggestion that the victim was targeted because of involvement in "drugs". No further elaboration is necessary. It's all in the name.

Certainly, nothing which could be construed as "evidence" is necessary. As the social control specialists of the Republican Movement are aware, such is the irrationality surrounding the issue of "drugs" that an insane atmosphere is easily, more or less automatically, generated once fear of a drugs problem is raised. As well might we have pleaded for a cool appraisal of proven facts in Salem, Massachusetts, in 1692.

Oppose Direct Action Against Drugs and you can be certain of a patriot in the corner who'll consider it a duty to denounce you as a danger to the children of the community.

PR-wise, "DAAD" is quite a trick.

The broad justification for the "DAAD" death campaign is that its targets are doing the community damage. The campaign is, therefore, being waged for the community's good, in a sense on the community's own behalf.

It's handy, of course, that there's no mechanism available for testing the extent to which the community freely endorses the campaign. But then, that's just part of the "policing problem", isn't it?

Strange all the same that we haven't heard from Direct Action Against Sweatshop Employers. Or Direct Action Against Pederast Priests. Or even Direct Action Against The Minister Responsible For Abolishing Lone Parents' Allowance and thus plunging thousands of the most vulnerable members of the community deeper into poverty.

Of course, that last one would be a breach of the ceasefire and we couldn't have that. Can't go around stiffing Tory Ministers.

Martin McGrory, though, Norglen Parade, no problem.

Although a number of commentators and a scattering of political back-benchers have argued that the DAAD killings should be regarded as a breach of the ceasefire, the official line of all the major parties, North, South and across the water, is that the ceasefire should be seen as unbroken, and that the killings of Mickey Mooney, Tony Kane, Saul Devine, Fra Collins, Sid Johnston, Martin McCrory and Ian Lyons should not be seen as an integral part of the conflict which came to, shall we say, a "cessation" in September 1994.

There is a logic to this.

The killings are not an expression of sectarian conflict, and have no relevance to any campaign against British imperialism. They have mainly to do with the relationship between the Republican movement and working-class Catholic communities.

And sure what would any of the major players in the peace process care about working-class communities?

The thought occurs to me that between stiffing people you see as a threat to your ability to boss an area physically, and stiffing people you see as a threat to your political control, isn't such a big jump that an agile organisation, with no compunction about killing people generally, couldn't manage it.

15 January '96

50

Hey Momma, We're All Tories Now!

THERE WAS A RALLY OUTSIDE the City Hall in Belfast at lunchtime on Friday, organised by the Irish Congress of Trade Unions and attended, the papers said, by 5,000 or 6,000 people. It could have been more.

The rally was for peace and to put pressure on anybody wanting back to war. But the notion that the Tory government should take a share of the blame for the Canary Wharf breakdown of the IRA ceasefire was banned. At an organising meeting three days previously, the majority view was that bad-mouthing Major would "alienate our Protestant members".

Protestant trade unionists were thus dismissed as Tory dupes. There's a lot of this about.

On Tuesday last week, I called in at a meeting of "community leaders" in the Rathmore Centre in the Creggan Estate, just in time to hear a senior member of Sinn Féin dismiss Protestant members of Derry Trades Council as "token Unionists". Scorn dripped from the words as he spoke. He was arguing against a suggestion that the support of community groups in Protestant areas and cross-community organisations should be sought, to put pressure on the British Government to move towards all-party talks.

The reason the trades council had come up in discussion was that earlier that day we'd had a rally in Guildhall Square, about 2,000 strong, at which the Tories were given a lashing that would have left welts on their hides if they didn't have rhino-thick skin. Protestant trade unionists and school students in the crowd roared out approval with the rest.

And why not? Shakespeare's Shylock said, asserting the humanity of Jews, if you prick me do I not bleed? And so do Protestants, if they are left with a leg hanging off them on a trolley in a hospital corridor for six hours because the medical staff are out on their feet trying to cope with staff shortages, and the facilities and equipment are being flogged off by the Tories to their fat-cat friends. And they draw conclusions. Most working-class Protestants I know hate the Tories with a passion.

But the Republican leader in the Creggan Centre was having none of that. Prods are reactionary bastards. Only political wierdos believe you can march forward in step with the Prods.

Another speaker at the same meeting referred casually to "Unionists, Orange Tories, Protestants, call them what you will."

So conservative union bureaucrats and right-wing Catholic nationalists agree on this at least: that working-class Protestants are hopeless reactionaries, and there's no point in trying to involve them in progressive political activity.

"Tory" seems to mean something different to Tony Blair, too, when it comes to Northern Ireland. Take any policy area other than the North, and Blair's lot will at least make a show of suggesting an alternative. Education, health, immigration, Europe, whatever: Labour will rubbish Tory plans and suggest they're motivated mainly by a grisly determination to hang in there by any means necessary, sucking down to low-lifes here, currying favour with a half-mad bunch of xenophobes there, in the quest for enough votes to keep their snouts in the trough for a few months more.

Blair being a blow-dried class of politician, these attacks are not mounted with nearly enough gumption or gusto. And the alternative New Labour offers will likely make little difference. The point is, though, that debate happens, and Labour even thinks it appropriate betimes to exaggerate the distance between the two sides.

But not on Northern Ireland.

There is a "Shadow" Northern Secretary – and never was the word "shadow" more appropriately applied – called Mo Mowlam, who has never been known to utter an original thought on the subject she supposedly specialises in.

When the Docklands bomb went off and the balloon went up, Mo went to ground before emerging to suggest a "negotiated amalgam" of John Major's idea of electing negotiators, John Hume's plan for referenda on peace and all-party talks and Dick Spring's wheeze for "Dayton-style proximity talks". Then she went away again.

And what was the line Blair laid out when he rose to answer Major on the day after the Docklands bomb? Posing gravely at the Dispatch Box, that grin which is usually superglued to his face replaced by an expression which facial consultants must have fondly imagined conveyed statesmanlike solemnity, and speaking in a voice which begged timidly for hush, he paused before declaring: "Me too."

He offered not even a tentative hint that the Tories might, even inadvertently, have put a foot wrong.

In the North, potentially the most decisive section of the population is dubbed "Tory" and dismissed. Meanwhile, in Britain, they are all Tories now.

The struggle continues blindly against the descent into darkness.

6 March '96

51

The Hundredth Monkey Puzzle

THIS IS SCARY. SOME READERS will remember a piece here a few weeks back commenting on John Waters and the monkeys of Koshima. John had revealed in his innovative column in The *Irish Times* that he'd been reading a book about scientists feeding monkeys on the Japanese island of Koshima in the '50s with seed potatoes dropped on the sand.

The book, *The Hundredth Monkey*, told how one clever young monkey, Imo, had begun washing the potatoes in a stream before eating. Then Imo's mum caught on and started washing her potatoes, too. Then other young monkeys, and their mums and so on. And then, suddenly, at a certain point, all of the remaining monkeys on the island simultaneously took to washing their potatoes as well.

The book suggested, and John was clearly entranced by the thought, that once, say, 99 monkeys had taken to washing their potatoes, it needed only one more to reach "critical mass". As he put it himself: "The added energy of the hundredth monkey somehow created a breakthrough".

An even more dramatic development soon followed. "The habit of washing sweet potatoes then spontaneously jumped over the sea – colonies of monkeys on other islands, and the mainland troop of monkeys at Takasakiyama, began to wash their sweet potatoes".

John spelled out the implications: "When a certain number achieves an awareness, this new awareness may be communicated from mind to mind. Although the exact number may vary, the Hundredth Monkey Phenomenon means that when only a limited number of people know of a new way, it may remain the consciousness property of these people. But there is a point at which, if only one more person tunes into a new awareness, a field is strengthened so that this awareness reaches almost everyone."

John applied this point to the political philosophy (I'm quoting here) of Tony Blair, and predicted that any day now Blairism would reach critical mass and sweep across Europe.

Fair enough. Far dafter things than that have been published in the *Irish Times*. But wait.

I'm passing through Dublin the other day when I bump into someone coming hot-foot from a briefing at the Department of Foreign Affairs, who tells me that a very senior official there is upset at myself and John Waters. Here's the story. I am not making this up.

It seems that the persons with the delicate task of devising and implementing policy in relation to the North have been operating for some time on a belief that Unionists are in the process of changing their attitudes to the South. Not noisily and *en masse,* you understand, but quietly, in ones and twos. The Department believes that if everybody is patient and just waits then, eventually, "critical mass" will be achieved and the Unionists will "come over" in an avalanche.

Department officials have been influenced in shaping this perspective by reading a book called *The Hundredth Monkey . . .*

As I was given to understand it, the reason for the upset has to do with a fear that if *The Hundredth Monkey* becomes the subject of raillery and skit in newspaper and magazine columns, progress towards critical mass among Unionists may well be disrupted. Presumably because the Unionists will cop on to what's happening.

The official whose thinking is here described, has played a key role in Anglo-Irish relations in recent years, and still does.

I walk away towards Toner's, backwards, resolving to get back up home across the border first bus in the morning.

Hey, scary.

* * * * *

I genuinely thought it was the joke story for the day that was in it when I read the off-lead headline in the *Irish News* of April 1st: "RUC pleased at capture of cannabis haul by IRA".

But no joke. The IRA in Newry had passed a bin-bag containing 15 pounds of cannabis resin to the RUC, using a local priest as intermediary. An RUC spokesman was quoted saying: "We are pleased that the drugs are off the street, and we are pleased that they have been handed in. It was a complete and total surprise. We would class this as a substantial haul, certainly".

The South Down Command of the IRA assured local "concerned parents" that it was ready to take "decisive action" against anybody continuing to deal in dope.

According to the Irish News, Sinn Féin councillor Brendan Curran accused the RUC of "putting little effort into combating the drugs threat, leaving the work to the paramilitaries".

All you who take the occasional toke when it's offered can let that one simmer in your minds and see what it reduces to. But nice to know in advance what sort of changed society we'd be living in if the armed nerds of the South Down IRA ever acquired real power.

24 April '96

52

The Provos Just Don't Think Big Enough

THE MARINE MAKES A BID, giving candy to the kids, his teeth are gleaming . . . Higher than O'Connell Street! Longer than Liberty

Hall! So huge in the water it will have to hove-to a mile and a half beyond the dock of the bay!

Come on without! Come on within! You ain't seen nothing like the mighly USS JFK, scheduled to make its majestic entrance into our unworthy Irish waters next week.

One hundred and seventy-thousand people panting to be picked to go aboard.

The cowards and the whores are waiting at their door to see who's winning . . .

And 22 VIPs have a zip in their step. Why? Because they are being flown down to Cork so as to sail back up the coast and actually be "on ship" (that's the technical term) when – Lawdy forgive me, I've just come in my pants – the "live firing exercise" is conducted.

If they want for their next thrill to come up this part of the country, I might be able to arrange a little live firing of a more homely kind. But I can't guarantee plain sailing back home.

Maybe the fellows on the JFK with the clear eyes and good skin will nuke Waterford for the craic (lovely authentically ethnic word there) as they sail past? There'll surely be no complaints except from begrudgers, if something of that sort happened to happen. We are the most popular people in the world, don't you know. That's actually been shown, in a survey. Everybody loves us and our lovable ways. If Waterford's reduced to a smear of ash on the map, we won't make a fuss to embarrass the visitors.

We'll clean the john with a rag, sir, we'll clean the john with a rag/If you like we'll use your flag, sir /If you like we'll use your flag.

What's the difference between the crew of the JFK and the celebs queuing up for invites to party on board?

One crowd kicks ass, the other crowd licks ass.

The crabs are crazy, they scuttle back and forth, the sand is burning/The fish take fright, poisoned in the night, the sea is churning.

The marines have landed.

And Michael D Higgins is nowhere to be found.

* * * * *

The JFK

Big, eh?

Tell me, a child once asked a wise old Flann, what manner of warriors must they be to be chosen for the band of Finn?

They must be warriors such as can run through the green places of Ireland with forty armed men standing upwards in the slack of their gut-hung drawers.

What manner of man, then, is Finn?

Such as man as when taking his rest at Mullingar, forty hirelings might play handball against the flat broadness of his buttocks.

As Finn put it himself and him amach ar na sléibhte: Big, me arse.

It is reported that, following the IRA bomb aimed at people provocatively shopping in Manchester, Dublin diplomats (now there's a paralogism for you: you don't meet them often these days) were animatedly in touch with the US Embassy to try to ensure that G. Adams was scrubbed from the JFK guest-list.

Can't allow somebody with second-hand car bomb associations to associate with chaps so respectable they are in charge of nuclear weapons.

It's like I've always said about the Provo bombers. They just don't think big enough.

So make a list of the ten people in the Dublin media most vehement in demanding that the government stop fudging and break off all links with Sinn Féin.

Now make a list of the ten people in the Dublin media most vehement in demanding that the government stop fudging and forge strong links with NATO.

There you are now.

26 June '96

53

Coogan's Bluff: The Arithmetic Of Sectarianism

TIM PAT COOGAN HAS BEEN studying the sectarian statistics of the North and drawing wrong and dangerous conclusions. A popular figure among political and media folk in Dublin, Tim Pat is a former editor of the *Irish Press* and the author of a history of the IRA, and of provocative biographies of De Valera and Michael Collins. He is regarded as something of an authority on the North, particularly on the development and course of nationalist politics.

In an interview on Radio Ulster and in articles in the *Irish Times,* Tim Pat has been arguing that there's no need for the IRA to persist with armed struggle in order to bring about a united Ireland. All they need do is wait for the Catholics to outnumber the Protestants.

In an article in the *Irish Times* recently he suggested the following: The census shows that, since 1993 the majority of new voters coming onto the North's register has been Catholic, and that Catholics are in a majority under the age of 15 . . . The famous 'million Protestants' are now under the 900,000 mark . . . It is as certain as anything can be that the next decade will show a marked growth in the Catholic population, with a corresponding effect on the numbers supporting nationalist parties . . . If the (IRA) . . . takes up arms again and goes to war for another 25 years, the very best it can hope for is to arrive by means of death and destruction at a situation which (they) would have arrived at in any case."

This is, at the least, an interesting thesis. If we were to be flippant we might characterise it as a new adaptation of the old '60s slogan "Make love, not war". But the situation it refers to is way too serious for that.

My basic problem with Tim Pat's view is that it's rooted in an assumption that Catholics and Protestants in the North are, naturally and necessarily, separate and distinct peoples, and that the problem has to do with which of these peoples predominates. This amounts to an acceptance, whole and complete, of the notion at the heart of Orange-Unionist ideology: it implicitly denies even the possibility of people identifying themselves in politics other than by reference to the religion they "belong" to.

This perception allows no acknowledgement of the old aspiration of Tone and Connolly, and of generations of unremembered radicals, who struggled against the stream of communal consciousness to proclaim that sectarianism is neither natural nor necessary. Instead, it envisages the sedulous preservation of the religious division while one community grows and gathers in strength to replace the dominance of the other.

This view dismisses the contribution to our political culture of the many thousands of Protestant people who, in good times and bad, have stood firm against Orange bigotry and for a sense of themselves which included Catholics. Protestants in every decade have taken this stand, often at some imminent danger to themselves.

Let us recall at this time the testimony of the sole survivor of the Kingsmills, Co Armagh, massacre of January 1976, the one Catholic man among ten Protestants who had been on their way home together when their minibus was stopped on a lonely road in the dead of night by an armed gang.

When the assassins lined the 11 workmates up at the side of the road and demanded that the Catholic stand out, it was assumed – very reasonably, given the appalling atrocities against Catholics in the area in recent times – that the gunmen were Loyalist paramilitaries intent on killing him as a Catholic. The ten Protestants gathered around the assumed victim, remonstrating with the gunmen and protecting him with their own bodies, and in so doing identified themselves as the Protestants. The gunmen, Republicans of a sort, slaughtered them all into the ditch.

That will have reduced the breeding population of Protestants by 10.

There's no place in Tim Pat's scheme of things either for my late friend, the "shipyard playwright" Sam Thompson, or for John Hewitt, or Louis McNeice, or Charabanc writer Marie Jones or actors Dan Gordon and Stephen Rea, or for Van Morrison for that matter, or the essayist Robert Lynd, or for scores of Protestants today who I know to abhor the evil divisiveness of Orangeism. I recall George Craig, who walked to his work from the Protestant estate he lived in through the barricades every day during the Loyalist stoppage in 1974 to proclaim trade union resistance to bigotry. George is a union official with the T&G now, and no better man to have in your corner.

We will outbreed *them?* That's the alternative to armed struggle!?

This may seem a harsh construction to put on Tim Pat's statistical jiggery-pokery, and an unfair attitude to attribute to him personally. I don't doubt he'd be appalled at any suggestion that he harbours hostility to Protestants, or to anybody on account of religion, and indeed he doesn't. But what is he saying in his prescription for the North other than that whichever community comprises the "greater number" has a right to impose itself on the other?

In what way is this different from the prescriptions of Trimble and Paisley, Cruise O'Brien and Billy Wright?

Incidentally, in his eagerness to anticipate the success of his strategy, Tim Pat gets his statistics in a twist. He told Radio Ulster's *Talkback* programme that Catholics will be in an electoral majority by the year 2005. No, they won't. On present trends, and, so to speak, giving the Catholics the benefit of every doubt, the earliest there could be a Catholic majority in the North in 2020. And even on the crass assumption that all Catholics are and will continue to be genealogical nationalists, this could not translate into a voting majority until 10 years later, at a minimum.

In the *Irish Times,* as mentioned, Tim Pat gave his readers specifically to understand that already "Catholics are in a majority under the age of 15". No, they aren't. At the last count, the number of 15-year-olds and under in the North was 418,275. Of these, 192,871 were designated Catholic.

The veteran nationalist writer Frank Curran, who knows more than Coogan and myself put together about the shifting demography of the North, has characterised Tim Pat's "analysis" as "mischievous and counter-productive", and commented: "Inaccurate figures like these . . . cannot contribute to a calm and reasoned debate on the future of Northern Ireland".

Tends to put things mildly these days, does Frank.

16 August '96

54

Inaccurate Reporting Of A Startling Kind

"FACTS ARE SACRED," MUSED AN editor of the *Guardian* so long ago it was the Manchester *Guardian*. That was the *Grauniad* then, this is the Indo now.

You can rant and rail to your heart's discontent against the values, opinions and what you take to be the biases of a person, a programme, a publication like the *Sunday Independent*. And so what? Comment is free.

But you don't make free with the facts.

The Sunday before last, on August 11th, the day after we'd survived a weekend of draining, debilitating worry in Derry, the *Sunday Independent* published a piece which gave the Bogside

Residents' Group a lashing for its hard-line approach to the Apprentice Boys' march in the city.

I have no problem with that. I lash them myself when I don't like what they are at, and do it at closer quarters. But even in anger, accuracy is all. Or should be.

You will have gathered, at the time, that the BRG had objected to the Apprentice Boys marching along a stretch of the City Walls overlooking the Bogside. As a result, the Northern Secretary, Patrick Mayhew, had ordered the closure of this section of the Walls. The *Indo* journalist suggested that the BRG had been unreasonable in the way it forced the issue.

She wrote: "As soon as the Walls are reopened, nationalists should go to Derry, walk the route intended by the Apprentice Boys, and then ask themselves if the demands which the BRG has been making of Protestants on their behalf in the past week can be justified. Half an hour on Derry's Walls ought to make nationalist Ireland thoroughly ashamed.

"Making such a circuit of the Walls, as I did for the first time last week, shows once and for all that the Bogsiders have made an issue out of nothing . . . The proposed route of the order does not go through the Bogside: one tiny section overlooks a tiny section of the estate, that is all. The nearest houses are 250 yards away . . .

"By getting the Walls closed off under threat of street violence, the Bogsiders also ensured that the Apprentice Boys could not get to their own headquarters before Saturday's proposed parade."

The piece also referred disparagingly to a "rally" against bigotry "organised on the Catholic side of the city".

To take the last point first: the "rally" consisted of a march and a meeting. The march route was from a mainly Protestant area to Guildhall Square in the city centre. At no point did the small number who attended enter any place which might be described as "the Catholic side" of the city. The organisers were, if it matters, both Catholic and Protestant.

More pertinently, the Bogside houses nearest to the contentious stretch of the Walls are not 250 yards away. The nearest houses

(at the top of Fahan Street) are the width of the street away –
maybe 20 yards. (The nearest Bogside residences to the relevant
portion of the Walls are flats on Waterloo Street which back
directly onto the Walls. The distance between these dwellings
and the Walls is, I suppose, nil.)

This is a major point only because the *Sunday Independent*
writer chose to major on it. It can be argued (although it's not an
argument I accept) that the Apprentice Boys and the other "loyal
orders" are authentic expressions of the culture of the Protestant
people and that they are entitled to march without hindrance
along any reasonable route, even ones which come within 20
yards of Catholic houses, as long as the marchers don't behave
offensively as they proceed.

But the *Indo* journalist based her argument squarely on the "distance factor" and got it as wrong as wrong could be. How, I
wonder, can this have happened?

The houses on Fahan Street are, well, obvious. Red-brick, two
storeys, small front gardens opening directly onto the pavement.
A couple have satellite dishes ornamenting the front gables. It's
hard, very, to understand how anyone could look down from the
Walls and miss them. But the woman from the *Sunday
Independent* managed it.

Remarkable.

Then there's the suggestion that the closure of the walls prevented the Apprentice Boys from reaching their own
headquarters. The building in question is the Memorial Hall. It
stands at the corner of Magazine Street and Society Street. To
reach it, you either go up Magazine Street from Butcher's Gate or
down Society Street from Bishop Street. You do not go onto the
Walls.

There is no access from any section of the Walls to the
Memorial Hall. This would be immediately apparent, literally at
a glance, to anyone standing in the vicinity.

What's going on here? This isn't a matter of getting the timing
or the sequence of a series of events wrong, of garbling a quote
or misidentifying an individual. This is inaccurate reporting of a
startling kind. The equivalent, in Dublin terms, would be report-

ing as the key fact in an important story that Burgh Quay can't be seen from Liberty Hall or that blocking off Middle Abbey Street denied citizens access to the GPO.

A couple of weeks previously, the same journalist had told *Sunday Independent* readers that residents of the New Lodge Road in Belfast had reacted to the Garvaghy Road affair by burning down a number of businesses, although they had not, she declared with heavy sarcasm, torched, for example, the local post office. That facility, she cackled, was where they collected social security benefits provided by the British tax-payer.

No businesses were burned in the New Lodge after Garvaghy Road. This wasn't an inaccurate, distorted or caricature version of something which had happened. It was an invention.

Sometimes, when events take a course which their mind-sets can't make sense of, people close their eyes and imagine things differently.

Close your eyes with the *Sunday Independent*.

20 August 1996

55

Horsewhip The Dole Cheats

MANY THOUSANDS OF READERS HAVE written in asking if I could tell them when and why Shane Ross went mad. I tell them not to exaggerate.

Ross is a Fine Gael senator and the business editor of the *Sunday Independent* and is involved in a number of financial and investment operations. He is also very upset.

Many might think that a fellow with such a portfolio of jobs would be too busy to get upset, but that's to miss the point. What makes Ross upset is that he can't enjoy the vast sums of money he makes because, all day, every day, there is the possibility that he may become conscious of the poor.

He might be sitting on cushions in his sumptuous abode on a leafy Dublin 4 avenue counting his incomes from the taxpayer, Tony O'Reilly and the London and Dublin stock exchanges, when suddenly a picture will form in his mind of hundreds and thousands of Irish people living in poverty. Why, wouldn't any stockbroker's happiness sicken and sour in an instant at the very thought of it.

He hates it when this happens. In fact, he hates the very notion of people living in poverty. He wishes they would go away. And if they won't go away he wishes they would stay quiet, be a little less obtrusive. And he wishes even more that bleeding-heart liberals who prattle on about the poor would give over.

One way and another, he thinks that if the poor and the prattlers about the poor don't stop bugging him right now, something will have to be done.

Take the dole. Off them. Because if there's one thing Ross feels strongly about (as a matter of fact there's more than one) it's the way the poor have gotten their grasping hands on so much of the money dished out by the State.

Why, he told anguished Sunday Indo readers a few weeks back, some of these people are raking in absolute fortunes (as window-cleaners, chimney-sweeps, dish-washers and the like, I understand) and drawing the dole as well!!!

Indeed, Ross may well have been in the vicinity of the Horseshoe Bar in the Shelbourne only the other week when the talk apparently turned to a man from Darndale (unlike Ross, we will come back to Darndale) who between a nixer on the build-ings and the money from the welfare was raking in as much as £250 a week, and no doubt using the loot brazenly to buy his children bags of crisps in broad daylight!

If that isn't enough to have decent citizens forming the Ballsbridge branch of the Michigan Militia, then I don't know what is.

If all this taxpayers' money wasn't being handed out willy-nilly to the poor so that they can stuff their children's faces with food, it might be possible to give senators a better daily rate for turn-ing up at Leinster House on the days when they aren't doing other jobs. But do the poor think about that, eh? No, they do not, the selfish bastards.

Then there's the residential property tax. If there's one thing makes Sen. Ross' thin blood boil (as a matter of fact there's more than one) it's the RPT. Think about it. If your house is worth more, in round figures, than a hundred grand, and there's more than thirty grand a year coming into the household, you have to pay RPT! Has anybody ever heard of anything so downright unfair? Did the blood-stained Bolsheviks of Soviet Russia ever propose anything so depraved?

But do the poor give a flying frig as they saunter arrogantly away from the hatch at the labour exchange weighed down with tens of pounds to fritter away on Bird's Eye fish fingers, ankle socks and Pampers? No bloody Pampers around when Ross was shiteing himself, I can tell you. As Sen. Shane sometimes says, the poor don't know when they are well off.

Which brings us to the point.

Although Sam Smyth swears on a Protestant bible that it's true,

I have never believed the story about Shane Ross shiteing himself in Darndale. But here it is anyway.

Ross had ventured into the huge working-class estate in north Dublin in search of votes in the 1984 European election campaign, travelling in one of those cars with a sliding roof so he could stand up on the passenger seat with the upper half of his body poking out, and wave, and use a loud-speaker to address passing voters.

Now Ross is what used to be called a Trinity Toff, and looks the part. Bad hair, eyes made for a monocle, a nose that looks lonely if it's not being looked down, the wrong waistcoat, yellow socks. If they'd been casting someone for the role of Ross in a movie forty years ago, they'd have thought first of Wilfred Hyde-White. Twenty years, Leslie Phillips. Ten, Penelope Keith. Nowadays, they'd wonder if Mark Thatcher would be too type-cast.

Wouldn't strike the people of Darndale as one of their own, would Ross.

Anyway, according to Smyth, Ross' talking head protruded through the roof of the car as it proceded slowly through the estate, articulating campaign slogans such as (I'm guessing here) "Horsewhip the dole-cheats!", "More money for people like me!" and "Hurrah for the British Commonwealth of Nations!" But Darndale folk didn't rally in droves.

No, I tell a lie, they did.

Indeed, in fact, it seems they poured from their homes and converged on the Ross-mobile with serious expressions on their faces and a suspicion of implements in their hands, at which the car took off like it was auditioning for the chase scene in *Bullitt,* causing Ross to slew backwards and forwards from the waist up across the roof, with his feet inside desperately threshing to find fixity and leverage to prevent himself being sloughed off and left as a thud and a bundle in the path of the impending horde. Small wonder he was in sore need of pampering by the time he reached the safety of a street of houses that nowadays you'd pay RPT on.

As I say, there's a theory that this was the defining experience of the rest of Ross' life, that it had a most awful effect on his mind, and that this is the awfulness now evident.

Does that answer your question?

31 October 1996

56

The Aftermath Of Bloody Sunday The South Recoils

25 YEARS AGO THIS MONTH, on January 30th 1972, Bloody Sunday, British soldiers stormed up the street where I was born and shot 13 people dead. I watched some of it happen.

Recently, I've been reading the newspapers of the period, per-paring a talk to mark the anniversary. What has intrigued me most is the reaction recorded in the South. It was on a much bigger, broader scale than I remembered. But at some levels it was shorter-lived, too, and perhaps not as deeply felt as I'd thought at the time.

For the three days after Bloody Sunday, the South was hit by a succession of work stoppages. On the third day, the day the vic-tims were being buried together in Derry, towns and villages across the country were paralysed by a general strike as effective as any in Europe since World War II.

This is commonly characterised in histories as a 'day of mourn-ing', which in a way is fair enough. But the mourning mainly took the form of massive walk-outs from work, which were called in Dublin, Cork, Dundalk, Waterford, Galway, Sligo and Letterkenny and quite likely in other places too, not mentioned in press reports – by the local trades councils.

Reports from Dublin on the Tuesday after the killings, for

example, tell of a succession of marches arriving at the British embassy in Merrion Square from mid-morning to late afternoon, to hand in petitions, or parade outside with placards, or shout protests or whatever.

500 workers from the Hammond Lane Group on the Bluebell Estate delivered a letter which each of them had signed. The entire workforce, it was said, from Beamish and Crawford in James Street, arrived next. Then "hundreds" behind an Electrical and Engineering Union banner from Murphy's Structural Engineers in Santry. After them, 120 marchers from the Agricultural Institute. Then "several hundred" from the Aspro Nicholas factory in Walkinstown. Then a contingent from Booth Poole and Co at Islandbridge. Then 500 agricultural students from UCD . . . and so on and so on and so on.

Reports from every other major centre of population were along the same lines.

Of the following day, the day of the funerals, the *Irish Times* account, by Dick Walsh and John Armstrong, began: "The British Embassy in Merrion Square, Dublin, was burned down yesterday, after the biggest demonstration the Republic has seen in a generation."

The report estimated that it took an hour for the parade, much of it workplace contingents, to cross O'Connell Bridge in an afternoon of driving rain and bitter winds. "Along the route, thousands joined the march and many thousands more waited in Merrion Square while, with muffled drums and black flags flying, the main body of protesters arrived".

The protesters eventually over-whelmed the Gardaí around the building and burned it down.

Around the rest of the South, the close-down of shops, offices, schools and factories was absolute. Few buses or trains ran and Aer Lingus aircraft were grounded. No British planes landed or took off at Dublin, Shannon or Cork airports. Estimates of the size of a rally in Cork city centre varied from 20,000 to 50,000.

This grief and anger was reflected also in an unprecedented contingent travelling to Derry for the funerals. Ten State cars in convoy crossed the border at Bridgend three miles outside the city. 14 members of the government, led by Tánaiste Brian Lenihan, a personal representative of President de Valera, 32 backbench TDs including Garret Fitzgerald, Conor Cruise O'Brien, Ray McSharry and Charlie Haughey, 17 senators, the mayors of Cork, Limerick, Waterford, Galway, Kilkenny, Drogheda, Sligo, Clonmel and Wexford, all in ceremonial robes, the general secretary of the ICTU, the president of the GAA, bishops, archbishops, and an estimated 200 priests, and many, many more, arrived from the South at St. Mary's in the Creggan for the requiem mass.

This was, in its way, the highpoint of 32-county nationalism in the history of the Southern State. Never, since partition, had there been such a deluge of emotion engulfing all of society, never before or since such a sense of oneness in shared, raging sorrow with nationalists corralled in the North.

But what's most remarkable, looking back on it now, is how rapidly and ruthlessly thereafter the Southern establishment moved to contain it, and to ensure that the aftershocks didn't unsettle political arrangements on their own patch.

Two days after the killings, on the day before the burning of the British embassy, alongside a series of lengthy reports from Derry, the *Irish Times* carried a single-column story which began: "The Army Chief-of-Staff, Major General TL O'Carroll, said yesterday that the force was well-equipped to deal with internal security and likened the morale in the country to that of the 1940 period when 40,000 men were recruited very quickly".

General O'Carroll was speaking at a press conference which almost certainly had been arranged before the massacre. But the tone and emphasis of his remarks are striking nonetheless. What was uppermost in his mind in the aftermath of the killings was the possibility of an internal threat to stability emerging in the South.

This same apprehension was repeatedly expressed in the Dail debate on Bloody Sunday, held on the day after the funeral deputation's return from Derry. Opening the debate, the Taoiseach, Jack Lynch, referred to "men who, under the cloak of patriotism, sought to overthrow the institutions of this State . . .

"Groups proclaiming themselves to be members of illegal organisations have gone about intimidating people," he said, "seeking to give the impression that these organisations are now to have a free hand . . . The institutions of this State will be upheld without fear or favour. The laws will continue to be enforced. Those who seek to usurp the functions of government will meet with no toleration".

Picking up the theme, the Opposition spokesman on Foreign Affairs, Richie Ryan of Fine Gael, declared that the lessons to be learned from the burning of the embassy was that "now the anarchists, those who hoped to destroy the institutions of the State, know that if they could get sufficient numbers of peope behind them, they could do untold damage".

Mr Ryan suggested that the government had not, until now, been "awakened" to the ominous possibilities. But the events of recent days had made the danger plain.

There were many expressions, too, of anti-British feeling, and of determination that the perpetrators of Bloody Sunday would and must not be allowed to unsettle the institutions of their own State.

The same note was dominant in a debate the following week on a Bill authorising an increase of 600 in Garda numbers. Fine Gael front-bencher Tom Fitzpatrick agreed with the Minister for Justice, Dessie O'Malley, that congratulations were due to the gardai who had tried to protect the British embassy. But, he went on, 600 new gardai wasn't nearly enough to rectify the deficiency the burning had revealed. At least 2,000 were needed. And "something would have to be done about training and equipping (them) to cope with crowd control and riot conditions".

Additionally, "any outstanding pay claims" by gardai should be conceded without further ado. Sean Moore of Fianna Fáil intervened to say that "any legitimate grievance under which the force laboured should also be removed".

At the Fianna Fáil Árd-Fheis held at the RDS on February 18th-20th, the same theme resonated through the hall. Justice Minister O'Malley announced "to prolonged applause" that a number of Northerners recently acquitted on arms charges in a district court would be re-arrested and charged with the same offences before a judge and jury. Mr O'Malley went on to say that the government "would not rule out 'Special Courts . . . if the new measures were not sufficient".

Mr Lynch's presidential speech, wrote the *Irish Times* political correspondent Michael McInerney, "was remarkable for its absence of attacks on Britain or the Unionists (and) for its appeal for an end to emotional reaction".

In his Árd-Fheis sketch, John Healy wrote: "By far the most significant thing, however – and one with far-reaching consequences – to strike me was the absolute absence of any feeling that the men of the North belong in the moral community of Fianna Fáil. The North to most of them, as a community, is half a world away . . .

"Sitting there listening to the speeches, you get the feeling that the North is nothing more than a functional historic claim: a thing so long reduced to standard clichés like our fourth green field that it isn't real any more".

There were many in the North, not all of them Unionists, including people like myself, who, then as now, had no wish to be enveloped in the embrace of Fianna Fail or included in any "moral community" of nationalism, and who will have found Healy's blood-and-soil rhetoric repulsive. The point is that, just three weeks after the North had seemed as never before to have become a visceral reality in the South. the main party of nationalism had disengaged from it, emotionally and intellectually, and resolved to crack down hard on anybody who showed disrespect for the Southern State by disregarding its border. The hundreds of thousands on the streets of the South were overwhelmingly wage-labourers. Whatever feeling they evoked in Britain or among Unionists in the North, they struck fear into Fianna Fáil – and all other Dail parties of the day.

Bloody Sunday had brought the North closer to home in the South than ever before. Once they'd had time to consider, the reaction of the South's ruling class was to ward it off, push it away, and to begin to devise solutions which would involve only such changes in the North as would mean no change in the

South.

The main effect of Bloody Sunday on Southern nationalism was to reconcile it to partition.

22 January 1997

57

A Horse Of A Different Colour

ROSA LUXEMBURG ONCE WROTE THAT anyone who steps needlessly on a worm on the road to revolution has committed a crime. But even she might be dismayed by how daft the British media sometimes go about animals.

The hysteria over the IRA's bomb-hoax disruption of the Grand National brought back memories of Sefton. You'll remember Sefton, the horse which survived a 1982 IRA bomb attack on bandsmen at Hyde Park, and instantly became a celebrity. Nobody outside their own family circles can now remember the names of the 11 human beings blown to bits in London that day, but the publicity which surrounded Sefton was such as to ensure he'll never be completely forgotten.

During Sefton's convalescence, tens of thousands of get-well cards and bunches of flowers were delivered to his stable. When he had recovered sufficiently, he was interviewed on ITN. Sefton's handler stroked his charge's shining flank as he told the journalist what a brave and true-Brit soldier this horse really was. Sefton would be back on parade soon enough. No way would he be intimidated from his national duty by cowardly terrorists. Not Sefton.

One thing, though: Sefton hadn't uttered a single sound since the bomb-blast. Nary a cough, snort, whinny, neigh nor ululation.

Upon receipt of this information, the journalist held the mike out at arm's length to Sefton's head and kept it there for long enough so the nation could hear Sefton not making a sound. The ITN man then himself looked silently into the camera for meaningful seconds before saying: "Somehow this sums up how so many people feel."

Myself, I felt gutted that Sefton couldn't speak, so the interviewer might have asked him, as they do, "Well, Sefton, what do you feel now about the people who did this?"

And Sefton might have answered: "They're fucking animals."

Then there was Moby, the sperm whale who fetched up in the Firth of Forth the week before the National, and who finally floundered on mud flats on a Monday morning. The *Mirror* reported Moby's "funeral", which took place after a "full post-mortem".

BBC reports of Moby's demise were couched in those hushed tones of gentle sadness which the corporation normally reserves for the death of ancient actors or music-hall turns that nobody under the age of 90 has ever heard of. Rescue workers were deeply moved. Some local people said it was akin to personal bereavement. Small children stood in tears. That sort of malarkey.

I have nothing against whales. They're enormous, and harmless to humans. We'd be hugely deprived if whales were let die. Roaming the oceans, they are a symbol of freedom and of concern for the global environment. My position on whales is unassailable.

Mind you, whales weren't so cuddly when Dopey Dick spent a week frolicking in the Foyle. Dopey was a big hit back in November '77.

He'd dandered up the river and in under Craigavon Bridge before he was spotted as he curled hugely through the water, seeming to revel in the mass acclamation. Whole schools filed into town to line the banks of the river, and thousands flooded in from all over the North West to get a glimpse of the impressive spectacle.

There were galleries of more than 5,000 some days, roaring approval of Dopey's dare-devil manoeuvres.

For a whole week, Dopey showed no inclination to leave. Some said that his radar equipment had gone wonky because of all the Brit radio traffic in the vicinity. Others reckoned he was afraid to run the gauntlet again of the security nets under the bridge designed to deter attacks on naval vessels. Dopey was recognised as a class of political prisoner.

Then there was the fact that coming up to Xmas, Derry people well knew the pain of separation from loved ones caused by circumstances arising from British imperialist domination.

But just as suddenly as he'd arrived, Dopey disappeared, making a dash for freedom and the wild Atlantic. The Journal reported "a deep sadness" in the city.

I mention all this so as to acknowledge that it isn't just the Brits who go doolally about dumb animals. Personally, I never believed that Dopey had a political motivation. I think he'd just been trying to get up the river to Strabane, to visit his cousins, the Sharkeys.

16 April '97

58

Gerry Adams And The Ditching Of Clause Four

AREN'T THE SIMILARITIES AND PARALLELS between Tony Blair and Gerry Adams interesting all the same?

Each took over leadership of a party which regarded its past with reverence, and led it into hitherto unexplored territory in search of support from elements who had never previously had time for its traditional beliefs. Each has had to be careful not to alienate long-standing supporters who remain vital to the party's organisational base.

So, symbolically, Labour switches from red to royal purple as its primary colour, while Sinn Féin selected an azure-blue backdrop for its Monaghan Ard Fheis. "Nationalise The Banks!" becomes "New Hope For Britain", even as "Brits Out Of Ireland!" gives way to "A Strong Voice For Peace".

Gone from the Sinn Féin gathering was the garish green-flaggery and the sulphurous sloganeering of years past, consigned to the same ideological graveyard as the "Red Flag" at the close of Labour conferences.

It's not just symbolism and song. Each of the parties now has a leadership with a pragmatic approach to ideas long regarded as fundamental to their political purpose. Labour's commitment to State enterprise wasn't just a matter of policy, it was written – Clause Four – into the party constitution.

Britain's claim to sovereignty over part of Ireland – long seen by Republicans as an intolerable illegality which must be removed as a prerequisite for peace – was rendered in Gerry Adams' Monaghan speech as "the key matter which must be addressed in any negotiation".

In the context of Republican history and ideology, that represented at least as daring a policy revision as Blair's ditching of Clause Four.

And thus to the apt questions: could Blair and Adams do business together? And would the business they'd do necessarily be of benefit to the plain people?

Yes and no.

* * * * *

A fortnight ago, on April 16th, the chancellor of the University of Ulster, Rabbi Julia Neuberger, speaking at the opening of an integrated primary school in Castlereagh, described single-religion schools in the North as "sectarian". All hell broke instantly around her.

Rabbi Neuberger didn't have Catholic schools or Protestant schools solely in mind. She hit out, too, at Jewish and Muslim parents in Britain who insisted on single-religion schools for their children.

Rabbi Neuberger was born in London in 1951. Her father's family had come to Britain in 1912 as refugees from poverty in Europe. Her mother arrived in 1937, fleeing Hitler. Her personal politics are moderate to the point of being boring: she once stood for David Owen's Social Democratic Party.

She must have been taken aback by the reaction of leading Catholics to her remarks at Castlereagh, and staggered by the response of the University of Ulster.

An *Irish News* editorial (April 17th) spluttered with anger against her. Two days later, the paper gave prominence to a report that "Catholic bishops . . . have been in contact with the university to lodge their protest". It revealed that the Council for Catholic Maintained Schools was "furious" and had demanded an apology from her "for the sense of hurt you have caused". A Catholic member of the University Court issued a statement to the effect that "either she goes or I go . . . " And so on.

Within two days, a spokesman for the University had issued what the *Irish News* accurately described as "an unprecedented apology". It read: "The university has taken immediate steps to reassure our many partners throughout Catholic education . . . that the views were unequivocally not the views of the university . . . We deeply regret any offence that has been caused and restate our commitment to what the Council for Catholic Maintained Schools has called 'respect for diversity in culture and heritage'."

The irony of a body which will not countenance Catholic children learning multiplication tables in the same room as Protestants calling for "respect for diversity in culture and heritage" was, obviously, lost on the spokesman for the University of Ulster.

What Rabbi Neuberger had said was right: the segregated schools of the North are sectarian, in the obvious sense that they reflect the existing sectarian division and in the ominous sense that they reinforce and perpetuate that division.

The episode illustrates the extent to which sectarianism has become accepted in the North. Orangeism is now defined – by many Nationalists as well as by Unionists – as an expression of "Protestant culture", entitled to the esteem of all who have "respect for diversity in culture and heritage". Increasingly, the main Nationalist objection to Orange marches concerns not the bigotry they celebrate, but the fact that they don't keep their bigotry to "their own areas".

The underlying theory is that Catholics and Protestants really are different peoples, and that separate development ("apartheid" in Afrikaans) is therefore normal and natural.

Thus, a university apologises for having caused "hurt" by its chancellor suggesting that children should be educated together.

Dear god.

30 April '97

59

Did I Hear Someone Saying That The British Should Withdraw?

HOT PRESS HAPPENED IN DUBLIN, but Belfast was more happening at the time. The Clash at the Ulster Hall never happened, though. Jittery officaldom junked the gig. But it was the moment the resentment of the Northern proto-punks found a focus.

Owen McFadden of Protex recalls: "Everyone who turned up got talking to each other. A lot of musical friendships were formed. It went on from there".

The current edition of the Cultural Traditions Journal Causeway, acknowledges that right from the start: "HOT PRESS was one of the few publications to champion the growth of the Belfast scene". Some say this was the first genuine music scene Belfast had known since the blues explosion of the '60s. But I think the blues explosion, like Wednesday week, never happened at all.

Stiff Little Fingers were a heavy metal outfit called Highway Star until punk came along and injected imagination.

Terri Hooley ran Good Vibrations records from his shop of the same name in Great Victoria Street. He thought that The Outcasts were the worst band in the world and signed them only because, "Well, they came into the shop". This is one of the best reasons ever for signing a band.

Feargal Sharkey tried to bribe me with a fiver not to mention his mother ordering him out of the kitchen when I was in mid-interview with him to make me a sandwich and then ordering him to take it back out again and cut off the crust. "He'd show you up," she sighed.

The Boomtown Rats made the big time. Elvis died. In 1977.

Plus ca change.

* * * * *

In June 1977 the Fine Gael-Labour coalition fell and Fianna Fáil leapt back into office. For months, the FFers had been sharply critical of Fine Gael's handling of the North.

"They've fumbled a real chance for peace," complained Liam Lawlor (FF Dublin West), "They have no feel for the national question. Nationalists in the Six Counties feel let down."

Still hear that.

A few months into office, new Taoiseach Jack Lynch called on the British government of James Callaghan to announce its intention to withdraw from the North. The Catholic archbishop of Armagh, Tomás Ó Fíaich, agreed: "I believe the British should withdraw from Ireland. It think it is the only thing that will get things moving."

Don't hear that.

* * * * *

In 1977, the Secretary of State for Northern Ireland hovered a thousand feet above the Antrim countryside singing 'Don't Cry For Me, Ballymena'. Then he had Ian Paisley arrested.

Roy Mason has described these lively events himself, in a BBC NI television programme called *The View From the Castle*. Paisley had organised a tractor blockade of Ballymena, part of an "all-out offensive" by an alliance of Unionist politicians and paramilitaries, the United Unionist Action Council. They wanted the British Government to crack down harder on Republicans, and to set up a parliament along the lines of the old Stormont.

Paisley issued a "solemn promise" to leave politics forever if the UUAC didn't succeed. It didn't, and neither did he.

Mason, a squat brute from Barnsley, whistled up an RAF helicopter so he could inspect the roadblocks, pickets and mobs of nerds who had answered Paisley's call. My own suggestion at the time, that Mason and Paisley should be tied together with barbed wire and made to fight it out between themselves with lump hammers, was ignored.

Mason is given credit by the usual miserable historians for taking a tough stance, which faced Paisley down. But the key factor was that the thousands that Paisley had been counting on didn't come out to support him.

Petrol tanker drivers and power workers at Ballylumford defied massive intimidation, including a specific UDA death threat against the Ballylumford night shift, the wounding by gunfire of a tanker driver and the shooting dead of a garage attendant.

The main reason we don't remember 1977 as a year of horror when Protestants rose up to demand a restoration of a sectarian parliament is that, overwhelmingly, and in many cases at some risk to themselves, they did no such thing.

* * * * *

The South African jaunt where David Trimble and Martin McGuinness didn't meet up and discover a common interest in fly-fishing wasn't the first event of its kind organised by the odd Irish-American academic Pádraig O'Malley.

Back in, I think, 1975 he brought Republican and Loyalist paramilitaries and Irish and British politicians of all sorts to Amherst in Massachussetts for a week-long talkfest. A mighty time was had by all. Andy Tyrie, Supreme Commander (didn't half fancy himself, Andy) of the UDA, was the hit of the late-night booze-ups with his light baritone voice and unsuspected repertoire of Republican ballads.

But, by common consent, the star of the main show was Seamus Costello. He had broken in 1974 from the Stalinist deadbeats of the Official Republican Movement (now split into the Workers' Party and Democratic Left) and, in the face of some difficulty, was in the process of piecing together the Irish Republican Socialist Party. He was a dab hand at putting a socialist spin on Republican politics.

Seamus, unfortunately, hadn't broken from the nationalist ideas and clandestine methods associated with physical-force

Republicans, which is what did for the IRSP as a serious party in the end.

Still, he was a class act in his day. The late Dr. Noel Browne was sufficiently impressed to write to the *Irish Times* on his return announcing, more or less, that he had discovered the leader for whom Ireland had been waiting so long.

We will never know for sure in what direction Seamus' ideas would have developed. I knew him well enough to feel certain he would have been sickened by the vicious sectarianism of some of the activities sanctioned over the years by the elements of the remaining IRSP.

But we can't be certain what he would have made of it all, or what difference he might have made himself. On October 5th 1977, the "Officials" had him murdered as he sat in his car just off the North Strand in Dublin.

* * * * *

People living in a small triangular area at the junction of counties Armagh, Louth and Monaghan speak with an accent in which "orchestra" rhymes nicely with "yesterday". As in: *"The Dundalk orchestra/Which wasn't born yesterday"*.

Likewise in Belfast, there is a specific New Lodge Road accent which makes a perfect rhyming couplet of *"Captain Nairac was a spy/Where is Captain Nairac now?"*

Robert Nairac, a British army officer working undercover in south Armagh, was captured by the Provos, "interrogated" and killed in May 1977. He was posthumously awarded the George Cross, Britain's highest award for bravery in peacetime. But everytime I hear his name it's the rhyme which springs into my mind.

* * * * *

1977 saw the first intervention by a US president in the Northern conflict. Under presure from the "Friends of Ireland", including Chappaquiddick Kennedy and Daniel Patrick

Moynihan, the man who gave Indonesia the go-ahead to invade East Timor, President Jimmy Carter, delighted nationalists by calling for a new peace initiative.

The US would buttress a settlement by helping to create jobs, he promised.

"A peaceful settlement would contribute immeasurably to stability in Northern Ireland and so enhance the prospects for increased investment . . . The US government would be prepared to join with others to see how additional job-creating investment could be encouraged to the benefit of all the people of Northern Ireland".

That was in August. The following month it was announced that Ms. Betty Williams and Ms. Mairead Corrigan had been awarded the Nobel Prize for having brought peace to the North.

Plus ça meme chose.

11 June '97

60

They Wanted The Bigot's Boot Off Their Necks And The British Army Off Their Backs

ON THE DAY IN 1983 WHEN he won the West Belfast seat for the first time, Gerry Adams told cheering supporters on the Falls Road: "Even de Valera couldn't win the Falls". It was an apt reference, with implications for the Republican Movement today, as it faces into negotiations which of their nature cannot deliver a united Ireland.

In the December 1918 general election, the constitutional nationalist Joe Devlin defeated de Valera, standing for Sinn Féin, in West Belfast. In the midst of that year's Sinn Féin landslide which transformed the political terrain, this was one of only two seats in Ireland (Waterford, where Captain William Redmond was returned, being the other) in which constitutional nationalism beat republicanism.

The four other seats won by the nationalists – Sinn Féin took 73 – were also in the North: these were among eight seats which might have gone Unionist had the Catholic vote been split. The head of the Catholic Church in Ireland, Cardinal Logue, "allocated" four each to the Nationalists and Sinn Féin.

Thus, in the last all-Ireland poll, the election Republicans still look to for validation of their struggle, it was the North which bucked the trend towards Sinn Féin and saved constitutional nationalism from wipeout. And it was the constituency now seen as the hardest-line republican area of all which dealt republicanism its most significant defeat.

This raises a question about the extent to which, historically, Northern Catholics have been wedded to republicanism – as opposed to embracing a broad oppositional outlook which, from time to time and depending on circumstances, has been expressed through the Nationalist Party, Sinn Féin, the SDLP and various independent, Labour and Republican-Labour groupings.

The question has relevance to the scepticism which has been expressed about the ability of Gerry Adams and those around him to keep both the renewed ceasefire and the movement intact. Predictably, the most strident sceptics have been extreme Unionists like Cruise O'Brien, who have been consistently wrong in their pronouncements and predictions about the North for 20 years.

* * * * *

But a number of objective commentators, and some generally sympathetic to the republican movement, have also doubted whether the ceasefire can hold. Their thesis is that the process which Sinn Féin has now been enabled to join is pre-pro-grammed to deliver a partitionist settlement – and that there's no way the republican movement could live with that, even if, which isn't certain, the current leadership were minded to.

Too much pain, too many deaths, too many years in prison cells for the movement to stop so far short of its objective. As John Hume put it a few years ago in an interview with Jim Dee of the US magazine, the *Irish Reporter*: what happens when a deal is announced and somebody stands up at the back and asks: "What did Jimmy die for then?"

This pragmatic consideration apart, the ideology of the Republican Movement also puts difficulty in the way of compro-mise.

Modern Republican activists have seen themselves as involved in a national liberation struggle, sharing perspectives with the ANC, the PLO etc. But they differ from the other movements in one respect which it is tempting to dismiss as arcane but which could be of critical significance for the playing of the end-game.

The Movement has seen the Republic not as an aspiration to be aimed at but as an already-existing reality which it is their duty to defend.

Thus, a settlement which might seem to outsiders to represent an honourable step forward might look to activists as shameful retreat.

The "theological" basis for this view has to do with the procla-mation of the Republic on the steps of the GPO in 1916, and its democratic endorsement in the 1918 election. The Sinn Féin MPs elected that year met in the First Dáil. The War of Independence was fought by the IRA in defence of the Republic, and to assert the legitimacy of the Dáil as its parliament.

It was logical, then, that the partition settlement which Michael Collins presented as a "stepping stone" to the Republic would be seen by others as a retreat from the Republic. And the IRA's episodic struggle since can be seen not as a matter of idealism, of keeping the faith, but of continuing in a practical way to assert the legitimacy of the Republic.

This may seem fanciful in 1997, even ridiculous, but it has been this conception of its role and its historic significance which sustained the Republican Movement through lean years when it could find little sustenance in the day-to-day world around it.

As important, it is this view of the Republic which has provided political and moral sanction for the armed struggle of the last 25 years. To abandon it would be retrospectively to withdraw sanction from those who carried the struggle on in the face of fierce denunciation and overwhelming odds.

In this view, obviously, any settlement based on the "principle of consent" would represent retreat and betrayal.

But is this the relevant perspective? To what extent has the republican struggle, now paused in ceasefire, been informed and guided by traditional republican ideology, anyway?

What pitched the Catholic working-class communities in which the movement is rooted outside constitutional nationalist politics and into militant republicanism was not mass conversion to a set of ideas or a conception of history, but more immediate and material considerations – the refusal of the State to concede equal citizenship, RUC and British Army brutality and murder, a corrupt legal system and so on.

The republican movement provided a natural and congenial channel for the deep anger of huge numbers of people who suffered these outrages. Many who joined the IRA, or became active in republican politics, did so not out of a sacred duty to "free Ireland" or a historic mission to vindicate the Republic, but because they wanted the bigot's boot off their necks and the British Army off their backs.

Viewed from the Falls or the Bogside, the question at the heart of the Talks is whether these deep-felt grievances can be removed short of the achievement of the Republic. If they can, then whatever purists might say about historical duty, and whatever sceptics predict, there will be a basis for a settlement in the communities which have borne the brunt of the struggle.

It's been clear from as far back as 1918 that there is nothing automatic or atavistic about the politics of places like the Falls.

If, on the other hand, it turns out that the Talks cannot deliver a settlement along these lines, that the Northern State is inherently democratically dysfunctional, then all who would rather the armed struggle were not resumed should be discussing now how, otherwise, social justice and equality might be achieved.

23 July '97

61

Oscar Wilde Was A Freedom Fighter

"OH WHO IS THAT YOUNG sinner with the handcuffs on his wrist?
And what has he been after that they groan and shake their fists?
And wherefore is he wearing such a conscience-stricken air?
Oh they're taking him to prison for the colour of his hair."
Thus A.E. Housman on the jailing of Oscar Wilde.

Wilde was freed from prison a hundred years ago. A film of his life, starring Stephen Fry, has sparked new interest in the man, and in his work.

Wilde was a man of extravagant talent and grandiloquent style. "A combination of Eric Cantona, Brendan Behan, Woody Allen and Liz Hurley", according to one commentator. It's said his last words were: "It's the wallpaper or me. One of us has to go".

No better man than the droll Fry to depict that gay indomitability. But there was more to Wilde, too, and we must wait and see what sort of fist Mr. Fry makes of the other aspects of his hero's persona.

Wilde was a socialist. Not many people – not enough, anyway – know that. He proclaimed himself a socialist years before there were Labour Parties in Britain and Ireland to drain the word of meaning.

Wilde had no personal experience of working-class life. He came from a comfortable, Dublin nationalist background, whence he moved with casual brilliance through Oxford, and onwards to the London literary society which he was to scandalise, dominate and delight for some 15 years.

He wasn't the only successful writer in London in his time to make the connection between artistic creation and political radicalism. But he was the only one to put his literary celebrity at the service of his politics and to carry his convictions onto the street.

Wilde marched alongside Eleanor Marx at the head of a huge demonstration to Hyde Park in support of the 1889 docks strike, one of the key events in the development of British and Irish trade unionism. And he was the only literary figure in London to speak up for and sign a petition in support of the Haymarket Martyrs, five radicals sentenced to hang in Chicago. His association with "the mob", and endorsement of an 1890s equivalent of the Birmingham Six, horrified the establishment.

It wasn't just his homosexuality, but the fact that it was combined, so to speak, with political attitudes of that sort, which was to have him denounced by the press at the time of his trial as "the most depraved man in England".

His essay, *The Soul Of Man Under Socialism,* published in 1892, is as much about the necessity of artistic freedom as about social and economic organisation. In parts, it is very much of its time. But it also has passages which could have been written here and now.

"As one reads history, not in the expurgated editions written for schoolboys and passmen, but in the original authorities, one is absolutely sickened, not by the crimes that the wicked have committed, but by the punishments the good have inflicted. A community is infinitely more brutalised by the habitual employment of punishment than by the occasional occurrence of crime".

And in days like these when journalistic dolts insist that we put dead princesses and brain-dead pop stars on pedestals because they have emoted in public, and that we join with the multitudes in gratitude for gifts bestowed upon them, is it not exhilarating to read: "We are often told that the poor are grateful for charity. But the best among the poor are never grateful. They are ungrateful, discontented, disobedient and rebellious. They are right to be so. Charity is a ridiculously inadequate mode of partial restitution, a sentimental dole, usually accompanied by some impertinent attempt on the part of the sentimentalists to tyrannise over people's inward lives"?

To emphasise Wilde's neglected socialism is not to deny that it was mainly because of his sexuality that he was dragged down in the end.

Although he had been sexually attracted to males since adolescence, Wilde's first homosexual act came in 1886, when he was 32. He then made up for lost time. It is far from coincidental that his creativity flowed in fullest spate in this period. But this circumstance ensured, too, that when he came to trial, his prosecutor, the future UVF leader Edward Carson, was able to call a succession of low-lifes, some from the gutters, others from great houses, some telling the truth, others bribed to lie, to ensure his destruction.

"Now 'tis oakum for his fingers and the treadmill for his feet
And the quarry-gang on Portland in the cold and in the heat,
And between his spells of labour in the time he has to spare
He can curse the God that made him for the colour of his hair."

It is commonly assumed that when Wilde went to jail, it was the end of him. And it is true there was scarcely a friend for him in the glittering world when he emerged in 1897, crushed in body and bruised in spirit. He was to die three years later in poverty and loneliness in Paris.

But his prison writings were not mere marginalia on the last chapter of his life.

It's interesting that they are so little known in his own country, where jail journals of questionable value are celebrated.

Wilde suffered horribly in prison, but there is a sometime

serenity about him there, too. "I have no desire to complain," he wrote to Lord Alfred Douglas in *De Profundis*. "One of the many lessons one learns in prison is that things are what they are and will be what they will be".

The letters to friends which have been published are full of delicate feeling. Two long letters he wrote to the Daily Chronicle suggest no self-pity, but concern for children and other innocents behind bars, and for the way the prison system can brutalise the jailers as well as the jailed. And, of course, his prison period yielded what some account his greatest work, *The Ballad of Reading Gaol,* a *cri de coeur* not at all against his own imprisonment but against the death penalty, and against all prisons, and all punishment.

I know not whether Laws be right,
Or whether Laws be wrong;
All that we know who lie in gaol
Is that the wall is strong;
And that each day is like a year,
A year whose days are long . . .
This too I know – and wise it were
If each could know the same–
That every prison that men build
Is built with bricks of shame.

If Wilde had been a fighter for Irish freedom only, he'd be better and more accurately remembered. But he was a freedom-fighter for the world, a wilde man altogether.

Jim Morrison is buried in the same cemetery in Paris, but Oscar opened wider the doors of perception.

15 October '97

62

Journalists And The Man Gardaí Believe Killed Veronica Guerin

PATRICK EUGENE HOLLAND HAS NEVER been charged with killing Veronica Guerin, but he seems to be serving time for her murder.

The implication of this for the rights of citizens before the law was scarcely mentioned in reports of the outcome of Holland's Special Criminal Court trial, which ended on November 28th. On the basis of a remark made by a garda in court, it was implicitly assumed that Holland had murdered Ms. Guerin. A number of commentators expressed satisfaction that he had been appropriately sentenced for the killing.

The only offence Holland was convicted of was possession of cannabis for sale or supply. No report or commentary that I saw or read has argued that 20 years was a reasonable sentence for this crime, or in line with precedent.

With remarkable unanimity, newspapers and radio and television news programmes identified Holland with the phrase: "the man gardai believe killed Veronica Guerin". Mention his name, Patrick Eugene Holland, in a word-association test now, and the answer would come, more or less automatically, ". . . killed Veronica Guerin".

There would be no possibility now of Holland receiving a fair trial for the murder of Ms. Guerin. But then, this will hardly arise. Untried, he's already doing time for it.

Many will have imagined the Irish public alert to the dangers of jailing people for crimes which the police believe they committed but haven't the evidence on which to build a prosecution. But in Holland's case it seems few care. To object to the conduct and coverage of his case is to risk being portrayed as insufficiently horrified at the murder of Ms. Guerin.

Thus, the killing of Veronica Guerin is used to stifle debate about the abuse of power by the authorities and the denial of rights to citizens. The complicity of a number of journalists and the media outlets they work for in this process is, or should be, a cause for concern.

Journalists like sometimes to claim a role for themselves in holding major institutions, including State institutions, accountable, and vindicating the rights of citizens in the face of implacable authority. Students on journalism courses, I'm told, still dream of the story which exposes wrong-doing in high places and remedies injustice visited upon ordinary citizens. But an alternative and more cynical view of journalism's function is now fashionable, too.

Back in the 1970s, the media played a major part in exposing the "Heavy Gang", a group of gardaí who interviewed suspects with boots, fists, threats and lying blandishments, and conspired to perjure themselves to pervert the course of justice. Meanwhile, other gardaí were abusing powers of detention and falsifying fingerprint evidence. It should be acknowledged that other gardaí, including the recent presidential candidate Derek Nally, alerted public representatives to these abuses and helped bring them to an end.

In the case of the falsifying of fingerprint evidence, indeed, it was whistle-blowers within the gardaí who contacted the media with their concerns and prevented the elaborate frame-up of an innocent person for a very serious crime.

The events came back to mind recently when a well-known journalist appealed on the RTE television discussion programme *Davis* for the re-formation of the "Heavy Gang" as a means of combatting an alleged "crime wave". Reminded by presenter Derek Davis that the methods of this unit had been found unacceptable, the journalist responded in the scornful manner of zealots for law'n'order everywhere: ask the victims of crime whether they were concerned about police methods!

Interviewed by Eamon Dunphy on Radio Ireland on the day Patrick Holland was sentenced, the same journalist sang a song of praise for the Special Criminal Court. Certain people, he explained, had suggested that the SCC was no longer necessary, now that the IRA had declared a ceasefire. (The no-jury court was set up in the early '70s ostensibly to deal with a specific threat to the State from the Provisional IRA).

The Holland trial proved, he maintained, that the SCC was still needed. Had Holland been able to claim the right to trial by jury, there might not have been such a satisfactory result. A jury, he warned, might well have been "nobbled". Special measures and special courts were still needed. His spake was well-studded with references to Ms. Guerin.

Campaigning for the return of "Heavy Gang" methods and justifying the continued denial of the right to trial by jury, even when the original reason for the denial no longer obtains, isn't considered outside the journalistic mainstream now.

Likewise, it isn't just this individual who regularly invokes the murder of Veronica Guerin to justify the view that journalism has an overriding duty to support the forces of law and order.

This is a view which, naturally, finds favour with senior gardai. Thus, common cause is established between journalists and elements in the State apparatus. The notion that it is the function of journalism to challenge and hold State authorities accountable begins to fray and unravel. Some come to accept it as part of a journalist's function to actively assist gardai, by, for example, acting as conduits for information which gardai want put into the public domain.

More than once in recent times, journalists favoured by gardai have been given and have published, presumably in good faith, items of accurate information interspersed with falsehoods, the combination having been designed to discommode and confuse the gardai's adversaries. A number of well-promoted crime exclusives have been of this character.

The relationship which can develop between some gardai and some journalists is seen in incidents in which senior gardai have suggested to witnesses in imminent cases that they talk to one of a small number of named journalists and not talk to other named journalists.

This is too close a relationship for journalistic comfort, indeed for anyone's comfort other than the Gardaí. It is, at its heart, a political relationship. The idea that there is a "crime-crisis" which can be dealt with only by tough new measures and new police powers and no old namby-pamby guff about civil liberties, this is a political idea advanced everywhere by right-wing elements who love good order and hate unruly freedom.

It is an idea which sits comfortably alongside the contention that crime is not caused primarily by poverty and alienation but by an absence of discipline and a refusal to accept authority. The answer, then, lies not in making society more equal but in making people more compliant.

It is possible that Patrick Eugene Holland pulled the trigger and killed Veronica Guerin. But he has never been charged with having done so. If the principle that a citizen is innocent until proven guilty has meaning, it means that Mr. Holland is innocent of Ms. Guerin's death.

We don't yet have a society in which people can be convicted of murder merely on the word of a policeman, much as some in journalism as well as in the security establishment might wish it were so. Or do we?

14 December '97

63

Billy Wright Was A Real Christian

"THOSE WHO PERPETRATED THIS murder are anti-Christian," declared the priest at the funeral of murder victim Liam Conway last month. Mr. Conway, the bread-winner for two disabled brothers, was shot dead as he sat at the wheel of a mechanical digger off the Crumlin Road in Belfast on January 23rd, another Catholic killed by loyalist paramilitaries in supposed retaliation for the INLA slaying of Billy Wright.

Most of those listening will have understood well what was meant. The word "Christian" is commonly used to convey decency, tolerance, mercy, love. It is taken to indicate the very antitheses of vengeance, bigotry, violence, hate. The majority of Irish Christians don't express their religious beliefs by deliberately doing evil to others. To characterise Liam Conway's killers as "anti-Christian" will have seemed no more than obvious common sense.

But the sectarian murder-gangs make just as much sense when they claim to act out of Christian conviction. Their view of what characterises the dominant religion in our society is at least as authentic as the assumption that Christianity is inherently benign.

The life and death of Billy Wright shows how naturally Christian fervour shades into evil. Wright was a religious man. He had been a lay preacher. He banned swear-words and other "unChristian practices" on his wing in the Maze. He left instructions that the emphasis in his funeral oration should not be on political salvation in this world, but on eternal salvation in the next.

Many took a cynical, not to say contemptuous, view of all this, reckoning Wright's protestations of a religious motive no more than a handy excuse for hate . . . Bernadette Martin, innocently asleep in her Protestant boyfriend's home when Wright's killers erupted into the room and riddled her head and body with bullets . . . Eileen Duffy, 19, and Katrina Rennie, only 16, shot to bits in a mobile sweet-shop by cowards . . . Charles and Teresa Fox, old-age pensioners, pitilessly dispatched in their isolated home in Tyrone.

To concede a religious motivation to such a man strikes many as throwing a cloak of respectability over sectarian thuggery.

But look at it in light of the slogan – shown on the television news after Mo Mowlam allowed the cameras into the Maze – in pride of place in the cell of Wright's friend, Johnny "Mad Dog" Adair: "Kill Them All – Let God Sort 'Em Out". Now from where did he come up with that?

From 1205 and the First Crusade against the Cathars.

The Abbot of Citeaux, head of the Cistercians, at the time one of the most powerful men in Christendom, was asked as the Crusaders prepared to set out from Montpellier how they could distinguish between heretic Cathars deserving of death, and innocent folk of the same stock who chanced to be in the same place at the same time. The Abbot decreed: "Kill Them All – Let God Sort Them Out".

It might seem ironic that Adair, a UDA commander from the Shankill, should adopt a slogan devised by a Catholic monk. But not really. He doesn't strike one as a fellow much concerned with historical niceties. And the point of the phrase– that followers of false versions of Christianity deserve death, and that only God can distinguish between the just and the unjust – is not specific to any particular Christian denomination.

The Crusade against the Cathars was itself undertaken by one Christian denomination against another. (The real purpose was to consolidate the power of the Duke of Burgundy in what is now southern France.) The Crusade was prosecuted with focussed ferocity: in the town of Beziers, 30,000 people, every man, woman and child the blood-drenched Crusaders could root out, were cut to death. Seven thousand were slaughtered where they had gathered for refuge, in the Church of the Magdalen in the centre of town.

Those who carried out the massacre were granted a plenary indulgence. As were those who took part in later Crusades against Muslims.

Over and over again, Christian convictions have been expressed in the mass murder of people identified as heathens or apostate. This has happened so frequently, and through so many centuries, that it makes no sense to present it as out of character for Christianity.

In Ireland, Protestantism has been associated since the 16th century with an anti-Catholicism so virulent as implicitly to deny the humanity of Catholic people. Again, as in the case of the Duke of Burgundy, material considerations have underpinned this stance.

In 1615, half a century after its foundation, the Church of Ireland rejected the 39 Articles of the Church of England, preferring a stricter version of predestination, one which held that those not "elect" were utterly irredeemable, their very existence offensive to the eyes of God. This provided a religious justification for cleansing the native population out of whole areas, suppressing their culture and exterminating them where "necessary".

The greater "need" for such measures in Ireland than in England dictated the difference in doctrine.

In seeing Catholics today as disposable people, Billy Wright was in harmony with this tradition. The Ulster Clubs will have had the same tradition in mind when they issued a statement describing his death as "Ulster's loss, Heaven's gain".

The few journalists who made it to his graveside report that it was, literally, a religious experience, no shouts of "No Surrender" but murmurs of "Halleluia" and ceaseless imprecations to "Praise the Lord!".

Respectable Protestant leaders, bishops and the like, portrayed Wright as having been beyond the pale of "proper" Protestantism. But the murderous attacks on Catholics which he inspired and organised were well in line with Protestant, and, more generally, Christian tradition. And those who went out with wholesale slaughter on their minds in retaliation for his death were rooted deep in the same authentic religious tradition.

This is not to say that the confict is mainly motivated by religion. It is to say that one of the most important ways in which Christianity has affected the conflict has been to render it more implacable, lend it greater ferocity, to make it more scornful of the sanctity of life.

The people who killed Liam Conway were Christians, not anti-Christians.

4 February '98

64

With Bill Clinton, There Are No Limits

THERE'S ANOTHER PADDY'S DAY GONE, and good riddance. What embarrassment. Even a stroll around town with a hand-spray of weed-killer for squirting on shamrock didn't ease my mortification.

Come March, they all wanna be in America. The UDP and PUP in America. Sinn Féin and the SDLP in America. The UUP and Dr. Mo in Amer-i-ca.

I understand that the International Aviation Authority has just declared the air corridor from Aldergrove to Washington DC a traditional March route.

A green-edged (literally!) invite to the White House hooley has become a ticket to political respectability. Bill Clinton has become chief arbiter of good behaviour in Irish public life. The pudgy fraudster who can cover up anything except pecker-stains and who was planning last month to make rubble of the Iraqi equivalents of Portadown and Moira marked St. Patrick's Day by sitting in judgment on the moral credentials of Irish political parties.

Norman Mailer has said that what makes Clinton particularly dangerous is that he has no bottom line. There are no limits of political behaviour which he will not exceed, no core of principle which he won't traduce, no moral boundaries beyond which he won't go. This, let us remember, is the guy who sent a mentally disabled black man to the chair – Rickey Ray Rector, half his brain blown away, who ordered dessert for his last meal and then didn't eat it because he wanted to save it for later – in order to garner the votes of the fry-the-blacks brigade in the 1992 Democratic primaries.

He's also the guy who – on the advice of the low-life Dick Morris (who continued screwing a hooker as he allowed her listen in on a telephone conversation with the White House) – cut welfare payments to millions of poor people, most notably single mothers, because they weren't leading sufficiently moral lives.

The mind boggles. The stomach churns.

Clinton will have appreciated the company of the Sinn Féiners, the breath-of-fresh-air Loyalists, the Orange and Green Tories and the rest of the crew. He likes having people on their knees before him, sucking up.

19 March '98

65

The Republican Leadership Have Accepted That The "Republican Analysis" Is Wrong

BOTH REPUBLICANS AND UNIONISTS will have to leave a lot of historical baggage behind in order to make the Belfast Agreement work, and it's the Republicans who'll have to abandon the more valuable items.

In the atmosphere immediately following the Talks breakthrough, there has been little patience with abstract argument about the ideas underpinning Republican and Unionist positions, and about how these will have to shift to provide the foundation for a new edifice of governance.

Fundamental realignments which have always been implicit in the Peace Process are about to show on the surface, and to be explored for the first time.

Acceptance of the Agreement, even on the basis of it being sufficient unto the day, will represent an admission by the Republican leadership that the "Republican analysis" has been wrong. The core of this analysis has lain in the contention that partition is the cause of the conflict, the end of partition the cure.

Pearse put it: "No 'half-way house' is possible as a permanent solution of the issue between England and Ireland. There were and are only two alternatives – an enslaved Ireland and a free Ireland".

The most hallowed figure in the Republican pantheon went on to warn, in his aptly-named *Ghosts:* "The man who in the name of Ireland accepts as a 'final settlement' anything less by one iota than separation from England is guilty of so immense an infidelity, so immense a crime against the Irish nation . . . that it would be better for that man (as it were certainly better for his country) that he had not been born".

Or, as Bernadette Sands put it more recently: "My brother didn't die for cross-border bodies."

There will be naught for the comfort of today's Republicans in trying to accept the Assembly and cross-border bodies as a temporary arrangement. If they endorse the Agreement, they will have to help secure it, and that can't be done while simultaneously seeking to put a time-limit on the durability of its institutions.

The ideological apparatus which gave the Republican Movement its context for survival through the years of the Troubles will have to be dismantled, or abandoned to others, for the Movement to assent, however grudgingly, to the settlement.

The wrench which this represents, and the practical dificulties involved in carrying it through, seem little understood by commentators, some of them well-wishers of the Republican leadership, who characterise debate within and around the Movement as analogous to disputation between New Labour and Old, or who present it as a rift between some who remain "wedded to violence" and others who have seen the error of their ways. Such a view belittles the role of ideology in Republicanism and in Irish nationalism generally.

The abandonment of core Republican beliefs was an unspoken addendum to the Peace Process from the outset. Although recommended to the Sinn Féin and IRA rank-and-file as a new road towards the old destination, the construction of a "Pan Nationalist Alliance", to use the Provos' own phrase, meant decamping from defensive positions around the idea of the Republic and adopting not just different tactics but new and more modest objectives. In terms which have come naturally to Ruairí Ó Brádaigh, Bernadette Sands and others, what's implied is desertion of the Republic.

The SDLP, the Dublin Government and corporate Irish-America were never available for recruitment to support of the armed struggle and Brits Out Now. Forging an alliance with these elements was always contingent on a readiness to leave armed struggle behind, and with it the associated all-or-nothing demand for British withdrawal.

The implications are profound for Republican perspectives, and are not at all of a theoretical nature.

How is Sinn Féin to respond to armed activity by the Continuity IRA, the INLA and, possibly, other emerging groups of Republican activists in the coming weeks? Hitherto, the view has been that such activities, while ill-advised and unwelcome in the context of the Peace Process, resulted inevitably from the unresolved nature of the constitutional question.

If the constitutional question has been settled, even if only for the time being, what's the line?

If assent is given to the institutions of governance put in place under the Agreement, is not outright hostility the only logical response to actions aimed at destroying these institutions? How is this to be finessed, and to be related to Republican tradition, on the ground in north Belfast, the Bogside, Fermanagh?

This raises a question which has lurked at the margins of nationalist politics throughout the Troubles. To what extent, in what sense, has the struggle led by the Republican Movement been fuelled by Republican ideas?

The Movement's intransigence, its unremitting hostility to the enclosure of the Six Counties within the British State, has matched the mood of communities whose experience of the State has been of belligerent contempt, brutality and murder. But there is a difference between a mood, however solid and well-rooted in experience, and conscious commitment to a set of ideas.

It may be that a dislocation between the ideology of Pearse and the practical needs of the moment reflects an underlying contradiction which is only now being examined.

If it is the case that Catholic working-class areas are minded to accept the settlement as, generally speaking, fair enough for the time being, what does this dictate to Martin McGuinness, the personal repository of enormous trust and even affection from the people he lives among, but mandated by history, too, to vindicate Republican ideas and guard them against the defilement of grubby practicality?

As I told him in the shop a while back, now comes the hard part.

15 April "98

66

Donnacha's Orange Dream

MY LATEST PLAN FOR EDUCATING the Northern masses in mutual understanding and harmony has had a vice versa effect in some quarters.

I had embraced a complaint in a local 'paper about the cultural imbalance involved in the Oscar-nominated Derry film *Dance Lexie Dance*. Why, the complainant wished reasonably to know, have we never had a film along the lines of *Dance Lexie Dance* but offering "the opposite point of view"?

Dance Lexie Dance, made for under £40,000 of the BBC's money by Pearse Moore and Dave Duggan, told the story of a widowed Protestant man whose winsome daughter has her heart set on entering the Irish dancing competition at Feis Dóire Colmcille. Dad, as might be imagined, is by no means ecstatic at his wee girl's grá for the Irish dancing. But his obduracy eases, as it must, in the warmth of her smile, and, awkwardly, in Easter Week, he escorts her, in her intricate Celtic-design dance-frock, to the Guildhall.

He takes his uneasy place in the hall and waits, shuffling on his seat, as she joins the other contestants back-stage. He's quite taken by the innocent simplicity of the performances and politely applauds each . . . and then his whole being melts into love when her number is called, and they catch one another's eye as she walks onto the stage, and hold one another's attention for a moment as she raises herself, poised on the tips of her dancing-pump toes, and the music strikes up for her set.

He dotes as she dances, then whoops, cheers and whistles at the end as they beam upon one another across the crowded Feis room.

She doesn't win, which doesn't matter. They join in a jig of joy along the banks of the Foyle as they make their way home. You can easily imagine Academy members feeling good.

But why not a reverse-angle version, the angry letter-to-the-editor demanded to know? And why not indeed, it occurred to me, maybe called *March Donnacha March?* In a twinkling, I had sketched, free, gratis and for nothing other than non-sectarian pleasure, an outline script.

March Donnacha March would tell the tale of a widowed Catholic dad and a son who has hitched his hopes of happiness to taking part in the Orange Order's Twelfth parade through Derry city centre. Initially, Dad won't hear of such heresy. But his spirit aches with sadness at the sight of little Donnacha after tea every evening strutting alone in the back yard. Eventually, of course, the sense of acrimony is sweetened with love. On the Twelfth, Donnacha's Orange dream is made real.

I envision the redemptive, climactic scenes. Dad, still uncertain, waiting behind the crash-barrier on the crowded pavement in the Diamond as the colourful parade swings into view. He observes, with a certain wonderment, the bright banners raised high, and scans the faces of the various contingents, until, at last, little Donnacha's lodge rounds the corner of the War Memorial. And, suddenly, there's Donnacha, well-scrubbed face blissfully aglow and proud Orange sash slung across his chest, arms swinging in jaunty time to the thump of the drum from the band just in front with its rollicking rendition of 'Dolly's Brae'.

Swept up in the exuberance of the moment, heart athrill from sudden elated understanding, dad finds himself shouting out in celebration of the little lad's splendid triumph over cultural curtailment and restriction. Later they march happily back home to the Bogside, in single file and strictly in step, their ears still filled with the rakish music of the fine flute bands.

Award-winning or what?

But let's ask ourselves this: Why is it that *Dance Lexie Dance,* notwithstanding the sentimentality and the obvious element of wishful thinking, is plausible enough to attract the production money, while *March Donnacha March* is ridiculous, to the extent that it wouldn't work even as fantasy?

Answer that, and you're a stretch further along the road to understanding why the attainment of peace is a more profound undertaking than a pact between political parties.

15 April '98

67

Is It Any Wonder The Fat Cats Are Purring?

THEY ARE CALLING IT A Peace Agreement. But this characterisation carries an implicit suggestion that anyone against it is an opponent of peace. Some of us, however, are against it out of opposition to the sectarian attitudes which have prompted atrocity heaped upon atrocity for the past 30 years and which are not challenged by the Agreement.

The Agreement envisages the reformation, not the removal of sectarianism. The structures are designed to contain sectarian rivalries, not get rid of them.

The document is based on an assumption that sectarianism springs naturally from the minds and hearts of Northern people.

On this view, the best we can do is to set in place an arrangement for ensuring that neither of the two tribes can dominate the other.

It's to be fair play between the Prods and the Taigs now, new rules, level pitch, objective referee. But the possibility of a settlement based on an outright rejection of tribalism doesn't rate a mention.

The Agreement is endorsed by some who fancy themselves as having long ago, personally, risen far above tribalism, but who fear that the brute masses on the Shankill and the Falls are incapable of such urbane elevation.

Paragraph six of the section dealing with the proposed new Assembly reads: "At their first meeting, members of the Assembly will register a designation of identity – nationalist, unionist or other – for the purposes of measuring cross-community support in Assembly votes".

Here at least the existence and possible presence in the Assembly of "others" is acknowledged. But acknowledgement is as good as it gets. A curt nod of the head rather than hail-fellow-well-met.

Paragraph 15 tells that: "The First Minister and Deputy First Minister shall be jointly elected into office by the Assembly voting on a cross-community basis, according to 5(d)(i)".

All "key decisions" will be taken on the same, cross-community basis.

This basis is set out in paragraph 5(d):

"(i) either parallel consent, ie a majority of those members present and voting, including a majority of the unionist and nationalist designations present and voting;

"(ii) or a weighted majority (60 percent) of members present and voting, including at least 40 percent of each of the nationalist and unionist designations present and voting".

The devil is in the detail – and sometimes in the absence of detail. Here, in relation to the making of the "key" decisions, "others" have disappeared from the text.

Not even in the darkest days of one-party Unionist rule under Craigavon and Brookborough has the sectarian basis of the

North's political system been so frankly proclaimed.

We are told that the choice lies between the Agreement and a return to all-out war. But acceptance of the deal won't guarantee peace, nor rejection automatically mean war. There is no stomach for a resumption of pro-active violence in the working-class areas, Catholic and Protestant, which have both provided the support-base and borne the brunt of paramilitary activity. A No vote next week won't change that one iota.

Among Republican supporters, rejection of the Agreement would make necessary a more fundamental re-examination of strategy than has yet been undertaken. If neither armed struggle nor attachment to the coat-tails of corporate Irish-America can deliver an acceptable outcome, what next?

Far from endangering the future, a result to prompt questioning along these lines would do nothing but good.

The allocation of the entire population into separate sectarian camps, and the institution of mechanisms for ensuring that all decisions are weighed to ensure sectarian balance, will make competition between the Catholic and Protestant communties the main dynamic for politics in the future.

It will be in the direct and compelling interest of the leaderships of nationalist and unionist parties to reinforce communal loyalty as the basis of political allegience, and to present themelves as the most forthright and uncompromising advocates of their own community's interests *vis-a-vis* the interests of "the other side". The possibility of abrasion at the interfaces generating new conflagration will be a permanent feature of the system.

The central purpose of the Agreement is to corall the working-class into separate camps, to pledge that neither side will be worse off now than the other, and to maintain an elaborate mechanism for ensuring than any imbalance which arises is speedily rectified. Each section of the working-class will have representatives watching like hawks to see that the other section doesn't gain an inch of advantage. Social justice will be defined as fair competition for scarce resources.

Small wonder that fat-cats North and South are purring with anticipatory pleasure at the Northern problem being settled along such lines.

14 May '98

68
___

Inside The Memorial Hall There's A Different Slant Of Light

"FÁILTE," SAID THE BIG BOY, welcoming a stream of Bogsiders into the headquarters of the Loyal Order for a celebration of Republicanism.

It was the witching night of May 1st and we'd gathered at the Apprentice Boys' Memorial Hall to kick off a weekend of songstering, speechifying and general jollification marking the 200th anniversary of the '98 Rising. About a hundred of us showed, many intrigued to be setting foot in the world HQ of an outfit generally encountered only in aggro and marching array.

A handful of members of the Boys themselves joined the audience for a talk on the United Irishmen in the Derry area, and a discussion on the apt theme: "Must we always walk like beasts of prey through fields our fathers stained with blood?"

Not many of us had known that Presbyterian Derry had been a hotbed of sedition in '98, that Oliver Cromwell Bond (the Dublin Corpo expurgated "Cromwell" when naming the flats) was a merchant from Ferryquay Street, that the Catholic Church in the town made it a mortal sin to make ready for revolution, that Paine's *Rights Of Man* had been published in Derry before its appearance in Belfast or Dublin, and so on and so forth.

We also learned that the Rev. James Porter was from our north west neighbourhood, Ballindrait just outside Lifford, which added resonance to the performance of his play, *Billy Bluff And Squire Firebrand,* on its belated Derry premiere.

The brilliant paradox about 1798 is that its stories are strikingly vivid and its lessons sharply relevant still, but none of it fits easily into the pattern of our politics today.

Tone, Neilson, Russell, Hope, the McCrackens and Grey believed with a transfiguring fervour that it was possible, and necessary, for Catholics and Protestants to identify themselves in politics by reference to an aspect of their existence other than the community they "belonged" to. Hardly anybody believes that now.

It's seen as so obvious that it hardly needs stating that "the two communities" naturally act and react separately, that "peace" means coexistence between two distinct camps, each respecting the integrity of the other. To the United Irishmen the exact opposite was obvious: that while separate camps remained, strife between them would be possible, and eventually inevitable.

The truth of that time holds good today. The only occasions in our history when Catholics and Protestants have abandoned rivalry and linked arms in sizable numbers have been those occasions when we linked arms against the prevailing power, to push together at privilege, the lower orders against ascendancy.

We had the Mayday march on the morning after the night out with the Boys, placards and speeches and a marching jazz band which gave us the style of a New Orleans funeral. We sashayed across Craigavon bridge, calling for a £5 an hour minimum wage, North and South. Now there's an idea for bridging the divide.

If an all-Ireland body took executive power to impose this modest provision, there would be few in Protestant working class areas of Derry or Belfast who'd object on the ground of its 32-county provenance.

But there would certainly be outpourings of anger and panic from propertied sorts across the divide, and the border.

Both sides in this conflict would transcend State and sectarian divisions. This is one road towards Irish unity. The other is via the Taigs outbreeding, outsmarting or outfighting the Prods.

Speaking in Guildhall Square at the end of the march, Jimmy McGovern, writer of *Cracker, The Lakes, Priest* and a number of splendid polemics against the hypocrisies of New Labour, said: "People may tell us that the things we have marched for today are impossible. They say that because they are afraid. These are things for the future."

* * * * *

The march hadn't set off on time. Nothing does in Derry. The Rev. Porter's play, for example, started 200 years late.

Porter, Presbyterian minister at Greyabbey in Co. Antrim, died in the torrent of vengeance which followed the failure of the Rising. He was hanged on a temporary gallows on a hill over-looking his own church. His wife, Ann, travelled with him in the carriage which brought him from prison in Newtownards, kissed him goodbye on the steps of the scaffold, then walked the short distance home.

Her husband's body was delivered half an hour afterwards to the doorstep where she waited, her seven children gathered around her. Her son, James, then 12, later attorney general of Lousiana, was to recall: "She had it carried into the room, and I remember that until the next morning no solicitation or entreaty could tear her from its side. Nor would she sit down. She stood and looked on it with her hands clasped. Not a tear fell, not a word escaped her lips".

Porter was hanged on the orders of Lord Londonderry, although he had taken no direct part in the Rising. It was personal. Londonderry had been lampooned to hilarious effect in Porter's play, *Billy Bluff And Squire Firebrand,* which had been published in 1796 in serial form in the United Irishmen's newspaper, the *Northern Star.*

The day before the hanging, Ann Porter had gone to Londonderry's home to plead for her husband's life. He gave her a letter confirming the hanging would go ahead. She said after-wards that "nothing in her life ever filled her with so much horror as his lordship's smile as he held out the letter".

Porter was executed for satirising the ruling class. He may be the only Irish writer ever to suffer this fate for this reason. He should be better remembered.

Billy Bluff And Squire Firebrand was written for public reading rather than for theatre performance. In an era when radical tracts were read out to largely illiterate audiences, it was designed for dialogue recitation in halls, taverns, homes, hillsides. It was, in modern parlance, a huge hit. Gales of plebian laughter wafted over the walls of the Londonderry estate at Mount Steward, filling the blue-bloods with murderous rage.

On a Sunday night in Derry in 1998, it was greeted with guffaws and hoots of recognition. Porter wasn't short of targets – tithes, the game laws, unfair leases, excessive drinking, the French war, the established church, the yeomanry, immoderate sobriety, the Orange Order, the persecution of Catholics, the government, the forced swearing of loyal oaths, capricious justice, informers.

Difficult as it is to know what a fellow might say were he alive now and not dead this two centuries, it's reasonable to surmise that Porter might add low pay and the lack of union rights to the list of targets for the pot-shots of a playright. Jimmy McGovern thinks so, too.

14 May '98

69

Why Should The RUC Be Allowed To Join The GAA?

MONICA MCWILLIAMS OF THE Women's Coalition says that Northern Irish society is "immature" and that this can be put down to the domination of politics and public life by people of the male persuasion. I'm told John Hume is livid.

John's views, like John himself, carry weight these days. As the most highly-regarded political operator around, he doesn't take kindly to any Jenny-come-lately rubbishing the efforts he's put in over the years.

It must be especially irksome at the moment for John to have to listen to nay-saying of this sort. This is his time of triumph. Small wonder the cameras cut to John in the King's Hall on May 23rd, immediately after the Northern Ireland Electoral Officer Pat Bradley announced a resounding 71.12 percent "Yes!" vote to the Agreement.

That reminds me that John and Pat Bradley had a disagreement during the last all-Northern Ireland count – for the Euro election of '94.

This disagreement arose after John had nipped out to the car-park for a series of inter-galactic television interviews – and had come back to discover fewer bundles of votes on his table than there'd been when he'd left. Fraud! he shouted, momentarily fearful that the bad old days of chicanery and subterfuge had returned. Gerrymandering!

Heads turned, jaws dropped, hearts leapt towards throats. Eager hacks espied a scandal.

It took all of Mark Durkan's powers of emollient phrase-making to calm John's frenzied tantrum. What had happened was that, in his absence, Pat Bradley had instructed counting staff to amalgamate 500-vote bundles into 1,000-vote bundles, beginning with John's table. But they hadn't yet started on Paisley's. Hence the disparity in the numbers of vote-bundles.

Nervous serenity re-established, the count continued.

Some time later, as candidates and senior aides drifted and hovered around the hall, Bradley eased himself alongside Durkan and wondered what had ailed John. Tense time, explained Mark, on edge, jumped to conclusion . . .

"I was in the same class at St. Columb's," confided Bradley, "and he was useless at counting even then . . ."

John finished a mere two-thousand adrift of perennial poll-topper Paisley. As candidates and close associates lined up on stage for Pat Bradley's formal announcement, he side-mouthed to Mark: "Saw you talking to Bradley . . .Did you know we were in the same class at St. Columb's?"

"Aye, he said."

"What were you talking about?"

"He said maths wasn't your subject."

Minutes passed as Bradley intoned the totals for each of the dozen candidates. John waited for a pause, then spoke again. If there's ever a re-run on television you'll notice the animated interchange, just stage left and slightly behind Returning Officer Bradley.

Said John at last, "I bet he didn't tell you we all used to call him goofy."

Thus do mature great men mark the pivotal moments in our history. What would the wet-behind-the-ears McWilliams woman know about it?

* * * * *

The controversy sparked by GAA president Joe MacDonagh's proposal to rescind Rule 21 gave us a glimpse of an aspect of the Belfast Agreement which hadn't hitherto been highlighted. (Rule 21 bars members of the RUC or the British Army from joining the association).

Most of the people in the North who voted Yes did so for thoroughly decent reasons. They wanted peace, and an end to sectarian hate. The most staggering statistic came from an exit poll which suggested that 99 percent of Northern Nationalists had backed the deal.

In the South, 94.5 percent voted Yes.

But in the minds of the most powerful elements behind the Agreement there's more to it than peace and an end to sectarianism.

Both before and after the special GAA congress, political and sports correspondents presented the proposal as an exact parallel and even an integral part of the Process, an essential ingredient of reconciliation between "the two communities". So to say No to the proposal to drop Rule 21 was to say No to peace and reconciliation.

A feature by the *Irish Times* Gaelic Games Corespondent Sean Moran on the Wednesday before the congress (May 27th) was typical.

If delegates voted against McDonagh's proposal, he warned, "The GAA will end up more politically extreme than the Provisional republican movement . . . It will need all delegates to stand up rather than abdicate their responsibilities, and refuse to allow their cultural and sporting association to be used to pursue a political agenda abandoned by 95 percent of nationalist Ireland".

Despite a flotilla of features along these lines, delegates didn't give the proposal the two-thirds majority it required. A compromise formula, whereby the association pledged to rescind the ban once the policing reforms promised in the Agreement were in place, was put and passed instead. The fact that Northern delegates were unanimously opposed to an immediate Rule-change had proved decisive.

In the aftermath, the *Times,* and the rest of the media, fulminated even more furiously. In his regular Monday column (June 1st), Tom Humphries laid into the delegates for their uncouth refusal to "(make) some sort of belated contribution to a prevailing mood which will benefit all its members".

He went on: "The GAA appears to be at least a step behind the nationalist constituency in the North. Apart from the intractably heavy metal elements of the republican movement, the thrust of nationalist philosophy in recent times has been compromise and forward movement."

It didn't seem to occur to Tom that since the Northern delegates who were 100 percent against the Rule-change had come from a community which had voted 99 percent in favour of the Agreement, maybe there was more to this matter than the media had cared, or dared, to acknowledge.

Overwhelmingly, Southern delegates had been ready to ditch the Rule. But support in the South for the Agreement, while huge, hadn't touched the dizzy heights recorded by the Nationalists of the North.

So were delegates from the South faithfully representative of grass-roots opinion in their areas – but delegates from North unrepesentative to the extent that they spoke for as few as one percent of their community?

This was the "explanation" provided in almost every Dublin newspaper and on RTE radio and television.

The alternative explanation – that the fault lay not in the composition of the congress but in an analysis which characterised the Rule 21 debate as a re-enactment of the Referendum poll – wasn't given an airing: not surprising in an intellectual climate in which it was assumed that critical thought had been rendered redundant on the instant of the Referendum result.

Let's look again at what was going on in the row over Rule 21.

Operating on an assumption that the GAA is representative of Catholic Nationalism (by no means a self-evident proposition), the media, the Government (David Andrews), the Opposition (John Bruton, Ruairi Quinn, Prionsias de Rossa), the Catholic Church (Archbishop Clifford), etc., demanded that delegates vote for a peace based on reconciliation with – not their Protestant neighbours – but the RUC and British Army. Which is not the same thing.

The grievances Northern nationalists have against the State security forces are not, either objectively or in the way they are felt, grievances against Protestants.

Humphries, implicitly but clearly, argued that Eilish McCabe, by protesting outside the congress against the murder by the British Army of her brother, Aidan McAnespie, on his way to play in a club football match, and against the refusal of the RUC to take the killing seriously, was setting her face against reconciliation between Catholics and Protestants and opposing peace. This is mendacious nonsense.

What critics of the Association were demanding of Northern delgates was that they signal reconciliation to the State. Unwilling to put this plain, they tried to bludgeon the congress into submission with moral cudgels labelled "peace".

The policy of the GAA now is comfortably within the requirements of the Agreement itself. What delegates rejected was the hidden agenda.

10 June '98

70

The Assembly: Nothing But The Same Old Story

IT'S BEEN A DIFFICULT BIRTH. But the Assembly is alive and fitfully kicking. With a bit of luck we can look forward to real politics.

Weary old arguments over parades, prisoners, police and partition will fade away. The new arena will ring out with speeches about hospitals, schools, jobs, the environment. No more the dull thud of Orange upon Green. Henceforth, Left will chime against Right.

So who'll be tolling for the Left, then, and who for the Right?

During the election campaign, the *Belfast Telegraph*'s business editor, Rosie Cowan, asked each of the five biggest parties to spell out its ideas for (a) encouraging investment and (b) combatting long-term unemployment – issues on which political forces anywhere might naturally assemble in Left-Right formation.

The result (*Telegraph,* June 20th) made interesting reading. It suggested that whether the Assembly turns out to serve Nationalist interests better than Unionists', or vice-versa, it's going to suit business-interests, big time: that if the Orange-Green axis fades away, it won't be replaced by a polarisation between Left and Right but, rather, by a Right-wing, or centre-Right, consensus.

The most common suggestion for encouraging investment was to give businesses bigger subsidies. The SDLP wanted "corporation tax . . . lowered to the same level as in the Republic". The DUP couldn't bring itself to plead for parity with the Republic but implied as much, calling for "a level playing field". Sinn Féin advocated a "common corporate and income tax regime . . . Disparity between . . . corporation tax rates in both states must be taken away". Alliance called for tax changes "to grow business". The Ulster Unionists, hardly buzzing with coherent ideas on any issue these days, suggested "more emphasis . . . on encouraging the growth of indigenous companies".

In relation to strategy for economic development, there was no visible gap between the parties.

On long-term unemployment, all five parties called for better education and training. Alliance wanted more emphasis on "enterprise", Sinn Féin spoke of the need to redress the legacy of decades of discrimination, the Ulster Unionists, again, underlined the importance of indigenous industry, the SDLP wanted a "long-term development strategy", the DUP warned against "ageism" (perhaps a reflection of the senior Paisley's septuagenarian status).

All of the ideas were conventional and, broadly speaking, conservative. No party advanced an idea which distinguished it from the others in Left-Right terms.

This suggests that members of the Assembly are not going to break ranks from their present array and reconstitute themselves in Left-Right formation when it comes to economic issues. How, then, is the realignment supposedly augured by the Assembly to be made manifest?

We are not dealing here with a local phenomenon. In Britain and Southern Ireland, as well as across Europe, the centre-Right stretch of the political spectrum has become uncomfortably crowded of late. The collapse of Stalinism, taken together with the evident inability of the free market to deliver stability or growth, has seen a scampering for the safety of "the middle ground".

In the North, this development has gone largely unnoticed – precisely because of the construction of politics around the idea of community. A tilt towards Green or Orange will instantly be noted and widely discussed. But a shift or convergence along the Left-Right continuum hardly registers. The result is that just at the time we are told to rejoice at the old political paradigm finally fading away, we find that the alternative axis has proven even more rapidly biodegradable.

It's not that a realignment along Left-Right lines is impractical in the North. But the Assembly may not be the best arena in which to achieve realignment. To "make the Assembly work" may turn out to mean no more than to make the politics of communal rivalry "work". Any serious challenge to the communal basis of Northern politics will have to come largely from outside the ambit of the Assembly.

Issues to provide a campaigning basis for challenging communalism are not hard to come by: the exclusion of young people from the minimum wage; the intimidation of the unemployed into demeaning jobs; the hounding of single parents and of social welfare recipients generally; the underfunding and understaffing of schools in working-class areas; the fact that the age of consent for gays and straights is a year older (17) than in Britain; the denial of abortion rights; arbitrary sackings, bullying bosses and no union organisation at work; the closure of hospital services on which people who can't "go private" depend, literally for their lives.

Etc.

* * * * *

Why is the Progressive Unionist Party popular among Catholics?

The PUP speaks for the Ulster Volunteer Force, the guys who gave us the Shankill Butchers. David Ervine is a convicted bomber, Billy Hutchinson a convicted killer. What an odd couple to be esteemed in Catholic areas. It cannot entirely be put down to the moist-eyed charisma of Mr. Ervine.

It has to do with a sense that the PUP, despite its origins, has an agenda which goes beyond the sectarian division. During the Assembly election the PUP was the only party to call explicitly for the extension of the 1967 Abortion Act to the North. The UDP spoke generally about women's rights, Sinn Féin, typically, dodged the issue, the Women's Coalition ran for cover. The SDLP and the mainstream Unionists were aligned with the "pro-lifers". Only the PUP, in the person of David Ervine on Radio Ulster's *Talkback,* publicly told the "pro-lifers" to SPUC off.

The significance of this lies not in the likelihood that a few Catholics-for-a-free choice may have warmed towards the PUP on account of this stand. What's relevant is that people feel more at ease making links across the divide when there's more to it than crossing the divide, when it's not a journey undertaken for its own sake.

The PUP's vaguely-formulated class line on economic matters, and generally progressive approach to issues of social morality, puts them into partial alignment with the thinking of some on "the other side". The larger these issues loom, the greater the extent of the common ground revealed.

It doesn't do to puff up the PUP. They are still wrapped in the Union Jack and bring horrible baggage with them from the past. They talk about the common interests of the working-class, while simultaneously presenting themselves as part of the

"Unionist family". Politically they are doing the double, and will be caught out unless they come clean.

But in the meantime, their relative popularity in Catholic areas hints at one of the most important political truths of the moment – that to say we must sort out the communal division before we can move on to "real politics", is to give up on ever reaching real politics.

8 July '98

71

Croppies Lie Down

THE WORLD IS FULL OF well-meaning people making things worse.

After the murder of the three Quinn children in Ballymoney, well-meaners jammed the lines to phone-in programmes with suggestions, for example, that a covered walk-way should be constructed along the length of the Garvaghy Road and various tableaux and artefacts installed so as to create a "memorial gallery" to all the dead of the Troubles, along which the Portadown District of the Orange Order might march every year.

A more interesting suggestion came in a call to Radio Foyle: wouldn't it be apt for the Orange Order to erect a memorial to the three children, so as to give permanent expression to the Order's feelings about their deaths?

What words might most appropriately be carved into a such a monument?

Remembering the huge banner displayed at Drumcree advising "Croppies lie down!", perhaps a chorus of the traditional ballad from whence the phrase comes?

"Poor Croppies ye knew that your sentence had come,
When you heard the dread sound of the Protestant drum.
In memory of William we hoisted the flag
And soon the bright Orange put down the Green rag.
Down, down, Croppies lie down."

Ms. Ruth Dudley Edwards would, I am sure, be happy to perform the unveiling ceremony.

23 July '98

72

They Haven't Gone Away You Know (Part One)

"BIGOTS OBSESSED WITH MEN'S BUMS". That was one commentator's apt description of the galoots who gathered in the House of Lords at Westminster last month to vote down a proposal to equalise the age of consent for gays.

Among odd-balls in ermine who managed to make it to London were Lady Saltoun of Abernathy, the Viscount L'Isle, Earl Kitchener, Baron (Norman) Tebbit, Lord Quirk of the Isle of Man and Baron Willoughy de Broke.

They haven't gone away, you know. Sadly, neither have bishops, imams or rabbis.

There is a bright side to it, if we look hard enough. It is, surely, gratifying to be able to remind ourselves from time to time that however quaint, whimsical or ignorant we Irish may sometimes be, we are no match for the aristos and bishops of Britland when it comes to hatred, unction and evil.

Baroness Trumpington wanted it known that she spoke as "the widow of a public-school headmaster", and knew well the "endess difficulties" lowering the age of consent would have created for her husband. Hmm.

Quirk of Man quoted extensively from the works of (who he?) Jeffrey Satinover: "Anal intercourse traumatises the soft tissue of the rectal lining which is nowhere near as sturdy as vaginal tissue . . . Even in the absence of major trauma, minor or microscopic tears in the rectal lining allow for immediate contamination".

Quirk went on to reveal that he doesn't know the difference between one ride and another: "If by law we protect motorcyclists from head injury, we must give a thought to protecting the sexually active from anal injury".

Some say there's a gene for it, that the ilk of Quirk were born like that and aren't personally to be blamed. But I say that a kick up the arse would do them no harm at all.

The Church of England's spokesman, the Bishop of Winchester, expressed "astonishment" that anybody could believe that "homosexual activity is as appropriate and as desirable as heterosexual activity". Which means, if meaning attaches to it at all, that His Lordship finds the existence of homosexuals astonishing. Which is fair enough. Personally, I find the existence of the Church of England astonishing, but I don't demand a law against it.

The leading Catholic peer Lord Longford said: "A girl is not ruined for life by being seduced. A young fellow is". Ah.

The Chief Rabbi of Britain, Lord Jacobovits, reminded the noble lords and ladies of the terrible things which had resulted from "the depravities of the biblical city of Sodom or the pagan Greek island of Lesbos". This is wrong. Sodom was zapped by the Lord God, right enough, but figuratively and literally the bible left Lesbos alone. Neither explicitly nor implicitly is there a single condemnation of lesbianism or of lesbian sex in the Old Testament or the New. This cannot have been an oversight. God knows everything.

The correct scriptural position is, then, that while the Judaeo-Christian god may have had a vicious attitude to gay men, she loved lesbians.

The House of Lords rag-bag of homophobe reactionaries managed to block the equal rights proposal by 290 votes to 122.

The following week, the Lambeth Conference – the world council of Anglican bishops, which meets every 10 years – was dominated by the issue of homosexuality.

"Repent, repent of your sin. You have no inheritance in the Kingdom of God. You are going to hell. You have made yourself homosexual because of your carnality," Bishop Emmanuel Chukwumu of Enugu, Nigeria, warned gay Christian lobbyists, expressing, as things turned out, the view of a huge majority of the 700-plus prelates present.

Chukwumu was recorded by *Guardian* journalist Madeline Bunting as he ranted outside the conference hall in Canterbury.

"We have overcome carnality just as the light will overcome darkness. God created woman for man. God did not create you as a homosexual . . . Your church is dying in Europe because it is condoning immorality. You are killing the church. This is the voice of God talking. I am violent against sin. Sodom and Gomorrah were destroyed."

Such intense hostility to homosexuality is one of the Anglican Church's selling points in Nigeria and other African and southeast Asian countries. The Church fears that if it weakened its stance it would lose out to Islam and to "independent" evangelical sects in competition to recruit from "traditional" homophobic areas.

There was an emissary from the Vatican on hand at Canterbury throughout, Cardinal Edward Cassidy warning that any mitigation of the line on homosexuality would put progress towards "Christian unity" in peril.

African and Asian bishops were further encouraged towards the fundamentalist position by a deal offered by the US evangelicals: we'll support an easing of the debt burden on the Third World if you back a tough stance against gays.

A caricaturist might be forgiven for rendering it thus: help us put the boot into homosexuals or we'll let your people starve.

By such means is the "Word of God" deciphered by Christians these days.

We would do well to take note of these developments, lest we fall into the liberal delusion that progress is assured. On gay rights, as on abortion and much else, it's easy to assume that the hate merchants have had their day and are being left behind, that there's a tide in the affairs of men and women inexorably ebbing and leaving twisted bigotry stranded. But it's not necessarily so.

In the US, abortion rights won 30 years ago are under renewed assault. In some States, women's right to choose is more constrained than at any time since the '70s. Under the guise of "anti-porn" ordinances, words and pictures presenting gay sex as normal have been outlawed in a number of cities.

The Lambeth Conference vote will have a material effect in boosting the morale of the bigots as they head back home. Anti-gay feeling will have been reinforced in countries like Zimbabwe, where homosexuality is already illegal and gay activists are routinely imprisoned.

Individually, the majorities at the House of Lords and the Lambeth Conference may have comprised doddering nonentities and purveyors of ridiculous superstitution. But their influence for evil when they operate together is not inconsiderable. We should keep a baleful eye on them.

* * * * *

They Haven't Gone Away You Know (Part Two)

On the day after the "Real IRA" bombing of Banbridge, a *Derry Journal* editorial summed up the consensus political view of the group.

They "represent nobody". They are "renegades, yesterday's men . . . with no agenda except to keep violence an ingredient in our society . . . No policies, no political philisophy, no contribution to make to the ideals of Republicanism as expressed in the 1916 Proclamation".

If that's all they amounted to, the *Journal* wouldn't have to worry about them.

During Easter Week in 1916, the *Journal* commented in forthright style on the Dublin events. The insurgents, it suggested, were not true Republicans at all, but followers of the anarchist Bakunin (!). Sinn Féiners who might be involved were "not really Sinn Féin as a compact force", but "desperate characters". The leaders of the Rising were men "without sufficient education to guage correctly the dire consequences of their behaviour . . . mad-headed . . . criminal, senseless, suicidal, deplorable . . .".

Not much change then . . .

Like every other movement or organisation which uses violence in the name of "the people" or a section of the people, the Real IRA should be called to account. But to suggest that their ideas and actions contradict "the ideals of Republicanism as expressed in the 1916 Proclamation" is plain wrong.

19 August '98

73

Search Out The Bombers - All Of Them

FRANCIE MACKEY, BERNADETTE SANDS and Michael McKevitt are sin-eaters for Ireland now.

It's a dirty job, but somebody has to do it. Otherwise, where would the rest of us be?

Damned, as like as not.

In Scottish pagan tradition, the sin-eater was an unkempt shaman, feared and revered in equal measure, who would attend at the home of the dying to perform an arcane ritual, a communion in reverse, to devour the sins of the soon-to-be deceased, ingest their evil into his soul.

Thus consuming others' evil, the sin-eater was consumed by evil himself. Rendered morally repulsive so that decent folk averted their eyes, nonetheless there was no-one more fervently needed, most of all at moments of face-to-face meeting with death, when thoughts tended towards the sacredness, or otherwise, and the meaning, of life.

The rich paid big money for the sin-eater's service.

Search out the bombers, shout the headline politicians. And don't dilute the purity of our ire. Don't dare cavil at curtailment of civil liberty. Bring them before us, unmask their faces so we can look into their eyes, and project onto them whatever is most troubling within us.

In the immediate aftermath of the bombing, Francie Mackey couldn't bring himself to say "I condemn", as he stood on the steps of the Omagh council offices. He has, it's reported, been declared anathema in the area as a result. It's said there isn't a pub would serve him, or a shop to sell him groceries.

Placed in the balance with the horror the bomb brought to Omagh, his discomfiture counts for nothing. But it's true, too, that nothing which he said, or refused to say, was without precedent. Directly to the contrary, it was par for this particular course.

If he departs the political scene now, if we don't have to meet his eyes ever again, will he have taken that moral memory with him, relieved all the rest of us of its burden?

Three national newspapers, British and Irish, used the word "nihilist" to sum up the Omagh bombers. Meaning people who believe in nothing except in destruction for its own sake, who reject all values, ideas, ideals.

So nothing any of the rest of us believe or have believed, much less said and done, can have helped prompt or have seemed to sanction the bombing? No need to search for the bomber inside ourselves, then.

Did anyone in the Real IRA pause, even for an instant, when

told of the plan to bomb Omagh on Saturday afternoon? Pause and say steady on, let's think?

We are told by the usual "sources" that Mr. Blair didn't pause, "even for an instant", when invited, within the octave of Omagh, to approve the no-warning bombing of Afghanistan and the Sudan. Of course, Clinton's bombs were programmed to deliver death to far-away countries, of which we know little.

Mr. Blair trembles his voice for the microphones in declaring the bombers of Omagh beyond human redemption. They represent an unintended alien growth in the moral community of democratic politics, he implies, which we must take sharp measures to extirpate.

He pledges to root them out, even as he assists in the scattering of the seeds of similar evil across landscapes elsewhere.

But the people who bombed Omagh are not of a qualitatively different moral order from Tony Blair or Bill Clinton. What the Omagh crime against humanity did was to confront us with the flesh-and-blood horror of war.

Forced to focus on that reality, we want it taken away. We load every ounce of blame we can retrieve from the debris onto designated outcasts, then claim moral credit for willingness to banish them to oblivion or imprison them, or anyone suspected of being of them, without pretence of due process.

The media line now, the line in establishment political circles on both sides of the border and across the water, is dictated by a notion that the harsher the measures which are brought in, the greater the disdain with which complaints about the destruction of civil liberty are dismissed, the more moral the system will have shown itself to be.

Meanwhile, arbiters of ruling-class ethics fret whether Clinton will be able to fit in a game of golf during his visit to our shores.

2 September '98

74

Omagh: The War Is Over

HISTORY MAY RECORD THAT THE armed struggle lifted off on Bloody Sunday, and fell to earth in Omagh.

It was Bloody Sunday which made the IRA campaign viable, Omagh which forced activists to see it as futile.

After Bloody Sunday, in Catholic areas of the North, it was sometimes hard to get a hearing for argument against reaching for bombs and revolvers. After Omagh, there was no argument.

And this despite the fact that the aim of the armed struggle clearly had not been achieved. But then it's questionable, as I have been at pains to point out before, whether "the Republic" had ever provided the main motivation of the people in whose name the struggle was conducted, and whose support was key to its continuance.

This dimension of the matter doesn't figure prominently in coverage of the current state of play within what we know as Republicanism. Security correspondents retail the leaks from the RUC and Garda Special Branches. Others prefer speculation about the psychopathology of individuals. Real IRA members suffer from "a twisted mentality" (Fintan O'Toole), or are "serial mass killers" (Mary McAleese), or "filled with blood-lust" (*The Sun*).

"The people", on the other hand, they all agree, want peace, and respectabilised Republicans are doing their best, or almost, to deliver it.

A sharper analysis came a few days before Omagh from a man who served with some distinction in the IRA at a high level, but who more recently has taken a wry view of political and paramilitary affairs. "Those fellows in Belfast were never Republicans at all," he observed, not in a disparaging way. "They were just fighting for their streets".

He had a point. The IRA didn't develop into a major force through Northern Catholics becoming consciously committed to a historical ideal and a militaristic tradition.

When the civil rights movement took to the streets in 1968, the IRA hardly rated a mention. Their last outburst of activity, the "Border Campaign", had ended in 1962 with a plaintive communique complaining that "The minds of the Irish people are being deliberately distracted from the supreme national issue".

The emergence on the streets of a new style of politics, drawing on the black civil rights and anti-Vietnam war movements rather than on tableaux from Irish history, was widely seen as underlining the irrelevancy of any who reckoned that broad black brimmers might make a fashion comeback in west Belfast.

It was when the movement for civil rights reform was met with murderous onslaughts against working-class streets, and with the armoured cars and tanks and guns of the RUC and British Army, that the mood in Catholic areas began to harmonise with the age-old, increasingly audible Republican message. Bloody Sunday set the seal on this transformation.

Republicanism became the vehicle through which raging anger, and the impulse to hit back, was expressed. Fr. Dennis Faul, who as chaplin at Long Kesh talked with hundreds of IRA prisoners in his time, has spoken of what typically propelled young Catholics to join "The Movement". Neighbours or relatives maimed or killed, constant harrassment on the way to work or play, a single instance of being battered senseless by sniggering cops or ignorant squaddies, the daily pin-pricking humiliation of being seen as second-class in your own home-place – these provided the engine for recruitment into the IRA.

It wasn't hallowed tradition but hard experience which dictated the decision to join up. This comes through clearly, too, in recent books by ex-IRA activists Eamonn Collins, Martin McGartland, Sean O'Callaghan and Raymond Gilmore. All four have good reason to misrepresent their own actions and relationships in the IRA. But the general picture they paint of life in the ranks is persuasive. Few political discussions are recorded, almost none at all about the supposed ultimate objective of the armed activity in which they were involved, at obvious risk to their liberty, lives and peace of mind.

On these accounts, and other evidence and experience confirms the view, there was a distinct pragmatism about the Republican enterprise, reflected eventually in the pragmatism of the Northerners who, in the '80s, came to lead Sinn Féin and IRA, and thereby alarmed and alienated those who held hard to the old road as a matter of principle rather than practicality.

Republican Sinn Féin and the 32-County Sovereignty Movement have a point when they say that the Provos have strayed off the straight Republican path. But it's as meaningful to see them as having travelled the straight road for a certain stretch of the way, before re-joining the higgledy route Northern Catholics were more used to.

Mainstream commentators still regularly represent Northern Catholics as rooted in a militant Republian tradition which, painfully, they must be weaned away from. The picture of plausible leaders striving to coax recalcitrant supporters to boldly go where they haven't ventured much before has become a common illustrative image. Pondering whether Omagh will help or hinder the peace-mongers in this process has filled thousands of column inches. But in the perspective of history, the scene makes little sense.

In rhetorical terms, through a quarter century of armed struggle, the IRA traced its democratic mandate to the December 1918 general election which gave Sinn Féin, standing for an all-Ireland Republic, a majority in the island. This is the mandate which Mr. Adams' true-Republican critics accuse him of breaking.

But the one part of nationalist Ireland which Sinn Féin didn't win in 1918 was the North. In West Belfast, de Valera was beaten two-to-one by the constitutional nationalist Joe Devlin, who in his eve-of-poll message had urged Falls voters to "tell Sinn Féin their phantom Republic is a fraud".

In Dublin, Tipperary, strongly Catholic areas along the border, the achievement of The Republic could be seen as a relatively unproblematic liberation. But Belfast was different.

Through the Stormont years, from 1922 to 1972, the only seats won by Sinn Féin in the North were in rural areas – Mid-Ulster and Fermanagh-South Tyrone in the '50s. It never came within an ass's roar of winning West Belfast.

When the party finally took the cockpit seat, with Mr. Adams' victory over Gerry Fitt in 1983, the victory was a reflection of the Republican Movement's prestige as having defended the constituency's streets and hit back hard against those who had attacked it. This was the product of well-founded communal anger, not an upsurge of revolutionary ideas.

Even at the angriest times, there has been an iffyness about the community's support for armed struggle. Many Catholics supported the IRA through gritted teeth.

A feeling of futility in relation to the armed struggle was the most powerful single factor behind the Sinn Féin "Peace Strategy" from the outset, and is the crucial factor now underpinning the IRA ceasefire, and militating against the construction of a base for a relaunching of the armed struggle.

Against this background, and unwilling to see class rather than community as the fundamental dividing line in Irish society, Sinn Féin has sought and found allies for a new strategy among the rich and powerful in the South and in the US. These new friends have bolstered the Movement as it has changed its ways. But the alliance has ensured that the new direction has been Rightwards towards respectability and accomodation with the status quo, not Leftwards towards a broader, better battle for change.

We must hope that Omagh marks the end of armed struggle. But it doesn't follow that struggle is ended. What the many Republicans who want the war over, but who sense that nothing adequate has yet been achieved, should do now is to begin to discuss which road other than Republicanism offers the best way ahead.

2 September '98

ALSO AVAILABLE FROM HOT PRESS BOOKS

U2: THREE CHORDS AND THE TRUTH
Edited by Niall Stokes
Critical, entertaining, comprehensive and revealing, *U2: Three Chords And The Truth* never misses a beat as it brings you, in words and pictures, a complete portrait of U2 in the process of becoming a legend.
Price: £8.95

THEY ARE OF IRELAND
by Declan Lynch
They Are Of Ireland is a hilarious who's who of famous Irish characters – and chancers – from the worlds of politics, sport, religion, the Arts, entertainment and the media. Written by Declan Lynch, one of the major new Irish literary talents of the '90s, this is one of those rare events – a book of comic writing that actually makes you laugh out loud.
Price: £7.99

MY BOY: THE PHILIP LYNOTT STORY
by Philomena Lynott (with Jackie Hayden)
The story of Philip Lynott as told by the woman who brought him into the world and who was at his side during the final days of his life, *My Boy* is not only an intimate and revealing portrait of an Irish rock legend, but an immensely moving account of a mother's devotion to her beloved son through the good times and the bad. A No.1 best-seller.
Price: £7.99

BEYOND BELIEF
by Liam Fay
There are parts of the world where religion is a contentious, fraught, grave business which ruptures families, rends nations, and causes fellow human beings to kill one another. In the island of saints and scholars, however, it's a lot more serious than that. Here, it is not God but His followers who move in mysterious ways. HOT PRESS writer Liam Fay has won a national journalism award for his investigation into the wild side of faith in Ireland. Uproarious, revealing and thought-provoking, *Beyond Belief* is an unforgettable exploration of a people and their faiths in late 20th century Ireland.
Price: £9.99 paperback, £16.99 hardback

U2: Three Chords And The Truth, They Are Of Ireland, My Boy: The Philip Lynott Story and Beyond Belief are available from Hot Press, 13 Trinity St., Dublin 2. Trade enquiries Tel: (01) 6795077 or Fax: (01) 6795097. Mail order, send cheques/POs or credit card details for £8.95 (U2) , £7.99 (They Are Of Ireland and My Boy), £16.99 (hardback), £9.99 (paperback) (Beyond Belief), incl. p&p, to the above address.

SUBSCRIPTION OFFER

Since 1977, HOT PRESS has established a reputation as Ireland's most lively and controversial magazine – as well as one of the world's most influential music publications.

With its roots in rock 'n' roll, the fortnightly HOT PRESS has become a forum for the most informed and intelligent journalism covering contemporary music, plus some of the best magazine writing available on current affairs, cinema, sport, fashion, sex, leisure and the environment. Contributors include columnists Eamonn McCann, Nell McCafferty, John Kelly and Sam Snort, as well as Joe Jackson, Adrienne Murphy, Niall Stokes, Jackie Hayden, Gaye Shortland and Liam Mackey.

Please photocopy this form

SUBSCRIPTION FORM

This is a... **renewal** ❑ **new subscription** ❑

NAME: _____

ADDRESS: _____

_____ Tel: _____

I wish to pay by [Cheque] [Postal Order] [Credit Card. My Card is (please tick) VISA❑ MASTERCARD❑ ACCESS❑]

Card No. ❑❑❑❑❑❑❑❑❑❑❑❑❑❑❑❑

Expiry Date _____

Annual SUBSCRIPTION RATES: Ireland IR£35, United Kingdom IR£40, Europe IR£55, North America $98US, Rest of World IR£105.
RETURN TO: HOT PRESS, 13 TRINITY ST. DUBLIN 2, IRELAND. TEL: 01 6795077